A Month-to-Month Guide

3

Third-Grade Math

A Month-to-Month Guide

3

Third-Grade Math   **Suzy Ronfeldt**

Math Solutions
Sausalito, CA

Math Solutions
150 Gate 5 Road
Sausalito, CA 94965
www.mathsolutions.com

Library of Congress Cataloging-in-Publication Data
Ronfeldt, Suzy.
   A month-to-month guide : third-grade math / Suzy Ronfeldt.
      p. cm.
Includes bibliographical references and index.
   ISBN 0-941355-56-X (alk. paper)
   1. Mathematics—Study and teaching (Elementary) 2. Third grade
(Education) I. Title.
   QA135.5.R663 2003
   372.7'049—dc22

                                        2003024386

ISBN-13: 978-0-941355-56-8
ISBN-10: 0-941355-56-X

Editor: Toby Gordon
Production: Melissa L. Inglis
Cover and interior design: Catherine Hawkes/Cat and Mouse
Composition: Argosy Publishing

Printed in the United States of America on acid-free paper
12 11 10 09   ML   3 4 5

A Message from Math Solutions

We at Math Solutions Professional Development believe that teaching math well calls for increasing our understanding of the math we teach, seeking deeper insights into how children learn mathematics, and refining our lessons to best promote students' learning.

Math Solutions shares classroom-tested lessons and teaching expertise from our faculty of Math Solutions Inservice instructors as well as from other respected math educators. Our publications are part of the nationwide effort we've made since 1984 that now includes

- more than five hundred face-to-face inservice programs each year for teachers and administrators in districts across the country;
- annually publishing professional development books, now totaling more than seventy titles and spanning the teaching of all math topics in kindergarten through grade 8;
- four series of videos for teachers, plus a video for parents, that show math lessons taught in actual classrooms;
- on-site visits to schools to help refine teaching strategies and assess student learning; and
- free online support, including grade-level lessons, book reviews, inservice information, and district feedback, all in our quarterly *Math Solutions Online Newsletter*.

For information about all of the products and services we have available, please visit our website at *www.mathsolutions.com*. You can also contact us to discuss math professional development needs by calling (800) 868-9092 or by sending an email to *info@mathsolutions.com*.

We're always eager for your feedback and interested in learning about your particular needs. We look forward to hearing from you.

*This book is dedicated to my grandsons, Michael and Kai,
and to my future grandchildren.*

*With special thanks to
teachers everywhere for their dedication,
my students past and present for their wonderful ideas,
my husband, Steve, for his caring support,
my daughters, Lara and Heidi, for their loving patience,
and my son, Matthew, for continuing our family's
teaching tradition.*

Contents

Foreword

One of the challenges of teaching mathematics is planning a coherent year of instruction. Not only must we address the important mathematics children need to learn, but we also need to help children learn to think, reason, and become proficient problem solvers. And we also want to inspire children to enjoy mathematics and see it as useful to their lives. Accomplishing this is a tall order that calls for understanding the full scope of the mathematics curriculum, having a rich repertoire of instructional options, being skilled at managing instruction in the classroom, and understanding the needs of the individual students in your class.

This book is a month-by-month guide for planning a year of math instruction. It is one of a multibook series, each book written by a master teacher to address teaching mathematics in the elementary grades. Each author acknowledges that her suggestions do not comprise the only approach to accomplish planning, or necessarily the best approach for others to follow. Rather, each suggests a thoughtful, practical, and very personal approach to planning that has grown out of her years of experience in the classroom.

The authors of this series are truly master teachers—experienced, caring, hardworking, and incredibly accomplished. They bring their wisdom and experience to their books in unique ways, but as teachers they share common experiences and outlooks. Each has offered many professional development classes and workshops for teachers while also choosing to make classroom teaching the main focus of her career. For all of them, mathematics was not their initial love or strength. However, they each came to study and learn to appreciate mathematics because of their need to serve their students. They are committed to excellence in math instruction, they understand children, they know how to manage classrooms, and they are passionate about teaching. It is a great pleasure to present these books to you.

MARILYN BURNS

Introduction

"Reasoning mathematically is a habit of the mind and like all habits, it must be developed through consistent use in many contexts."

Principles and Standards for School Mathematics
NCTM 2000, 56

Late every summer, as part of getting ready to return to school, I plan the mathematics program for my next year's students. Even after twenty-seven years of teaching, I am energized as I think about how I can best teach so my students have an opportunity to think and reason as they learn mathematics. I am excited as I plan meaningful and interesting contexts from money and measurement situations to games and story problems for the children's problem solving. In this book, I share my planning process with you.

Each year, my classroom plan differs as a result of incorporating my previous year's teaching experience, ideas from classes or workshops I have attended, and information from new books I have read. Also, I realize that my plans must be flexible as they always change once I meet the children and as the year progresses. This book is filled with suggestions for you to consider, but I expect that you will refine, reject, and expand on these ideas according to your own good teaching instincts.

As I create a mathematics program that encourages children to make sense of mathematics, I draw on the teaching I do in reading and writing. For example, when a child says that Henry Huggins is a hard worker, I ask the child to find proof for his idea in the words of the story. He may reply that in the story Henry spent hours catching earthworms to earn money to purchase a football for Scooter. Then I turn to the other students and ask if they agree and why or why not? I ask if there are other places in the story that prove that Henry is a hard worker. Learning in this way takes place through the give and take of children's ideas. This should happen in the mathematics classroom, too.

During writing instruction, when a child writes about the fun she had at recess, I ask that she explain in detail why recess was fun. When the child reads aloud about going down the twirly slide and feeling dizzy, the other children respond enthusiastically with comments and questions. The learning takes place in the midst of conversations about the children's own ideas based on their everyday experiences. In writers' workshop, I honor the voices of my students. And I do the same in our mathematics program.

As you open up your mathematics classroom to the wonderful ideas of children, think about planning for and providing engaging problems and explorations to spark students' thinking and reasoning and help them bring meaning to mathematical ideas and skills. Instruction in literature is not limited to sounding out lists of words outside the context of stories. Instruction in writing is not limited to learning the rules for capitalization outside the context of writing personal narratives. The same needs to be true for instruction in mathematics. Learning mathematics should not be limited to memorizing facts and practicing computation. Rather, students should use their mathematics to make sense of the money, measurement, and story problems they are solving daily, and they should explain why their answers make sense by using words, numbers, and pictures.

As you plan your third-grade mathematics curriculum, I hope this book helps you open up your mathematics classroom to your students' wonderful ideas and supports you in choosing worthwhile problems and mathematical tasks that engage your students in learning and meaning-making.

Chapter 1

BEFORE THE CHILDREN ARRIVE

"Representing numbers with various physical materials should be a major part of mathematics instruction in the elementary grades."

Principles and Standards for School Mathematics
NCTM 2000, 33

Before the first day of school, you need to plan your math program and set up the classroom to support that program. ■

Planning Your Math Program

As you begin planning your math program, remember that this book is not a program for you to adopt. Rather, it presents mathematics concepts you want your students to make sense of and a learning environment that supports this sense making. Before you map out your year and set up your classroom, page through the entire book to become familiar with its contents. Then spend time reading Chapters 2 and 3 to better understand the book's structure and intent.

There are many programs available that you can follow step by step, replacement units you can use at your discretion, and problem-solving lessons you've already gathered from a variety of sources. This book can help you weave all these threads into a meaningful whole in your mathematics classroom. Here's how:

Chapter Focus and Time Span

A Month-to-Month Guide: Third-Grade Math contains nine chapters. In Chapter 2, you'll find ideas for addition and subtraction problem solving. In Chapter 3, I've offered suggestions for introducing children to multiplication. Each of these two chapters is designed to be used over six weeks—to give children time to settle into the school-year rhythm. These chapters also allow plenty of time for you and the students to build the learning environment suggested in this book. Feel free to reverse the order of these two chapters if you wish.

The last chapter, Chapter 9, focuses on geometry. It covers the end of the school year and could be six weeks in length. On the other hand, this could be the time of year when you do other math activities you have been eager to introduce or math problem solving that you did not get to during the rest of the year. (The book contains one other geometry chapter—Chapter 4.)

Each of the remaining four chapters cover a specific month and is designed to be used over four weeks. These chapters focus on arithmetic: addition, subtraction, multiplication, division, and fractions. If you also want to introduce probability and statistics, data collection, or algebraic thinking to your students, you can easily supplement this book with other resources that focus on those items.

Chapter Structure

Most of the chapters in this book follow a similar pattern and include similar sections. I describe these sections below.

The Learning Environment

Each chapter begins with a section called "The Learning Environment." This section is intended to help you align your teaching priorities with the classroom climate. For example, if you want students to communicate freely and frequently about math, you'll need to build an environment in which your questions get at children's thinking, students risk sharing their reasoning, and mistakes are treated as opportunities to learn. "The Learning Environment" sections help you cultivate such a classroom.

If you decide to begin the year with multiplication (Chapter 3), you might still want to read "The Learning Environment" section in Chapter 2. Why? That section discusses teaching and learning issues that need addressing during the first six weeks of school. If you decide to use the other chapters in a sequence that differs from the structure shown here, read, "The Learning Environment" section that addresses the particular time period in the school year on which you're focusing.

As you survey "The Learning Environment" ideas, select one or two suggestions on which to concentrate. That way, you'll keep things simple. You can always address the remaining ideas later in the school year if necessary. The key is to think about learning-environment issues as rigorously as you think about the mathematics you're teaching.

The Mathematics

"The Mathematics" section follows "The Learning Environment" section in each chapter. This section presents the main math concepts covered by the chapter. You may decide to substitute some of these "big math ideas" with others that you consider more appropriate for your class, or to focus on only a few ideas at a time.

If you want students to make sense of mathematics using their own strategies, you'll need to listen carefully to how they figured out their answers. Have them represent their thinking by first using concrete models, then using words, numbers, and labeled pictures. Eventually, some children will think numerically by breaking numbers into familiar parts ($45 = 40 + 5$) or going to nearby friendly numbers (think of 39 as 40) as they add, subtract, multiply, and divide. These ideas are discussed more fully in "The Mathematics" sections.

These sections help you think about the connections between addition and subtraction (one can "count up" to find the difference between two numbers), addition and multiplication (one can multiply instead of add to find the total number of items in several equal-size groups), multiplication and division, and division and fractions. "The Mathematics" sections also discuss subtraction as both take-away and comparison and division as both sharing and grouping.

The mathematics thinking and reasoning explored in this section of each chapter comes to life through the children's problem solving in the contexts explained next.

Problem-Solving Context

Except for the two geometry chapters, this book's chapters present problem-solving suggestions in the following order of contexts—"Mathematics Throughout the Day" (routines and activities), games, measurement, money, children's literature, and story problems. Some problems require work that extends over three or four days. Others can be dealt with by using quick classroom routines, such as figuring that day's outdoor temperature and comparing it to the previous day's temperature. Many of the problems have extensions that you can use for extended classwork problem-solving or for homework assignments.

Once you have selected the chapter you want to cover first, read through these sections to see which activities and problems are best suited to your class or to your interests. As always, you may want to substitute some of these suggestions with activities you've used in the past. Remember: You are the decision maker in your own classroom.

Whatever you decide, you may find it helpful to make a rough draft of your plans for the month—realizing (of course) that the plan will likely change as the weeks unfold. As you draft your plan, aim to include learning experiences drawn from more than one context. (See Figure 1–1.)

In this book, you and the children are encouraged to revisit some problem situations over and over again, each time with a different emphasis. For instance, my division plan for January has students revisiting the *Circles and Stars* multiplication game from November. Like reading a favorite book again and again, revisiting familiar activities can foster deeper understanding of the concept presented.

Additional Sections

Most chapters also include several "Teacher-to-Teacher Talk" sections. In these sections, I share ideas and teaching insights that I hope you'll find useful. Some chapters also end with suggestions on how to design mathematics menus (a list of problem choices) and set up stations (activity areas) as alternatives to whole-class and partner work. A few chapters end with parent newsletters. Other chapters touch on various kinds of assessments— from listening to classroom discussions and taking anecdotal notes to reading classroom problem solving that students wrote step by step, from assigning specific written assessment problems to conducting one-on-one

Monday	Tuesday	Wednesday	Thursday	Friday
6 • Individual Written Assessment: What is division? • Share Paper Cookies Dividing cookies 6 cookies 4 people 5 cookies 4 people (discuss fractions)	**7** • 16 pieces of paper shared at table • Share Paper Cookies Dividing cookies, continued 3 cookies 4 people 2 cookies 4 people 1 cookie 4 people (discuss fractions)	**8** • 18 pieces of paper shared at table (discuss remainder/leftover) • Share Paper Cookies Do one of the extensions	**9** • 24 pencils grouped by 3s • Raisin Box (estimate) - group and count individual $1\frac{1}{2}$ oz box 2 ways	**10** • 16 books grouped by 3s (discuss remainder/leftover) • Raisin Box (estimate) - combine all raisins at a table to get total - share the total
13 • *The Doorbell Rang* - Begin to write follow-up seven part story	**14** • *The Doorbell Rang* - Complete follow-up story	**15** Station Time • Story Problem • Teacher—Revisit *Things That Come in Groups* Story Problem: Write companion grouping and sharing problems $(\div)$ • Paraprofessional—Teach *Leftovers* with 15 tiles • *Circles and Stars* with number cube (4, 5, 6, 7, 8, 9)	**16** • Classroom Groups Problem - Twenty children grouped into 2s, 3s, 4s, 5s, and so forth, up to 10s	**17** • Classroom Groups Problem, continued
20 Martin Luther King, Jr. Birthday Holiday	**21** • Individual Written Assessment: What does $20 \div 4 = 5$ mean? • Share $5.00 equally among 4 children (2 strategies)	**22** • Share $.50 equally among 4 children	**23** • *One Hungry Cat* - Share 12 cookies among 3 people - Share 8 cookies among 3 people	**24** • Menu Time
27 • *Two Tickets to Ride* - Share 25 tickets among 4 people, then among 5 people	**28** • *One Hundred Hungry Ants* - Make different arrays for 100 ants	**29** Station Time • Story Problem • Teacher—Revisit or reteach areas of confusion • Paraprofessional—*Leftovers* with 18 tiles • *Circles and Stars* with division notation, too	**30** • Menu Time	**31** • Individual Written Assessment: What is division? • Menu Time

FIGURE 1–1 ▲

I created this rough draft of January's plan, which featured division.

interviews. Two chapters end with brief discussions of standardized test preparation.

The quotes from the National Council of the Teachers of Mathematics (NCTM) that begin each chapter are meant to set the stage for that chapter, validate your efforts, and inspire you in your work.

Setting Up Your Classroom

As you arrange your classroom before the children arrive, think about ways to set up physical materials so students have easy access to learning tools, and arrange spaces so they can communicate their sense-making easily with you and one another.

Furniture and Spaces

The Rug Area

Communication plays as central a role in mathematics as it does in literature, so have a rug area large enough for your entire class to sit next to the white board or the chalkboard. That way, students will be able to hear one another's thinking and respond easily. The rug area also affords a much-needed change of scenery during a long day of learning. When children leave their desks and come to the rug area, they flex their brains *and* bodies.

Desks

Arrange students' desks in groups of four—two desks facing two desks. Or, have children sit in table groups of four—two students facing two students. These seating arrangements encourage children to talk about their ideas with one another. Typically, children will work on math problems with partners sitting next to them, but they may also share their thinking with classmates sitting across the table.

Monthly Math Area

Designate an area in your classroom as the monthly math area. Set this area aside for students' open-ended exploration of and experimentation with various materials that you provide. (Look at the "Teaching Materials" section of this chapter on pages 10–14.)

During September you could put out the tube of pattern blocks. As the children build flat designs in the monthly math area when they have completed their other assignments, watch and listen to what they are doing and saying. Pick up on the children's ideas for investigations they might do with the pattern blocks later in the month or let them continue to explore freely. Perhaps they could investigate designs that are symmetrical or asymmetrical. The children will use these concrete materials more formally as they make sense of fractions in February.

In October, the children could explore with wooden cubes (either 2 cm or 1 inch) or plastic Snap Cubes ($\frac{3}{4}$ inch) and fit those cubes into a variety of small boxes of different sizes. After a period of free exploration, you might come up with some investigations for the children to do based on their experimentation talk. For example, which boxes of different sizes hold the same number of cubes? Which box holds the greatest number of cubes? Which box holds the least number of cubes?

Through their pattern-block explorations, children informally get a feel for how the different geometric shapes fit together. With the cubes and boxes, they gain a tactile understanding of volume. This sense making may be enough without your having to assign specific tasks.

Of course, you and the children will need to decide on some ground rules. In my class, the manipulatives are not to be used as weapons or objects catapulted through the air.

Wall and Board Spaces

Arranging your classroom includes designating spaces on the wall and board for displaying materials essential for particular activities and routines. Also designate spaces accessible for children's observations and work.

Today's Number and the 1–100 Chart

In the *Today's Number* routine, you propose a different number each day and display it in a reliable location on the wall. Until the end of September, use the calendar date as the daily number. This allows you and the class to write equations for numbers from 1 through 30. After that, use the number of school days in the year so far. In many districts, children attend school for 181 days each year.

During the *Today's Number* routine, the children generate equations relating to that number. For example, if the date is September 8, students might say "four plus four is eight" or "ten minus two is eight." List these words in equation form ($4 + 4 = 8$; $10 - 2 = 8$) on the board near the displayed number. (You might want to check *Mathematical Thinking at Grade 3* [Russell and Economopoulos 1995] for additional ideas.)

Place the 1–100 pocket chart next to the daily number so children can easily make connections between the two. For the child who suggests the equation $4 + 4 = 8$, have him come to the pocket chart and show the accompanying moves on the 1–100 chart. He explains, "First you take four steps on the chart and land on four, then you count up four more steps and land on eight." For 10 – 2 = 8, another child comes to the 1–100 chart and says "Start at ten and count back two steps. You land on eight."

The 1–100 pocket chart is a meaningful tool for many other mathematical moments in the classroom as children build their sense of numbers. For instance, if a child says that you can skip-count by 20s and land on 100, have the child use the pocket chart to show her thinking by skip-counting 20, 40, 60, and 80, and landing on 100. It took five skip-counts by 20s to land on 100 exactly.

Attendance Graph

Find an area on the wall or on the board for posting a daily attendance graph. (See Figure 1–2.) When school begins, you might want to have students take turns recording the attendance using tally marks. Again, you could also use color-coded bars (e.g., red for girls, green for boys) or have just one bar that represents all the children in attendance for each day.

Temperature Graph

Post a graph on the wall that you'll use to record the daily temperatures during each month. (See Figure 1–3.) Write the days of the month across the graph's x-axis and temperature in five-degree increments along the y-axis. Make sure the graph is large enough so the children can see and discuss it. To add even more information to the graph, you may also wish to use different colors for the various bars. For example, you could use black for rainy days, blue for sunny days, green for cloudy days, and so on.

Lunch-Count Graph

Some students will buy a school lunch every day; others will bring bag lunches. These differences provide additional opportunities for students to work with numbers and graphs. Consider posting a weekly lunch-count graph on the wall or on a board showing how many are buying and how many are bringing. (See Figure 1–4.) You can have students take turns adding tally marks, Xs, or some other marks to the graph.

FIGURE 1–2 ▶

This class has recorded attendance for September 10 through September 12 so far.

	Mon. 9/10	Tues. 9/11	Wed. 9/12	Thurs. 9/13	Fri. 9/14
Girls	卌 lll	卌 lll	卌 lll		
Boys	卌 卌 ll	卌 卌 ll	卌 卌		

Week Two

FIGURE 1–3   ◄

This class has recorded the temperature on the first three days of school so far, and is using color-coded bars.

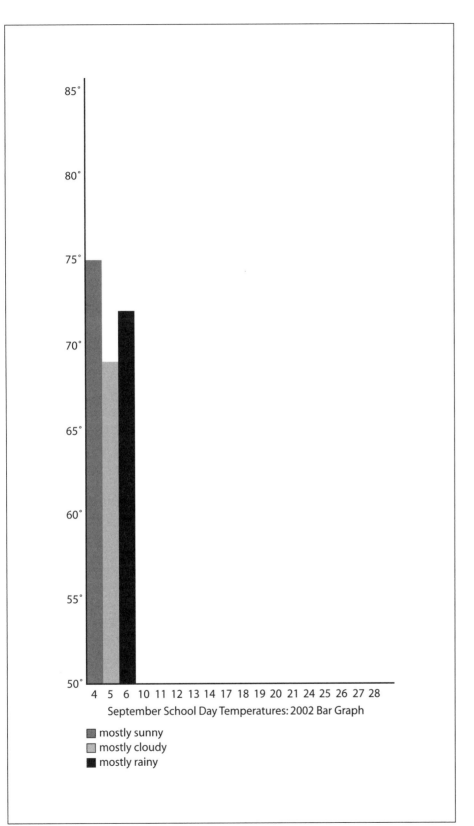

September School Day Temperatures: 2002 Bar Graph

■ mostly sunny
■ mostly cloudy
■ mostly rainy

FIGURE 1–4   ▶

This class has used red and purple *X*s to indicate who brought lunch on September 10–12.

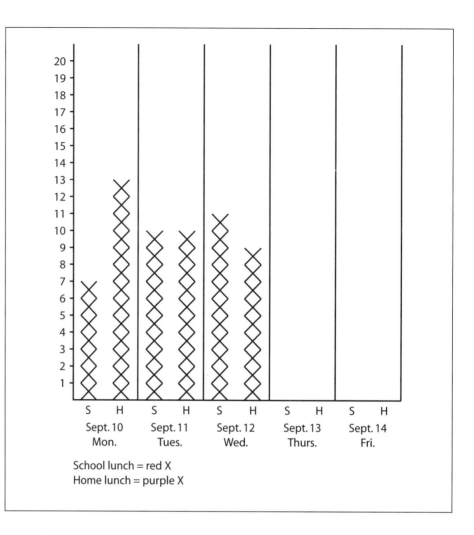

Teaching Materials

Math Manipulatives

Some teachers throw out manipulatives without knowing how expensive they are and without understanding their value to children. If you can find such materials hiding in supply closets, your colleagues' classrooms, or some other corner of the district, ask if you might borrow or keep them. Here are the materials you'll definitely need this year, with amounts adequate for about twenty students shown in parentheses:

- 1-by-1-inch colored tiles (about two thousand)
- interlocking cubes such as Unifix cubes, which connect on one side of each cube (about one thousand); or Snap Cubes, which connect on all six sides of each cube ($\frac{3}{4}$ inch; about one thousand)
- pattern blocks (about one thousand)
- wooden cubes (2 centimeter or 1 inch; about one thousand)

- plastic or real coins and dollar bills (200 pennies, 200 nickels, 100 dimes, and 80 quarters)

Get catalogues of math learning materials from companies such as ETA/Cuisenaire or Nasco and talk to your administrator about ordering before school begins. (To order learning materials, see the References section at the back of this book.) If there is no financial support for buying these items, look to grants and parent groups such as the PTA or turn to donations from your students' parents when school begins. Try to obtain these materials as soon as possible.

Also see if you can find the following materials hidden away in your school or in some other corner of your district:

- attribute blocks
- Cuisenaire rods
- geo blocks
- tangrams
- pentominoes
- base-ten blocks
- scales and weights

These items are not essential for your math program, but they will add richness to your students' mathematical experiences, especially your monthly math area, if available. Again, look in math catalogues to acquaint yourself with these materials.

How should you organize and store essential materials? It helps to put sets of manipulatives in gallon plastic bags, and then store them in big plastic tubs (such as dishpans). You could put each set of pattern blocks in one bag and then put the bags in a tub. This system will make it easier for you to provide materials for students. For example, if your students are seated at five tables of four and will be working with pattern blocks during a particular activity, you would want to have five gallon bags filled with pattern blocks—one bag per table. You can store these tubs on open shelves in the classroom when they're not being used.

With coins, consider filling small Ziplock plastic bags each with the following real or pretend coins: 20 pennies, 20 nickels, 10 dimes, and 8 quarters. Also include five one-dollar bills. Ideally, you'll have one "money bag" for every two children.

Store any nonessential materials—such as Cuisenaire rods, base-ten blocks, and so on—on designated shelves in the classroom where the children can easily retrieve them. Additional shelves should house essential materials such as rulers, dice, string, markers, pint and quart canning jars (at least ten of each size), small empty boxes (such as boxes for checkbooks, mugs, scarves, gloves), and so forth. All materials mentioned in this mathematics manipulatives section should be easily accessible tools for the children's mathematical problem-solving.

Blank Chart Paper

Some teachers use flip charts to write math concepts and vocabulary, equations, and children's responses to questions or problems. Others write on a single sheet of chart paper taped to the board and then roll up and secure the paper with clothespins until it's needed again. Still others write quickly on the white board and then transfer the writing to chart paper after school. The next day they post the chart paper on the board and unroll it for further math discussion.

Chart paper enables you to record the variety of strategies children use to make sense of different math problems and concepts, making it easier for students to see one another's reasoning. When appropriate—and with the children's permission—you can copy some of this "math talk" into parent newsletters so families can see the power of discussion in the mathematics classroom.

Playing Cards

Many of the activities described in this book require the use of playing cards. Before school begins, obtain enough sets of cards to hand out to table groups of students. For example, if you're planning to have five table groups of four students, obtain ten sets of playing cards, one deck for each partner pair.

Lined, Unlined, and Grid Paper

Store reams of lined, three-hole-punched paper on a shelf for your students. Some children may want to use it to back up their oral responses to math problems with drawings and, diagrams. Also provide stacks of unlined, three-hole-punched copy paper in white and other colors. If you ask students to draw or write something on unlined paper, children who have difficulty writing without lines can put a piece of lined paper behind the unlined page and use the lines to guide their work. Finally, provide stacks of 2 centimeter grid paper, $\frac{1}{2}$-inch grid paper, $\frac{3}{4}$-inch grid paper, and 1-inch grid paper (see Blackline Masters). Children will find grid paper helpful for drawing rectangular window arrays (see Chapter 3) and building boxes (see Chapter 9).

Math Folders

Obtain colored folders with inside pockets for children to organize their work. Select a color for math that's different from work folders used for other work (such as language arts or science). Each child will get one math folder. Before school begins, write each child's name on the cover of his or her folder. Students will store loose papers in their folders, putting their names and the date on each page. They can keep the folders in their desks when they're not using them, or put them in hanging files in an open, moveable cabinet in the classroom.

Plan to collect these math folders from students at the end of each day and look over their contents. You'll gain valuable insights into each child's understandings and misunderstandings, as well as the various strategies the children are using to make sense of math problems. You can then use your observations to plan the next day's lessons. Periodically, you can also review a child's folder contents in chronological order to assess progress and trouble spots. The resulting insights can prove handy during parent/teacher conferences. Children can also use the folders during parent/student/teacher conferences, pulling out work samples showing their favorite assignment, their strongest work, or their most difficult problem.

You'll likely want to create your own confidential folders for your students, and keep them in the top drawer of your file cabinet. In each folder, record observations and thoughts about the child's progress and needs, and store work samples.

Class List

Prepare photocopies of your class list to keep track of students' accomplishments. Organize names in a way that works best for you. I like to list my students alphabetically by first name down the left side of an $8\frac{1}{2}$-by-11-inch sheet. I then create five or six columns across the sheet. I enter the name of an assignment at the top of each column, then fill in each box with brief anecdotal notes about the child's understanding of the activity—for example, uses skip counting; counts up to compare; lost when adding four numbers. I also use these lists to quickly check off work completed and work not completed.

Sticky Notes

You may want to obtain a stack of 2-by-2-inch sticky notes to keep nearby at all times. These come in handy when you want to jot down observations about children's mathematical "ahas" or mathematical misunderstandings. For instance, when I notice that a child has suddenly grasped a key math concept, such as skip-counting instead of adding, I quickly record the concept, the child's name, and the date on a sticky note. I also record confusions a child exhibits in his or her work or through questions asked in class. For example, a child who keeps writing an addition story problem and thinks it is a multiplication story problem.

At the end of the day, I reread these notes, decide which students will need attention the next day, and stick the notes in chronological sequence inside the front covers of the confidential folders I've prepared for my students. I review these notes at the culmination of each unit to remind myself of who needs my attention during menu time. I also use the notes to refresh my understanding of each child's strengths and struggles before filling out report cards and having parent/student/teacher conferences.

Of course, you'll develop your own systems for tracking important moments in your students' math learning. This is just one approach that I've found helpful.

Rather than write directly on children's written work, I often use sticky notes. When I begin asking children to explain their reasoning in mathematics using words, numbers, and labeled pictures on paper, I make comments on the notes about what is clear and convincing and ask questions about what is not clear. I attach the notes to the students' papers. I expect children to use my comments to go over their written work and make it stronger. This is the same process I use in writers' workshop with first drafts.

Children's-Literature Titles

Each chapter of this book describes activities you can draw from titles published in Scholastic's Hello Math Reader children's-literature series. (See the References section at the end of this book.) I've recommended these books because they're small, reasonably priced paperbacks (less than $5.00 per title). Each volume also includes an "About Activities" section in which Marilyn Burns discusses the story's mathematics and suggests problems relating to the story. You may find many of these suggested books are in your school library, colleagues' classroom libraries, or your district curriculum center. Plan to allow children to borrow these books and take them home to share with families.

Chapter 2

September/ October

ADDITION AND SUBTRACTION

"By allowing time for thinking, believing that young students can solve problems, listening carefully to their explanations, and structuring an environment that values the work that students do, teachers promote problem solving and help students make their strategies explicit."

Principles and Standards for School Mathematics
NCTM 2000, 119

Before school begins, even the most seasoned teachers have doubts about whether their plans for teaching mathematics are the best possible ones and whether their students will be excited about their learning. Take heart. Use this anxiety to focus on getting to know your students as you build a community of learners. ▪

The Learning Environment

Listen carefully and ask questions to get at each child's sense making.

It takes practice to ask questions that help children open up and explain how they're making sense of a problem. But the rewards are great, as you open up the mathematics classroom to children's ideas. You step away from being the teacher who "tells" the child how to do the math and become the teacher who "facilitates" each child's unique approach to sense making. Your curiosity about your students' ideas makes the mathematics classroom come alive.

Here are some questions to include in your repertoire. You will likely augment or substitute these with your own ideas as the month progresses.

"How did you figure out your answer?"

"How do you know that your answer makes sense?"

"Who can explain what _____ said in your own words?"

"Who did this problem another way? How did you do it?"

"How have you made sense of this problem?"

"Do you have any questions you want to ask about the problem or about someone's solution?"

Build a caring community of active listeners and questioners who look at mistakes as an opportunity to learn.

Most children will not risk sharing their thoughts if they feel they might be laughed at for mistakes or if they feel ignored. Thus it's your job to insist on active listening to and acceptance of each child's ideas. Stop everything if some children are not listening, and re-engage them by asking "Who can explain what _____ said in your own words?" Sometimes having children first share their strategies with a partner before sharing with the whole group can be helpful. Make sure the children understand that, in your classroom, mistakes are considered opportunities for learning.

At the beginning of the year, your students will be more eager to share their very own ideas than listen to others' ideas. Insist that children put their hands down when someone is speaking and that they turn and look at the speaker. Keep math discussions short and fast paced—aim for ten to fifteen minutes at the most. In *Teaching Arithmetic: Lessons for Addition and Subtraction, Grades 2–3* (2001), Bonnie Tank and Lynne Zolli suggest giving students a job to do while they're listening during class discussions. For example: "Your job is to listen to Kim's report and see if her strategy is like yours," "Listen to Brian's strategy so you can describe it in your own words," or "Collin's strategy is similar to one we've already heard; see if you can figure out whose strategy it's like."

You will also find that some students are reluctant to speak up during whole-group discussions but share their ideas in small groups. Perhaps you can encourage reluctant children to share their small-group idea with the whole class the next day or ask them if it's OK for you to share their ideas.

You might also post a list of class rules and refer to them regularly during the first few weeks of school. Engage the children in discussions about what they think each of the rules means. Redirect the children's attention to certain rules when you notice that the rule is being followed especially well or when problems arise. Examples of rules might include:

- Be fair and friendly to one another.
- Quietly look at, listen to, and learn from one another.
- Work thoughtfully and stay on task.
- Ask questions when you do not understand.

Provide a variety of problem-solving experiences in meaningful contexts.

Children do not all follow the same route on their journey to understanding addition and subtraction. For that reason, you will want to provide a variety of problem-solving experiences through which children add and subtract in contexts that have meaning for them. Some children will gain a sudden understanding when working with manipulatives. Others will have "mathematical moments" while playing games. Some children construct their understanding while writing story problems, and others make sense of mathematics by listening to and reading children's literature. Still others find meaning by measuring things or dealing with money. This book provides suggested problem-solving activities for each context.

The same is true for you, the teacher. You may be drawn to using children's literature in mathematics instruction, or perhaps you find games a natural fit for your teaching. Begin by teaching to your comfort level or your passion. Remind yourself that *your* excitement and interest feed those of the children.

Celebrate each child's voice in the mathematics classroom.

When you show curiosity and enthusiasm for a child's insights or strategy, other students will follow your lead. As you record a strategy on chart paper posted on the white board or on an easel, write the child's name. Other students and their parents will soon realize that children's ideas count in this classroom. As mentioned in Chapter 1, you can share these charts of strategies with parents during conferences and/or "Back to School" night.

When someone presents a "never before shared" strategy, refer to it by the child's name for the rest of the year. For example, early in September, Nan decided that skip-counting was a meaningful way to group and count how many stars she could draw in a minute. For the rest of the school year, I referred to skip-counting as Nan's Strategy, and recorded it on the wall chart titled *Addition Strategies*. Later, I added it to the *Multiplication Strategies* wall chart.

Ray discovered that he could make sense of subtraction by breaking up the subtrahend into smaller numbers. In the problem where there were 37 birds and 19 flew away, the question was how many were left? Ray thought of the subtrahend, 19, as 10 + 9 then he first subtracted the 10 from 37 (37 – 10 = 27). His next move was to take the 9 away from 27. To do this, he thought of 9 as 7 + 2. Next he took the 7 from the 27 (27 – 7 = 20). Finally he reasoned that 20 – 2 = 18. This became Ray's strategy, and it was added to the wall chart titled *Subtraction Strategies*. Notice how Ray first decomposed 19 then 9.

Early in the school year, you'll find that several of your third graders are beginning to reason mentally when they add and subtract. When asked to share their strategies, they may say, "I just know." Explain that you cannot hear and see what is going on inside their minds, so you need to hear and see words, numbers, and perhaps pictures to understand how they figured out their answers.

The Mathematics

Children use a variety of strategies to make sense of numbers up to 100.

Youngsters initially add and subtract by counting things one by one, then they group objects or quantities as they count by using models, such as manipulatives or pictures. Eventually, they begin to think numerically with the help of words and pictures. Finally, they reason numerically in their heads by using mental computation. Different children will reach different stages in this journey at different times. To build a firm foundation for this eventual numerical thinking, all children need to add and subtract using numbers up to 20 before moving on to numbers up to 100. Students practice the *repeating* patterns of counting (1, 2, 3; 11, 12, 13; 21, 22, 23) and the *growing* patterns of counting (1, 2, 3; 10, 20, 30). Guard against moving the children too quickly into operations with larger numbers. You'll have sufficient time for this when the class revisits addition and subtraction in the spring. Even then, you will want to support children's reasoning with numbers in the 100s before jumping to numbers in the 1,000s.

Children need continued counting and grouping experiences.

To grasp that numbers stand for quantities or relate directly to things in the real world, children need experience counting tangible or visible objects. Working with numbers on a page is not enough. Students make sense of numbers by seeing how many of their classmates are wearing tennis shoes and how many are not, how many beans in their right hand versus beans in their left hand, how many stars they can draw in a minute, and other counting activities. When you see this kind of activity going on, notice which children count objects one by one and which group objects by 2s, 5s, or 10s. Ask yourself, "Do the children who count one by one realize that the last number counted represents the quantity, so they can count on instead of starting all over again?" (For example, Jarod knows that there are 15 tiles here, so he counts on: 16, 17, 18, 19.) Once children are comfortable counting on, encourage them to group as they count. For instance, it's more efficient to count thirty-six cubes by grouping the cubes into 10s or 5s first, compared to counting one cube at a time. By grouping the cubes into 10s, students can come up with 10 + 10 + 10 = 30 cubes, with 6 cubes remaining—and 30 + 6 = 36.

When children group things by 2s, 5s, 10s, or other numbers as they count, they begin to skip-count. Instead of adding three groups of ten cubes by thinking "ten plus ten plus ten equals thirty," students skip-count by thinking "ten, twenty, thirty," adding as they go. When children count objects by first organizing them into equal-size groups (three groups times ten cubes in each group equals thirty cubes), they begin to make sense of multiplication. They also build the groundwork for division (thirty cubes divided into three equal groups means there are ten cubes in each group).

Children make sense of numbers by breaking them into familiar or "friendly" parts.

After children have had many counting and grouping experiences with manipulatives, they represent these experiences with pictures and numbers. They begin making sense of addition and subtraction by decomposing or partitioning the numbers, as Ray did when he subtracted 37 – 19 on page 18.

Eventually children rely less on counting real objects or drawing pictures, and begin reasoning numerically both mentally and on paper by breaking numbers into familiar parts. When adding 25 + 19, they might think of 25 as 20 + 5 and 19 as 10 + 9. They are breaking the numbers according to place value. They are *using* place value to make sense of the numbers instead of just *naming* the place value of 10s and 1s. Then they add 20 + 10 to get 30 and 5 + 9 to get 14. Finally, they figure out that 30 + 14 = 44 because 30 + 10 = 40 and 40 + 4 = 44.

Presenting problems horizontally enables children to decompose and recompose numbers more easily than presenting them vertically.

$$25 + 19 = \qquad \begin{array}{r} 25 \\ + \ 19 \\ \hline \end{array}$$

In looking at a horizontal equation, students often make sense of the numbers by dealing with the 10s before the 1s. Many of us adults also reason this way, even though we were taught the paper-and-pencil procedure of always starting with the 1s and carrying to the 10s.

As your students solve problems, they will arrive at different places in their meaning making at different speeds. Some need manipulatives to count as they make sense of an addition or subtraction situation. Others find that pictures and words help them sort out their thinking. By recording their strategies, you model how children represent their thinking numerically. Remind yourself that the child who reasons numerically most of the time may turn to manipulatives or pictures to tackle new problem-solving situations. We adults do the same thing. Also, be aware that a child who works mostly with pictures or manipulatives might reason numerically for some problem situations. Continue to accept and celebrate all strategies that make sense.

Children make sense of numbers by going to nearby friendly numbers.

A child might figure out 25 + 19 by thinking that 19 is close to 20, a friendly number. Then she adds 25 + 20, getting 45. Finally, she compensates by taking away the 1 added to the 19 by reasoning that 45 − 1 = 44. This child went to a nearby friendly number rather than breaking the two addends into familiar parts.

When Ray subtracted 37 − 19 on page 18, he first broke each number into familiar parts or friendly numbers by place value. Then he went to nearby familiar or friendly numbers in his second step when he subtracted 27 − 9. He thought of 9 as 7 + 2 and began by taking 27 − 7 to get to 20, a nearby familiar number. From there he took away the 2 and thought 20 − 2 = 18.

Friendly numbers are often multiples of 5 or 10. This makes sense in a number system based on 10. When adding 23 + 75, a child might think of 23 as 25. She then thinks that 25 + 75 = 100. Then she compensates by taking away the 2 added on to 23, making it 25. She concludes that $100 - 2 = 98$.

Children think and reason as they make sense of the addition combinations.

So often, we assume that children must learn their basic addition combinations up to 20 by memorizing through rote repetition. Instead, we need to encourage youngsters to think and reason—to use number sense as they learn these combinations and apply them to larger numbers. Here are some strategies that support such meaning making:

- *Doubles + 1, – 1:* Children find doubles, such as $3 + 3 = 6$ and $9 + 9 = 18$, meaningful. They use their understanding of doubles to make sense of other combinations. For example, to make sense of $3 + 4$, the child reasons that $3 + 3 = 6$, then you add 1 to get 7. To make sense of $9 + 8$, the child thinks that $9 + 9 = 18$, then you take away 1 and get 17. The student can then apply the same thinking to $33 + 4$. She knows that $33 + 3 = 36$, so 1 more equals 37.

- *Going for the nearest 10 or multiple of 10:* The number 10 is a friendly number that helps children make sense of other addition combinations. For instance, $8 + 3$ becomes $8 + 2 = 10$, then add 1 to get 11. (Notice how the 3 has been decomposed into $2 + 1$.) And $9 + 7$ becomes $9 + 1 = 10$, then add on the remaining 6 to get 16. (The 7 has been decomposed into $1 + 6$.) This thinking makes sense for larger numbers as well. To illustrate, $49 + 7$ can be $49 + 1 = 50$, plus 6 more gets you 56.

- *Putting the larger number first when adding:* Because addition is commutative, the addends can be placed in any order and the sum will remain the same. This characteristic of addition provides students with a valuable strategy if they like to add by going for the nearest 10. For example, $3 + 8$ becomes $8 + 3$, then you reason $8 + 2 = 10$, then 1 more gets you 11. And $7 + 9$ becomes $9 + 7$, so you think $9 + 1 = 10$ then $10 + 6 = 16$. This works for larger numbers as well. For instance, $3 + 28$ becomes $28 + 3$, then you reason that $28 + 2 = 30$, then $30 + 1 = 31$.

Children make connections between addition and subtraction.

For $11 - 9 = 2$, some children might write eleven tally marks, then cross out nine. Others might start at 11 on the 1–100 chart, then "count back" nine squares. More and more children connect addition to the inverse operation, subtraction. These children reason numerically that $11 - 9 = 2$ because they know that $2 + 9 = 11$.

Many children make sense of comparison subtraction problems ("how many more," "how many less," "what is the difference") by using addition or counting up. For example, if one child has sixteen pencils and another child has seven pencils, a child might figure out the difference by thinking 7 + 3 = 10 then adding 6 to get 16. Then the child adds the 3 to the 6 and gets 9 as the difference. Another child might reason that since 7 + 9 = 16, and 16 is 9 greater than 7, then 9 is the difference. Still another child might draw 16 pencils in one row and 7 pencils in another row directly underneath, then count the difference between the two rows.

Your job is to accept and celebrate each strategy. Gradually, your students will be able to reason mentally and numerically because it is more efficient. However, you will want them to bring concrete experiences and understanding with both take-away and comparison subtraction to the more abstract numerical strategies.

TEACHER-TO-TEACHER TALK The rest of this chapter is filled with possible problem-solving situations to consider for your mathematics program. The ideas come from many sources. Go gently, using only those ideas that make sense to you and interest you. Be sure your students are solving combining problems (cubes in a jar, handfuls of beans) as well as comparing (temperature) and separating or take-away problems (the *Give and Take* game).

As you plan, think about providing a balance of math experiences through games, money and measurement problems, situations drawn from children's literature, and the writing of story problems. And remember that any mistakes you might make are also learning opportunities. Provide time for meaningful math conversations with a few selected problems, rather than trying to do them all.

Mathematics Throughout the Day

Classroom routines such as daily attendance, lunch count, and daily temperature readings provide a real-world context for math problems. They also give children opportunities to practice their addition and subtraction skills within contexts that interest them.

Daily Attendance

If your classroom has twenty children and they are all present when you take attendance, create an addition/subtraction problem from this situation. For example, point out that "all twenty of you are here today and twelve of you are boys. How many girls are present and how do you know?" Encourage the children to use paper and pencil, beans and interlocking cubes, or mental figuring to solve the problem. As the children share their solution strategies, record each strategy on chart paper. Some children may think of this challenge as an addition problem ($12 + \_\_ = 20$). Others may use subtraction ($20 - 12 = \_\_$). After students have offered their solutions, you could have them come up and stand in groups of boys and girls for a data check.

When you feel that students have gained confidence in their reasoning with these smaller numbers, help them make the connection to larger numbers. For example, "If there were thirty of you in the class and twenty-two of you were boys, how many girls would there be?"

On subsequent days, you may identify other problems to pose. For instance, if seventeen of your twenty students are present when you take attendance, and eight of them are girls, ask how many boys that leaves. After a few days of posing these sorts of problems, invite students to come up with their own attendance questions. Also, start showing attendance data on a graph like the one shown in Chapter 1.

Extensions

If the children tire of gathering attendance data from your classroom only, consider combining your class data with that of another third-grade class. Eventually, you could do attendance graphs for all the third-grade classrooms at your school.

Lunch Count

The daily count for school lunch provides another real-life opportunity for mathematical thinking as your class determines how many children brought a bag lunch and how many will order a school lunch. Designate a "classroom data collector" to record the information on a graph like the one shown in Chapter 1. This same student could record that day's attendance and temperature.

Pose questions similar to those you present for attendance. For example, "Eleven of you brought bag lunches, and twenty of you are in class today. How many of you are going to buy lunch?" If the children tire of experiences with numbers 20 and under, you can present word-problem extensions for classrooms with 30 students.

Today's Number

As we saw in Chapter 1, you can make *Today's Number* a daily routine in your classroom in a variety of ways. For example, the date could serve as the special number for each day during the first month. For each date, students could try coming up with as many different equations as possible to arrive at that number. Revisiting the September 8 example, the children might offer the following responses:

$$6 + 2 = 8$$

$$4 + 4 = 8$$

$$5 + 3 = 8$$

$$(100 - 100) + 8 = 8$$

$$10 - 2 = 8$$

$$100 - 92 = 8$$

Some children might write equations in systematic patterns; e.g., $1 + 7 = 8$, $2 + 6 = 8$, $3 + 5 = 8$, and so forth. Or $9 - 1 = 8$, $10 - 2 = 8$, $11 - 3 = 8$, etc. TERC calls this approach modifying numerical expressions systematically. (See Figure 2–1.)

As the children offer equations, record them (with their originators' names) on the board under the date. The next day, ask a student to review the list and identify children who have not yet offered equations. Encourage those children to suggest equations for the next round of *Today's Number* (the date).

You can also suggest some interesting rules for *Today's Number*. For the 9th day, for example,

- Use only one operation (addition *or* subtraction) today: $2 + 7 = 9$; $11 - 2 = 9$
- Use three numbers today: $2 + 3 + 4 = 9$; $(20 - 17) + 6 = 9$

After every *Today's Number* session, ask the children to write the resulting equations in their math notebooks or on loose pages that they can then store in their math folders. Consider collecting the notebooks or folders periodically and checking the equations.

Today's Temperature

On the day before school starts, record the outdoor temperature during the early afternoon. Put the information on a temperature graph like the one shown in Chapter 1. Then, on the first day of school, ask a student or the "daily data collector" to record that day's temperature right after lunch and add his or her finding to the graph. Invite the class to discuss which temperature is higher and how much higher, or which temperature

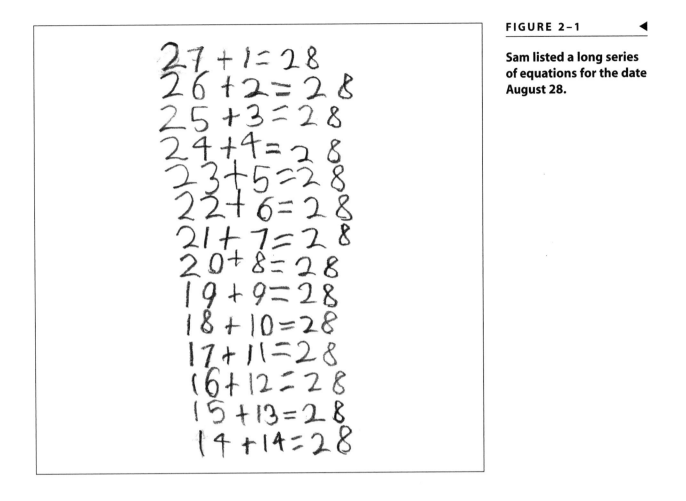

is lower and how much lower. You could also ask students to determine the difference between the two temperatures.

As the children share their answers and how they got them, record their responses. Point out solution strategies that involve addition or counting up numerically, as well as those entailing subtraction or counting down numerically. If children use 1–100 charts and interlocking cubes to arrive at answers, record these more concrete strategies with diagrams and pictures on the board.

Your students will use a variety of strategies to compare temperatures. For example, suppose the temperature is 56 degrees one day and 70 degrees the next. In this case, some children will go to the daily-temperature graph and count the grid squares from the 56 up to the 70 on the y-axis. Other children will reason mentally by thinking of 56 as 60. If they know that 10 is the difference between 60 and 70, they might add the 4 needed to go from 56 to 60. The total difference they arrive at is 14.

Others might use paper and pencil to "count up" in number-line fashion from the smaller number to the larger. They find the difference between the two numbers by going from left to right on the imaginary number line or by adding up using two steps. (See below.) This number-line approach was a strategy used first by Marcus, Eun-Jin and Janet. It became a strategy which made sense to many children. (See Figure 2–2.)

$$+\,4 \qquad +\,10$$

$$56 \longrightarrow 70 \quad or \quad 56 + \quad 4 = 60$$

$$\qquad 60 \qquad\qquad\qquad 60 + \underline{10} = 70$$

$$14$$

Some children might "count down" from 70 to 56 by going from right to left on an imaginary number line or counting down using two steps. (See below.)

$$-\,4 \qquad -\,10$$

$$56 \longleftarrow 70 \quad or \quad 70 - 10 = 60$$

$$\qquad 60 \qquad\qquad\qquad 60 - \underline{4} = 56$$

$$14$$

Still other children might decompose 56 into 50 + 6 and reason that 70 minus 50 equals 20, and 20 minus 6 is 14.

A child may also use the traditional borrowing procedure shown below:

$$\begin{array}{r} {}^{6\;1}\!\!\!\not{7}0 \\ +\ 56 \\ \hline 14 \end{array}$$

After recording this traditional procedure, ask the child why the 7 is crossed out and 6 is written above it, and why a 10 is written over the 6 in 56. Then ask yourself, *Does she realize she decomposed 70 into 60 plus 10? Does she think 10 minus 6 and 60 minus 50, or is she thinking 6 minus 5 without a sense of the magnitude of the numbers or an understanding of place value?*

Extensions

Have children work in pairs to solve temperature comparison problems using two different strategies. Being able to use more than one strategy helps children build flexibility with numbers and check their work. Also, working in pairs encourages each partner to participate in the problem solving.

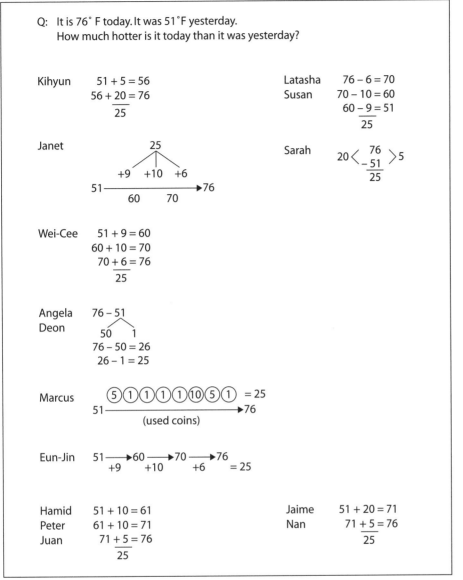

FIGURE 2–2 ◀

This class generated a variety of creative solutions to a temperature comparison problem.

Q: It is 76° F today. It was 51°F yesterday.
How much hotter is it today than it was yesterday?

Kihyun
51 + 5 = 56
56 + 20 = 76
—
25

Latasha
Susan
76 – 6 = 70
70 – 10 = 60
60 – 9 = 51
—
25

Janet
25
+9 +10 +6
51 ——————→76
60   70

Sarah
20 ⟨ 76
     –51
     —
     25 ⟩ 5

Wei-Cee
51 + 9 = 60
60 + 10 = 70
70 + 6 = 76
—
25

Angela
Deon
76 – 51
50   1
76 – 50 = 26
26 – 1 = 25

Marcus
⑤①①①①⑩⑤① = 25
51 ——————————→76
(used coins)

Eun-Jin
51 ——→60 ——→70 ——→76
  +9   +10   +6   = 25

Hamid
Peter
Juan
51 + 10 = 61
61 + 10 = 71
71 + 5 = 76
—
25

Jaime
Nan
51 + 20 = 71
71 + 5 = 76
—
25

TEACHER-TO-TEACHER TALK In your classroom, you might see some or none of these strategies emerge. You may also see new strategies that you've never encountered before. Give yourself permission to listen to all your students' ideas rather than feeling compelled to present the ideas you see here. Remind yourself that rather than teaching by telling, you are facilitating the ways your children make sense of their mathematics. When children feel free to do their own thinking and reasoning, you never know *what* you're going to hear and see! If the strategies make sense, encourage their use. Sometimes you might want to write up the variety of strategies children used on a particular problem and post the chart for the children to examine and discuss. (See Figure 2–2.) This same chart can be useful during discussions with parents about honoring children's meaning-making.

FIGURE 2–3 ▶

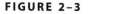

Deon used two strategies to find the difference between 86 and 52 degrees.

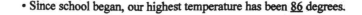

• Since school began, our highest temperature has been <u>86</u> degrees.

• Since school began, our lowest temperature has been <u>52</u> degrees.

1. What is the difference between these two temperatures? <u>34</u> degrees
Explain step by step how you figured this out.

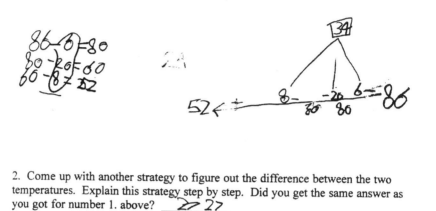

2. Come up with another strategy to figure out the difference between the two temperatures. Explain this strategy step by step. Did you get the same answer as you got for number 1. above? <u>27</u>

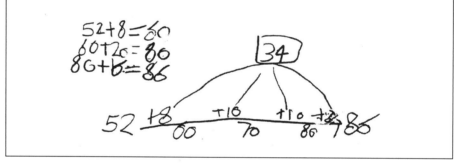

Later, you can assign the same types of story problems as homework, again asking for two solution strategies. (See Figure 2–3.)

Snack Time

Snack Time is a good opportunity for children to practice grouping and counting, using raisins, fish crackers, or other snacks you provide. To leverage this context, first model on the overhead projector how you plan to group and count your own handful of twenty-seven raisins.

First, place your thirty-five raisins on the overhead, then group them by 10s. You'll have three groups of ten and five leftovers. Turn to the board and show the children a picture of these groupings. Draw three circles, each with ten dots inside. Draw the five leftover dots off to the side without a circle. Now add numbers to your pictures. Either write *10, 10, 10,* next to each circle or write skip counts *10, 20, 30.* Write *R5* by the leftovers. Explain that when we make equal-size groups for counting, we call the leftover pieces *remainders* (R). Later, this wording will help children make sense of division. With help from the children, write the equation *30 + R5 = 35.*

Place a clean $8\frac{1}{2}$-by-11-inch sheet of paper on each student's desk. Then give each child a handful of raisins for counting. Leave your demonstration equations on the board for the children to use as references. Invite the children to group, count, and record the number of raisins they received from you. When the children finish, help them check the accuracy of their work. If their reasoning makes sense, give them permission to eat the snack.

Then use the overhead projector to model another way to group and count your own raisins. For example, consider organizing your raisins into seven groups of five. Draw seven circles with five dots inside each. Note that there are no remainders. Then write a *5* by each circle or use skip-counting to arrive at the 35: 5, 10, 15, 20, 25, 30, 35. Point out how your second grouping and counting lets you check your first way of counting. By getting the same answer each time (35), you can feel more confident that your answer is correct.

Offer an extension that children can do after they consume their snack, so those who work more slowly or need more support will not feel rushed.

Extensions

- Have each child who finishes the snack group and count his or her raisins a second way.
- Have the children figure out a way to group, count, and record their raisins in a way that doesn't involve counting by 10s or by 5s.
- After the children have completed their work, write up some of their findings as problems. (See Figure 2–4 on the following page.)

Games

Games provide a welcome context for children to practice addition and subtraction. During math games, children interact socially as they explain and listen to one another's reasoning. In the games described below, the mathematical thinking the children engage in is more important than who wins and who loses.

You already have favorite addition and subtraction games; this section suggests others. Be sure to play each game yourself so you have a sense of the mathematics involved.

FIGURE 2–4   ▶

Aaron's strategies for grouping and counting his raisins became the data for these story problems which Sarah did as homework.

1. Aaron grouped his raisins into 2 groups with 10 raisins in each group. He had 7 raisins leftover. Show his groupings with a picture then represent the math with an equation.

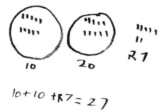

2. Then Aaron grouped his raisins into 5 groups with 5 raisins in each group. he had 2 raisins left over. Show his groupings with a picture then represent the math with an equation.

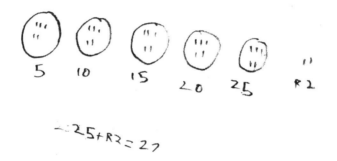

3. Now you group and count Aaron's raisins in a different way. Show your groupings with a picture then represent the math with an equation.

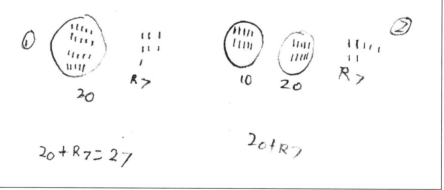

Guess My Rule

This is a great sorting and classifying game that's ideal for the first week of school, when children are fidgety and are getting to know one another. In *Mathematical Thinking at Grade 3* (Russell and Economopoulos 1995) you will find further ideas for gathering and recording data during this game.

TEACHER-TO-TEACHER TALK Games are a great way to make mathematics a positive part of family life. If you play some games with parents during Back-to-School Night, model the importance of having each player explain his or her thinking, and celebrate the variety of ideas being shared by pointing to the strategy charts in the room. Families can become meaningful partners in children's math learning and enjoyment. Perhaps you could ask that each family invest in two dice and one deck of standard playing cards (not pinochle).

Some families do not approve of dice, but are willing to use number cubes (cubes with a number written on each face) or index cards cut in half with numbers written on them—four 1s, four 2s, four 3s, four 4s, four 5s, and four 6s. (See Dice Number Cards, in Blackline Masters.) These number cards can be mixed up and drawn from a bag or a bowl.

Have children play games often in class before they introduce the games at home. You may want to send home 1–100 charts for regular use as the children count up (add or compare) and count down (take away) during the games. Also encourage the use of manipulatives such as beans or pennies.

Instructions

1. Think of a secret criterion for your students, such as "children wearing watches." Some students will fit your "rule," while others will not.

2. Invite several students who fit the rule to come up and stand in a group on one side of the room. Then invite others who don't fit the rule to stand in a different group.

3. Ask class members to carefully observe the two groups and try to guess your rule.

4. Once people have figured out the rule and you've grouped everyone into one category or the other, enlist the children's help in counting the number of students in each group and comparing the results.

In conducting this activity, make sure your students understand that some of them will fit your secret rule and some will not. Point out that those who do not fit the rule will be just as helpful in figuring out the secret rule as those who do fit. The purpose of the game is to *figure out* the rule, not to *fit* the rule. To get this message across, you might suggest that mathematics is like detective work. Each child will need to reason and observe.

Also set some standards for responding to the activity. As you bring up students and put them in categories, insist that class members take some quiet time to "observe and think inside your own head." No one is to raise his or her hand yet. Next, have side-by-side partners talk quietly with one another about what they think the rule might be. Finally, ask for a volunteer who fits the rule to come up and join the appropriate group. *At this point, insist that no one call out the rule.* Class members may only respond to the volunteer's choice of group by saying, "You fit the rule" or "You don't fit the rule." Repeat the process with several more volunteers, some of whom fit the rule and others who don't.

Only after most of the children are standing in one or the other group and seem to have an idea about the rule should you invite the class to guess. Ask several children what their guess is and why they guessed it.

As you play your first rounds of *Guess My Rule*, encourage the children to record their counts using stick figures to represent the numbers of children in each group. After several rounds, suggest that students express their findings more abstractly, using tally marks or check marks. Once the data are graphed, ask some *comparison* questions, such as, "Which group has more members—the group with watches on or the group without watches? How *many* more? How do you know how many more?" You could also ask *combining* questions: "If we combine the numbers in both groups, how many children would we have altogether? How did you figure that out?"

Race for a Dollar

The children can play this game in partners or in a group of four at their team table.

Materials

- 2 dice and 1 money bag for group (see Chapter 1 for instructions on preparing money bags)

Instructions

1. Players remove the contents from their money bag and put them on the table.

2. Players take turns rolling the dice. The sum of the dice tells the child how much money to take from the pile. If a player rolls a sum higher than 5, he or she can exchange five pennies for a nickel.

3. As players accumulate money, they keep "trading up"; e.g., two nickels for a dime, two dimes and a nickel for a quarter, etc. The game ends when one player has enough coins to exchange for a dollar.

Give and Take

This card game is similar to the familiar game called *War* or *Snap*. Children practice their addition and subtraction combinations when they play.

Give and Take

You need:
   a deck of playing cards per pair of players (with jokers removed)
   a sign that reads Jack = 11, Queen = 12, King = 13, Ace = 1
   a 1–100 chart

Rules
1. The dealer shuffles the cards and deals them one at a time, starting with the partner.

2. Each player takes the top card off his or her pile and turns the card face up for the partner to see.

3. If Player 1 has a 10 and Player 2 has a 3, Player 1 gets to take both cards *after* he or she explains how much bigger 10 is than 3 by using addition ("I know that three plus seven equals ten.") or by using subtraction ("Ten take away three equals seven so ten is larger than three."). Or the child might place his or her finger on 3 on the 1–100 chart and count up seven spaces to get to 10. Player 2 listens to Player 1's thinking to be sure it makes sense.

4. If both players turn over cards of equal value, they turn over one more card each.

5. Play continues until players have used all the cards in their original pile. The winner is the player with the most cards in their Take pile.

6. Keep the emphasis on the addition and subtraction thinking that is shared between two players.

Extensions

In *Teaching Arithmetic: Lessons for Addition and Subtraction* (Tank and Zolli 2001), there is a game called *More*. In this version of the same game, Player 1 collects 7 interlocking cubes which represent the difference between 10 and 3. The player with the most cubes at the end of the game wins. You might want to refer to this resource for two other games—Fifteen-Number Cross-Out and Addition Tic-Tac-Toe.

Double Give and Take

In this version of *Give and Take*, the children practice their double-digit combinations by drawing two cards from the deck on each turn and adding to get the numbers they compare.

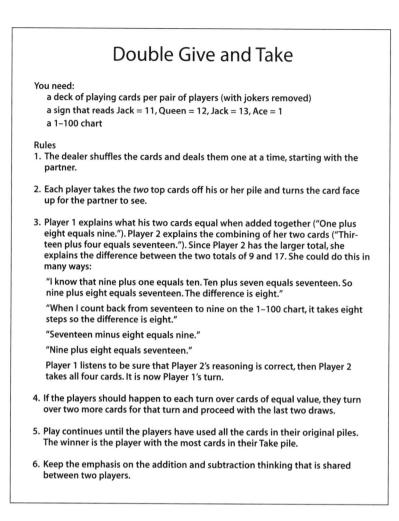

Double Give and Take

You need:
   a deck of playing cards per pair of players (with jokers removed)
   a sign that reads Jack = 11, Queen = 12, Jack = 13, Ace = 1
   a 1–100 chart

Rules
1. The dealer shuffles the cards and deals them one at a time, starting with the partner.

2. Each player takes the *two* top cards off his or her pile and turns the card face up for the partner to see.

3. Player 1 explains what his two cards equal when added together ("One plus eight equals nine."). Player 2 explains the combining of her two cards ("Thirteen plus four equals seventeen."). Since Player 2 has the larger total, she explains the difference between the two totals of 9 and 17. She could do this in many ways:

   "I know that nine plus one equals ten. Ten plus seven equals seventeen. So nine plus eight equals seventeen. The difference is eight."

   "When I count back from seventeen to nine on the 1–100 chart, it takes eight steps so the difference is eight."

   "Seventeen minus eight equals nine."

   "Nine plus eight equals seventeen."

   Player 1 listens to be sure that Player 2's reasoning is correct, then Player 2 takes all four cards. It is now Player 1's turn.

4. If the players should happen to each turn over cards of equal value, they turn over two more cards for that turn and proceed with the last two draws.

5. Play continues until the players have used all the cards in their original piles. The winner is the player with the most cards in their Take pile.

6. Keep the emphasis on the addition and subtraction thinking that is shared between two players.

TEACHER-TO-TEACHER TALK   To understand the importance of 10 in our number system, third graders need to know how to add 10 to and subtract 10 from any number up to 100 at this time of the school year. When children break numbers into their familiar parts to add or subtract, knowing how to add and subtract 10 becomes critical. For example, when adding 28 blue cubes and 13 orange cubes, children often think $20 + 10 = 30$ before they reason that $8 + 3 = 11$. And when figuring the difference between temperatures of 56 and 70 degrees, children often count up by adding 10 ($56 + 4 = 60$, then $60 + 10 = 70$), or they count down by subtracting 10 ($70 - 10 = 60$, then $60 - 4 = 56$). You may want to refer to *Plus, Minus, Stay the Same* in *Mathematical Thinking at Grade 3* (Russell and Economopoulos 1995). In this game, children make moves based on adding 10 to a number, taking 10 away from that number, or staying with the number as is.

Measurement

Children love to measure things as they connect mathematics to their own environment. In this context, they actively use addition and subtraction.

Cubes in a Jar (Volume)

In addition to volume, this activity also involves counting, adding, and subtracting.

Materials

- 2 pint-sized canning jars per pair of students
- 28 blue interlocking cubes and 13 orange cubes per pair of students

Instructions

Part 1: Demonstrate with Blue Cubes

1. Place the twenty-eight blue interlocking cubes into one of the canning jars. Place the thirteen orange cubes in the other canning jar.

2. Show the class the jar with the blue cubes in it. The jar should be pretty full.

3. Invite the children to guess how many cubes they believe are in the jar, and how they arrived at their guess.

4. Record the guesses on the board and discuss their range. To find the range, subtract the smallest guess from the largest one. If the smallest guess is "20 cubes" and the largest is "62 cubes," then the range is 42.

5. As the children watch, remove ten cubes from the jar and snap them together. Explain that now that the children have some data to use in their reasoning, they can estimate instead of guess the number of cubes in the jar.

6. Ask for their estimates, and record their responses on the board. (Ideally, the range of estimates will be smaller than the range of guesses. If not, students may need more experiences with estimating the number of objects in containers.)

7. Remove ten more cubes from the jar and snap them together. Then remove the eight leftovers. Write *28 blue cubes* on the board.

Part 2: Demonstrate with Orange Cubes

1. Show the children the jar containing thirteen orange cubes. The jar should be about half full.

2. Ask the children to estimate the number of cubes in the jar. (Based on their experience with the jar of blue cubes, some children will reason that this jar contains about half the number of cubes that were in the first jar. But don't be surprised if some children estimate twenty-eight cubes or more. Children often need many more concrete experiences like this before they start making connections between one jar that is full and another jar that is partially full.)

3. Encourage each child who volunteers an estimate to talk through his or her thinking.

4. Remove six or seven of the orange cubes from the jar and ask for revised estimates. Then, have the children help you count the thirteen cubes.

Part 3: Working in Pairs to Combine Cubes

1. That same day or the next, have the children work in pairs using their own table sets of twenty-eight blue cubes in one jar and thirteen orange cubes in a second jar. But explain that this time, their job is to figure out how many cubes they would have altogether if they combined the cubes from both jars.

2. If you think it appropriate, you might ask the children to figure out their total by using two different strategies. Below are some strategies you might hear. (Notice how the children and I represent the words with numbers and/or pictures.)

Strategy 1: Break Both Addends into Friendly Parts

I know that twenty-eight equals twenty plus eight. And thirteen is ten plus three. I am going to add the bigger numbers first: twenty plus ten is thirty. Then I'll add the smaller numbers: eight plus three is eleven. Then I'll add those two totals together: thirty plus eleven gets me forty-one as the final total.

$$
\begin{array}{r}
28 = 20 + 8 \\
+\ \ 13 = 10 + 3 \\
\hline
30 + 11 = 41
\end{array}
$$

This child has a good sense of number. She understands place value and puts the larger number first when adding. Many children do this so they can think and reason mentally in this way. ("I know that eight plus three equals eleven because eight plus two equals ten, then I add on one more. I know that thirty plus eleven equals forty-one, because thirty and ten equals forty, then I add on one more.")

Some children suggested that I use this representation on the board:

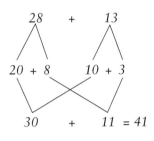

Strategy 2: Use Manipulatives to Go to Friendly Numbers

I made two ten-trains of interlocking cubes plus eight extra cubes to show twenty-eight cubes. Next I made one ten-train plus three extras to show thirteen. I put the three ten-trains together, then I took the extras, which were eleven, and made a ten-train plus one extra. I ended up with four ten-trains and one extra, and that equals forty-one. (See Figure 2–5.)

This child is more comfortable making sense of the numbers using manipulatives. Notice how well he makes sense of the place value idea of 10s. I did ask him how his strategy was like Strategy 1. He did not see the connection yet, so I didn't push it.

Strategy 3: Break the Smaller Addend into Friendly Parts

I think about the smaller number, which is thirteen, as ten plus three. First I add twenty-eight and ten, because ten is a friendly number to add, and that equals thirty-eight. Then I add on the three by thinking three equals two plus one. Next I add on the two to thirty-eight to get to another friendly number, forty, then I add on the one and get forty-one.

$$13 = 10 + 3 \qquad 28 + 10 = 38$$

$$3 = 2 + 1 \qquad 38 + 2 = 40$$

$$40 + 1 = 41$$

As you can see, this child reasons numerically by decomposing and recomposing numbers.

FIGURE 2–5   ▶

Jaime made ten-trains out of interlocking cubes to add 28 and 13.

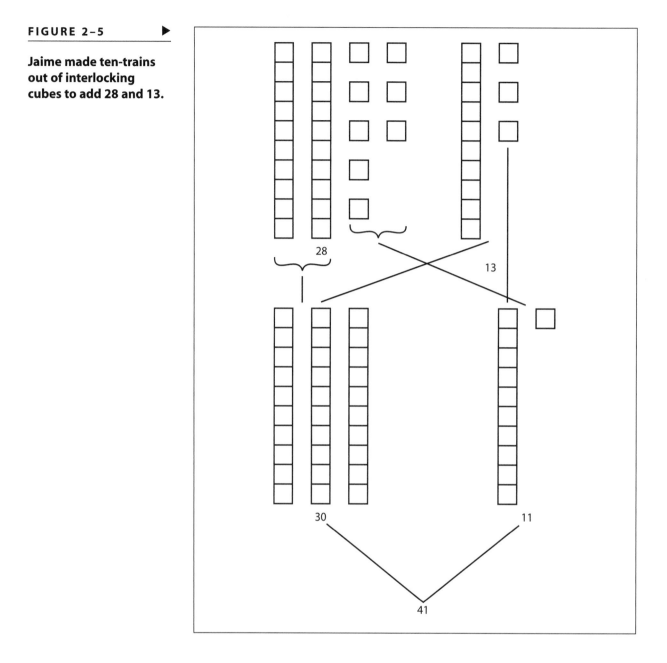

Strategy 4: Use the Traditional Carrying Procedure

I just put the twenty-eight above the thirteen and added by writing one below the eight plus three and one above the two plus one. When I added one plus two plus one, I got four and put it down here.

$$\begin{array}{r} \overset{1\,1}{2\!\!\!/8} \\ +\ 13 \\ \hline 41 \end{array}$$

This child followed the traditional procedure of carrying when adding. But notice how he does not talk of "ten plus twenty plus ten." He lacks a sense of place value. Perhaps you could have the children help you connect this traditional procedure to the use of the interlocking cubes in the previous strategy.

Sometimes children gain a better sense of place value when adding vertically by arranging the numbers in this format:

$$30 < \overset{28}{\underset{\;}{\underline{+\;13}}} > 11$$
$$41$$

TEACHER-TO-TEACHER TALK Notice how I am modeling different ways in which students' words can be represented with numbers. When children have their own way of using the numbers to explain their thinking, I add those to the strategies list. Also notice that I am not prioritizing which strategies are "best." I want the students to look, listen, and think about which strategies make sense to each of them. My hope is that each child will find a couple of the strategies useful and will employ more than one strategy when approaching a math problem.

Part 4: Working in Pairs to Compare Cubes

1. Now challenge your students to figure out the difference between the twenty-eight blue cubes and thirteen orange cubes. Ask the question in one of the following ways: "What is the difference between twenty-eight cubes and thirteen cubes?" "How many more blue cubes do you have than orange cubes?" "How many fewer orange cubes do you have than blue cubes?"

2. Again, ask students to use two different strategies. (See Figure 2–6.) (You might want to take a second look at the temperature section, pages 24–28, where children find the difference between two numbers which remain constant.)

Extensions

Have students each take a handful of lima beans in their right hands and count and record the number of beans. Then have them take a handful of lima beans in their left hands and record the number. They can next combine the totals and show their figuring, using two strategies in order to double check their work. Then they can figure the difference between the two totals by using two strategies.

FIGURE 2–6 ▶

Aaron showed how he figured out the difference between 28 and 13.

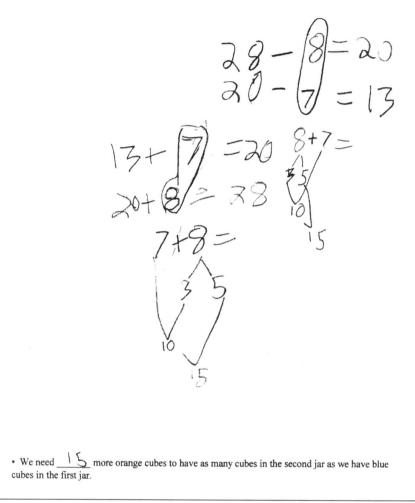

2. How many more orange cubes would we have to add to this other pint jar so it would have as many cubes as the jar with blue cubes? Or, what number is the difference between the two groups of cubes? How did you figure this out. Show your thinking or how you figured this out step by step.

- We need ___15___ more orange cubes to have as many cubes in the second jar as we have blue cubes in the first jar.

TEACHER-TO-TEACHER TALK As you and the class relax into the rhythm of whole-class math discussions, you will begin noticing that some children are using certain strategies over and over again, other children are often confused, and still others who are often quiet. This ongoing assessment can inform your next teaching steps for the class and for individuals.

You may wish to record these observations, as well as note moments when a child suddenly grasps a concept or struggles with an idea or approach. These observations, coupled with the child's work filed chronologically as mentioned in Chapter 1, provide a clear picture of growth over time and help you conference with parents and write report cards.

Stars in a Minute (Elapsed Time)

This activity involves assessing elapsed time, counting, and adding.

Materials

- wall clock
- 3 different-color markers
- drawing materials for students

Instructions

Part 1: Demonstrate the Activity

1. Have the children sit with their eyes closed. Ask them to raise their hands when they think a minute has passed. Keep time on the wall clock and say, "Stop" when a minute has passed.

2. Ask the children to cite examples of things they do that they think take about one minute.

3. Tell the children that you're going to draw stars on the board for one minute. Ask them how many stars they think you will be able to draw.

4. Select a quiet student to watch the clock while you draw stars on the board, and to call out "Stop" when a minute has passed.

5. Now explain that you're going to count the stars you just drew. Ask the children how they would approach this task. They might suggest that you count by 2s, 5s, or 10s.

6. Using a different color pen or chalk than the one you used to draw the stars, circle the stars into equal-size groups. For example, let's suppose you drew a total of 49 stars. If the children suggested counting by 10s, you could circle four groups of ten stars and have nine stars as leftovers. Do not draw a circle around the leftovers or remainders. Help the children recognize that grouping by 10s goes with our place-value system. So, we write 9 in the 1s place and 4 in the 10s place, and the resulting number is 49.

7. Take a third color pen or chalk and group the stars in another way to see if you get the same total. For example, you might get nine groups of five, with four leftovers. You could then use skip-counting to count the groups: 5, 10, 15, 20, 25, 30, 35, 40, 45. On the board, you would write *45 + R4 = 49* below the 49 you wrote earlier. Someone else might want you to write *9 times 5 equals 45, plus 4 leftovers equals 49*. When you record this thinking, do it on two lines as well.

$$9 \times 5 = 45$$

$$45 + R4 = 49$$

Many children would write $9 \times 5 = 45 + 4 = 49$ to show this thinking. If you see this happening, remind your students that we write a different number sentence, or equation, for each equal sign. Some children find this easier to understand when each equation is shown on its own line. The same is true for adding instead of multiplying:

$$5 + 5 + 5 + 5 + 5 + 5 + 5 + 5 + 5 = 45$$

$$45 + 4 = 49$$

Part 2: Conduct the Activity

1. As you time a minute, have a couple of students draw stars on the board and count and record their totals using two strategies.

2. Discuss the various strategies as a class.

3. Have each child draw stars on his or her own paper while you keep time. Each child then groups and counts the resulting stars using two strategies.

   Notice children's reactions if they get different totals using different strategies. Some think nothing of it when this happens, and move on. If you see this occurring, stop everything and take time to discuss as a class what it means when you get different answers to the same problem. Point out that getting two different answers to the same problem does not make sense—and things need to make sense in mathematics.

4. Have students pair up and take turns timing one another to see, first, how many stars they can draw in a minute and, second, how many times they can write the ten digits (0, 1, 2, 3, 4, 5, 6, 7, 8, 9) over and over in a minute. (See Figure 2–7.) The partners then separately

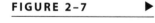

FIGURE 2–7 ▶

Angela grouped stars by 4s and numbers by 2s. She miscounted the leftovers, but still got the correct answer.

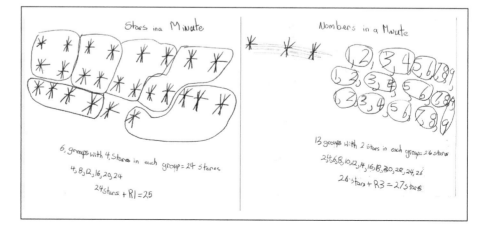

figure out the difference between each of their totals (stars in a minute, digits in a minute).

Extensions

- Write story problems related to the children's own *In a Minute* data (both Stars and Numbers) and have the class solve these problems. (See Figure 2–8.)
- Modeled after story problems you wrote, have partner pairs write story problems about their own *In a Minute* data. With the children's permission, you could use their story problems as homework assignments.

Estimate and Measure (Linear)

This activity has children using nonstandard tools such as interlocking cubes or Popsicle sticks to measure things. (In the spring, they'll use standard measurement tools.)

1. Eun-Jin drew 64 stars in a minute, and she wrote 41 numbers in a minute.
How many more stars than numbers did she draw?
Show your work.

41 + 9 = 50
50 + 10 = 60
60 + 4 = 64
23

64 − 4 = 60
60 − 10 = 50
50 − 9 = 41
23

64
−41
23

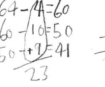

A = 23

2. Peter wrote 40 numbers in a minute, and he drew 51 stars.
What is the difference? How did you figure it out?

40 + 10 = 50
50 + 1 = 51
11

51
−40
11

A = 11

3. Juan drew 35 stars in a minute, and he wrote 20 numbers in a minute.
What is the difference between these two numbers?
How did you figure it out?

20 +10 30 +5 → 35 (15)

A = 15

FIGURE 2–8

Susan showed how she worked out these three story problems.

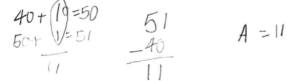

TEACHER-TO-TEACHER TALK   To give children practice with telling time, have them record the time they begin every written assignment at the top of the page, next to their name and the date. This process affords mini-lessons throughout the day. For example, if the time is 10:10 when you ask children to start a new assignment, hold up your model clock and ask the children if it is "before ten o'clock" or "after ten o'clock." Ask how many minutes after 10:00 it is, and how they figured this answer. Then have the children put the time on their papers and begin their work.

Materials

- various objects that could be used as nonstandard measuring tools such as interlocking cubes, Popsicle sticks, paper clips, marking pens, etc.

Instructions

1. Ask the children to select an object in the room that they would like you to measure.

2. Ask them to select another object in the room with which to measure the first object.

3. Suppose the students have suggested that you measure a bookcase using a ten-train of interlocking cubes. Explain that you can measure the width and record your findings—then do just that. Add the word *width* to your chart of *Measurement Words*. Then do the same for the bookcase's height. Add *height* to the chart.

4. Now ask the students to select another object for you to measure. Invite a volunteer to estimate the new object's width, height, or length in terms of total number of cubes.

5. Measure the new object using your ten-train.

6. Record the estimate and your findings on a chart like the one shown below. Reassure the children that it's OK if an estimate is approximate; the point to estimating is to come up with a reasonable assessment, not the exact answer.

What We're Measuring	How Many Cubes We Estimated	Actual Number of Cubes	How Far Off?
Height of bookcase	50	42	8

7. Have students measure additional objects themselves using the nonstandard measurement tool you used and have them record using

a similar chart. They can work individually or in pairs. As they work, circulate among them and see whether they're adjusting their estimates based on their previous experience measuring with this tool.

Extensions

- Students use the same nonstandard tool they used in the earlier part of this activity, but this time they measure parts of their bodies or objects outside.
- The children select a different nonstandard tool to measure other things in the room.
- The children take a nonstandard measurement tool home to estimate the dimensions of objects at home, measure, and figure the difference between their estimates and their actual findings.

Money

Children think of money problems as real-world mathematics. Because they have many problem-solving experiences, such as buying school lunches and paying for book orders, they love pretending they are buying or selling things using real or play coins and bills.

Selling Bookmarks

Materials

- colored card stock cut into 3-by-8-inch rectangles; several per student
- drawing and coloring materials per student
- several pieces of different-color construction paper per student
- money bags

Instructions

1. Have students design bookmarks on the card-stock rectangles. They might cut the book marks further into shapes such as ice-cream cones or pencils, then decorate the shapes with colorful pen work. Or they might like to cut out shapes from colored construction paper and glue them onto the rectangles.

2. As a class, decide on a price for the bookmarks. Select pricing that gives students opportunities to make change; for example 11 cents for one bookmark, and 19 cents for two.

3. As a class, decide on a worthy cause for your profit and get permission from your principal. Advertise the purpose, time, and prices of the bookmark sale in the weekly school newsletter and on student-made posters.

4. Have students pair up and practice buying and selling bookmarks to one another.

5. Now have the children sell their bookmarks to students from other classes during lunch recess, making change as necessary.

Although this activity provides valuable practice with adding and subtracting, it of course doesn't generate any real profits. But your students can still learn important values from it. For example, this past school year, my class made $12.42 profit selling bookmarks. We decided to send the money to UNICEF, because we learned that $3.00 bought a five-day course of antibiotics for a sick child, $1.00 bought polio vaccines for four children, and $10.00 bought a set of school supplies for four children.

Selling the bookmarks yielded some surprising math investigations as well. For instance, we sold bookmarks over five days, so we were able to add up the profits from each day.

Classroom-Supply Shopping

Materials

- 1 pretend dollar per student
- 1 money bag per pair of students
- Supply order form, 1 per student (see Blackline Masters)

Instructions

1. Give each student one play dollar to spend on school supplies found in the classroom.

2. Post the following kind of price list.

Eraser	$.10
Ruler	$.29
Pencil	$.20
Glue stick	$.35

3. Have students fill out order forms for items they plan to purchase.

Supply Order Form		
Quantity	Item Name	Price
		$.
		$.
		$.
		$.
		$.
	Total	$.
	Change	$.

Here is how I figured the total:

Here is how I figured the change:

4. Have the children pair up. Give each pair a money bag.

5. One child acts as shopper while the other acts as cashier. The shopper hands his order form to the cashier. She checks his total and his change. If she agrees that his figures are correct, he hands her the dollar. She counts up from his total to one dollar to calculate how much change she owes him. For example, if the shopper's total is $.88, the cashier counts back his change with two pennies and says "89, 90." Then she hands him one dime and says, "One dollar." Then the cashier places the supplies the shopper purchased into a brown-paper lunch bag with the order form stapled to it.

6. Next the partners switch roles.

If this activity is meaningful to your students, you may want to look in *Teaching Arithmetic: Lessons for Addition and Subtraction* under "Billy Goes Shopping" for further suggestions.

Coins in Two Pockets

Materials

- 1 money bag per pair of students

Instructions

1. Write some money riddles on cards. Here are some examples:

   I have some coins in my two pockets. I have exactly $.35. I have one dime and one nickel in one pocket. What coins could I have in my other pocket? Show your answer and how you figured it out step by step.

   Or

   I have $.60 in my two pockets. I have eight nickels in one pocket. What coins could I have in my other pocket? Show your answer and how you figured it out.

2. Have children pick out cards and solve the riddles on them using the coins in their money bags.

Extensions

Have the children write their own *Coins in Two Pockets* riddles. Send the riddles home for homework after they have been class tested. Be sure to have the riddle writers' names connected to their problems. Look in *Mathematical Thinking at Grade 3* by Susan Jo Russell and Karen Economopoulos for further ideas.

Literature-Based Activities

To introduce the literature-based activities described below, first read the stories for enjoyment. Then take a close look at the math. Have the children take turns retelling the story, then ask them to think of math questions connected to the story. Reading a story as a context for problem solving enables you to make mathematics a positive experience in the classroom and at home. You might consider establishing a system for letting students borrow the books and take them home.

During your regular classroom read-aloud time or your classroom literature hour, you will come upon sections or sentences in stories that easily spark a mathematics question or investigation. Take advantage of these moments. For example, in the book *Matilda,* a chapter book by Roald Dahl, Matilda is five years old. Point out to your students that the book was written in 1988. Ask, "If Matilda were a real five-year-old girl in 1988, how old would she be today?" And in *Caps for Sale*, a picture book by Esphyr Slobodkina, you can invite students to figure out how many caps the peddler was carrying on his head.

Spending a Dollar

Materials

- 1 money bag per pair of students
- 18-by-24-inch blank newsprint or manila-folder paper; several pieces per student

Instructions

1. Read Judith Viorst's *Alexander, Who Used to Be Rich Last Sunday* to the class.

2. Reread the book, stopping each time Alexander spends some of his dollar. After each stop along his spending route, have the children figure out how much money Alexander has left. Some children might be able to figure mentally; others may want to use their money bags or the 1–100 chart. Take time to have children explain their thinking at each stop. You might record subtraction sentences to describe Alexander's spending.

3. With the class, brainstorm different ways students could spend one dollar. List items they would like to buy, and have them estimate the cost of each. Of course, these days it's difficult to find anything that costs less than a dollar! But use your imagination. For example, perhaps an older teacher could share his or her memories about the cost of ice-cream cones (5 cents?), movies (15 cents?), comic books (10 cents?), and penny candy when he or she was a child. The children could use these numbers to do the activity.

4. Next have students use lined paper to document their story, starting with how they got the money on the first day to how they spent the last of their dollar on the eighth day. They should show the math in each situation, so you can check their thinking.

5. Ask students to write a final draft of their story, using the following process: With your help, the children fold a large 18-by-24-inch piece of newsprint or manila paper into eight sections. They title the first section with their name; e.g., *Amy, Who Used to Be Rich Last Tuesday*. In the first section, they write a sentence explaining how they got their dollar. In each succeeding section, they write a sentence telling where the money went that day and how much money is left. They also write an equation to show this transaction. Then they draw a picture to go with the situation. (See Figure 2–9.)

Measuring Girth and Height

In *The Fattest, Tallest, Biggest Snowman Ever* by Bettina Ling, Jeff wants to be the best at something. Other boys and girls hit and catch balls better than Jeff does. Others sled better than Jeff. Finally, Jeff builds a snowman. His friend, Maria, builds one, too. Jeff thinks his snowman is the fattest, so the two friends measure the snowmen's girth with string and paper clips to find out who's right. Then Jeff thinks his snowman is the tallest, requiring more measurement. The story ends with Maria telling Jeff, "When it comes to ideas, you're the best!" Eventually, the snowmen melt.

This story provides a jumping-off point for measuring things at home with arm spans and string or measuring body parts with paper clips.

FIGURE 2–9 ▶

Eun-Jin drew her *Used to Be Rich* story, showing an equation for each day.

Counting by Grouping

In *The King's Commissioners* by Aileen Friedman, the king has appointed so many royal commissioners that he is having trouble counting them all. He tells his commissioners to file into the throne room to be counted by his two royal advisors. One advisor counts by 2s, and the other counts by 5s. The king becomes confused. It's up to the clever princess to convince her father that there is more than one way to count.

This book helps children think about grouping as they count and about place value. You could have your children work alone or in pairs to complete the following sentences:

"The first royal advisor made sense because . . . "

"The second royal advisor made sense because . . . "

"The princess made sense because . . . "

Extensions

Have students recommend the names of a few more commissioners the king needs and count the new total number of commissioners. They then explain how the first and second royal advisor and the princess would count the new total by 2s, by 5s, and by 10s. You might find that your students use a wide variety of strategies—from counting and grouping pictures to skip-counting or multiplication.

Counting Feet

In *The Napping House* by Audrey Wood, one creature at a time joins a snoring granny in her cozy bed. After reading the story, ask the children to figure out how many feet are in the bed when it is filled with the granny, a dreaming child, a dozing dog, a snoozing cat, a slumbering mouse, and a wakeful flea. Students could draw a picture of the people and pets who live in their own homes and count the number of feet there.

Story Problems

You'll find many opportunities to write story problems relevant to your students' school and home lives. Children, too, can create their own story problems. As they devise such problems and connect numbers to the real world, they gain a deeper understanding of addition and subtraction. Why?

They must envision a context that makes sense for combining numbers (addition) and for comparing or separating numbers (subtraction).

Teacher-Generated Story Problems

As your students compare temperatures, group and count raisins, or do their stars and numbers during whole-class problem solving, you can write story problems connected to their work in these activities. You can then assign these problems as class work or homework. (See Figures 2–10 and 2–11.)

You can also find ideas for story problems in other sources. For instance, the following problem from *Putting Together and Taking Apart, Grades 2 and 3* by Karen Economopoulos and Susan Jo Russell (1995) encourages students to use a variety of addition and subtraction strategies (see Figure 2–12 on page 54):

A class of 29 students is going on a trip to the science museum.

There are 12 adults going with them.

How many people are going?

FIGURE 2–10 ▶

Rebecca worked on problems related to the *Stars in a Minute* activity.

1. Jerry wrote 27 numbers in a minute, and he drew 41 stars in a minute. What is the difference between the two numbers and how did you figure that out?

$$41 - \text{\textcircled{11}} = 30$$
$$30 - \text{\textcircled{3}} = 27$$
$$14$$

$$27 + \text{\textcircled{3}} = 30$$
$$30 + \text{\textcircled{11}} = 41$$
$$14$$

$$27 + \text{\textcircled{10}} = 37$$
$$37 + \text{\textcircled{4}} = 41$$
$$14$$

$$A = 14$$

2. Eun-Jin drew 50 stars in a minute, and she wrote 35 numbers in a minute. How much more is 50 than 35 and how do you know that?

$$A = 15$$

$$35 + \text{\textcircled{5}} = 40$$
$$40 + \text{\textcircled{10}} = 50$$
$$15$$

$$50 - \text{\textcircled{10}} = 40$$
$$40 - \text{\textcircled{5}} = 35$$
$$15$$

3. Jaime wrote 24 numbers in a minute, and he drew 33 stars in a minute. What is the difference between these two numbers and how did you figure it out?

$$24 \underset{30}{\overset{+6 \quad +3}{\longrightarrow}} 33$$

$$A = 9$$

FIGURE 2–11 ◄

Wei-Cee made sense of
these story problems
about temperature.

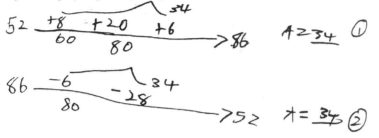

• Since school began, our highest temperature has been <u>86</u> degrees.

• Since school began, our lowest temperature has been <u>52</u> degrees.

1. What is the difference between these two temperatures? ___34___ degrees
   Explain step by step how you figured this out.

   $52 \quad \overset{\overbrace{\qquad}^{34}}{\underset{60}{+8} \quad \underset{80}{+20} \quad +6} \longrightarrow 86 \qquad A = \underline{34} \ ①$

   $86 \quad \overset{\overbrace{\qquad}^{34}}{\underset{80}{-6} \quad -28} \longrightarrow 52 \qquad A = \underline{34} \ ②$

2. Come up with another strategy to figure out the difference between the two
   temperatures. Explain this strategy step by step. Did you get the same answer as
   you got for number 1. above? ___Yes___

   $52 + 8 = 60$
   $60 + 20 = 80$ $A = \underline{34} \ ③$
   $80 + 6 = 86$
   $\quad 34$

   $86 - 6 = 80$
   $80 - 28 = 52$ $A = \underline{34} \ ④$
   $\quad 34$

Student-Generated Story Problems

After a field trip to a nearby wetlands, my students wrote addition and
subtraction problems based on the trip. I then wrote down some of these
problems and assigned them as homework. (See Figure 2–13 on page 55.)

Some children are eager to write problems relevant to their outside-of-
school interests. For example, one of my students picked his own numbers
and drew on his interest in basketball to write a comparison problem. (See
Figure 2–14 on page 56.)

Students can also ask their own questions about math situations in children's literature. For instance, after reading *Alexander, Who Used to Be
Rich Last Sunday,* have the children help you go through the book and
create story problems based on Alexander's situation.

29 students + 12 adults

• Strategy: Going to nearby friendly number such as 30

Sam	$29 + 1 = 30$		Sarah	$29 + 1 = 30$
Rebecca	$30 + 10 = 40$		Jaime	$30 + 11 = 41$
Deon	$40 + \underline{1} = 41$		Marcus	
Ray	12		Hamid	

• Strategy: Breaking both addends into familiar parts: $29 = 20 + 9$
$12 = 10 + 2$

Latasha   I know that $2 + 9 = 11$ Peter   29   +   12
and $20 + 10 = 30$. Then   Angela
you take 10 from 11   30   11
and add it to 30 which
makes 40. Then $40 + 1 = 41$ $30 + 11 = 41$

Aaron $20 + 10 = 30$
$30 + 10 = 40$
$40 + 1 = 41$

• Strategy: Breaking smaller addend into familiar parts: $12 = 10 + 2$

Eun-Jin	$29 + 2 = 31$		Susan	$29 + 10 = 39$
	$31 + 10 = 41$		Nan	$39 + 1 = 40$
				$40 + 1 = 41$

• Strategy: Counting up by ones

Jarod   I had 29 then I counted on in my head 12 more to 41.

• Strategy: Traditional

Yousif   29
Janet $+ 12$
                    41

FIGURE 2–13   ◀

Hamid used several strategies to solve two story problems written by Aaron and Deon drawn from the wetlands field trip.

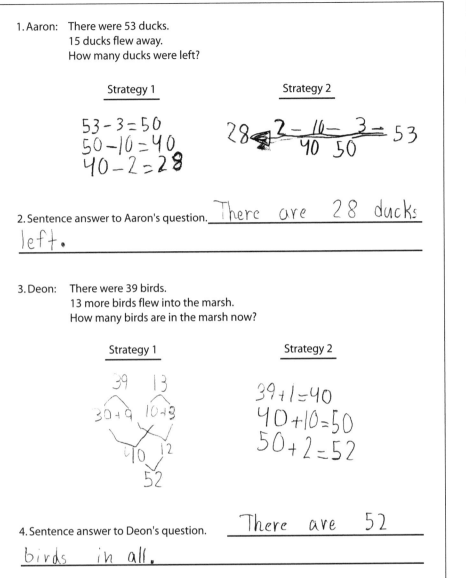

1. Aaron: There were 53 ducks.
15 ducks flew away.
How many ducks were left?

Strategy 1

$$53 - 3 = 50$$
$$50 - 10 = 40$$
$$40 - 2 = 28$$

Strategy 2

$$28 \longleftarrow 2 - 10 - 3 = 53$$
$$40 \quad 50$$

2. Sentence answer to Aaron's question. There are 28 ducks left.

3. Deon: There were 39 birds.
13 more birds flew into the marsh.
How many birds are in the marsh now?

Strategy 1

39   13
30 + 9   10 + 3
40   12
52

Strategy 2

$$39 + 1 = 40$$
$$40 + 10 = 50$$
$$50 + 2 = 52$$

4. Sentence answer to Deon's question. There are 52 birds in all.

TEACHER-TO-TEACHER TALK When children write story problems, they practice writing sentences that are statements (telling) and sentences that are questions (asking). This is appropriate for third grade. Even in the mathematics classroom, this writing practice is valuable. In your own classroom, you'll need to decide whether written story problems need correct capitalization, punctuation, and spelling. Some teachers feel that such standards become important only when work is made public on bulletin boards, in menu work, or at parent conferences.

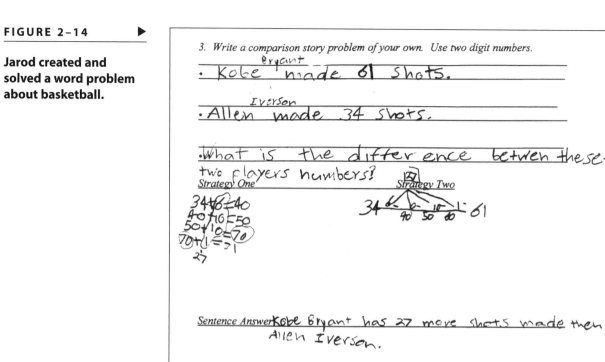

Also encourage students to write problems paralleling problems they have just solved in class. To illustrate, after doing *Stars in a Minute*, one student wrote this three-sentence word problem following a model her teacher had written on the board:

I had 9 groups with 5 stars in each group.

I had 3 stars as leftovers.

How many stars did I draw in a minute?

Many third graders seem to find it easier to sort out their story-problem thinking when they write their sentences on three separate lines. The first two sentences are "telling" sentences. The last sentence is an "asking" sentence; thus it needs a question mark.

Many story problems challenge children to find *unknown results*. For instance, in story problems involving combining, or addition, students might know the quantities to be combined and must use that information to find the sum. (See Figure 2–15.)

In separating, or subtraction, problems, students may know the initial number and the number to be taken away. They must then use their knowledge to find the result of the subtraction. (See Figure 2–16.)

When the children revisit addition and subtraction in the spring, you will want them to work on problems with *known results*. That is, they

It.. have 36 baseballs.
My friend gave me 15 baseballs.
How many do I have?

36   15 $15 \underset{20}{+5} + \underset{50}{30} +1 \rightarrow 51$

30 + 6   10 + 5

40   11

51

~~That~~ I have 51 baseballs.

· There are 56 books in the library.

· The kids borrowed 29 books.

Q. How many books are left in the library?

A.   A.
Strategy.   strategy
  56   29 = 20 + 9
 -29
 ───   56 - 20 = 36
  27   36 - 9 = 27

A. Sentence: There are 27 books in the library right now.

TEACHER-TO-TEACHER TALK Make sure your students have many opportunities to write *comparison* subtraction problems involving questions such as "What is the difference?" "How many more?" "How many less?" In such problems, the two quantities remain the same; neither of them is decreased. In take-away problems, the initial quantity is decreased. For example, during September and October, students compare the number of cubes in two jars, the number of beans in two hands, the numbers on two playing cards, two different daily temperatures, and estimates and actual measurements.

may know a sum or a result of a subtraction, and need to fill in a number to be combined or a number to be taken away. Here are some examples:

Twenty children were seated in the cafeteria ready for lunch. Ten minutes later, there were fifty-five children in the cafeteria. How many students came to the cafeteria during that ten minutes?

There were thirty-five newly sharpened pencils in the classroom at the beginning of the day. At the end of the day, there were only eighteen sharpened pencils. How many sharpened pencils did the students take away and use that day?

Menu Time

During menu time, children have some choice about the problems they're going to work on, the amount of time they'll spend on a problem, and the individuals they'll work with. They work independently of the teacher. Menu thus differs from whole-class teaching followed by partner or small-group work.

Through the menu format, you can meet the math needs of a range of students. While children work independently on menu problems, you're free to work one on one with children who are struggling with a math concept or guide a small group of students with similar mathematical needs. Menu time is also great for days when a substitute teacher will be filling in for you—the children will know what they need to do during menu, and they can work quite independently.

What do menus consist of? Most problems on a menu are extensions of what the children have done in whole-class lessons. Some problems arise from questions students ask. For example, one of my third graders asked, "When you add an even number to an even number, do you always get an even answer?" This question led to a valuable menu investigation. Other problems may include story problems written by the students or problems drawn from children's literature.

I've designed a "dinner" menu focusing on addition and subtraction for children who need practice in these areas. A "dessert" menu is available for students who have a firmer grasp of these concepts and want further challenge. Only those children who have completed the problems in the "dinner" menu can move on to "dessert." Here's what I offered for "dinner":

Handful of Beans: Grab some lima beans beans with your right hand, then grab some with your left hand. Group and *count* each of these handfuls separately. Next *compare* the two counts. Finally *combine* them to get a total.

Subtraction Story Problem: Write a take-away subtraction word problem using the question "How many are left?" Then show how you solved the problem. Finally, write a sentence answer to your word problem.

In One Minute: Have a partner time you to see how many letters you can write in one minute. Then have a partner time you to see how many numbers (0, 1, 2, 3, 4, 5, 6, 7, 8, 9) you can write in one minute. Time your partner in both. Next, individually group and *count* your letters and numbers. Finally, *compare* the numbers by finding the difference.

Penny Count: The pennies each of you brought for the Families of the World Trade Center Victims are in pint jars. Each jar is about half full. Group and count the pennies in one jar two different ways.

Estimate and Count: Use interlocking cubes to estimate then measure the length of five different objects in the classroom. Finally, figure the difference between your estimates and your actual measurements.

Addition Story Problem: Write an addition problem in which you combine two quantities. Use two strategies to solve the problem. Show each step in your thinking. Finally, write a sentence answer to your word problem.

Menu work can be ongoing throughout a unit or can be done as the culmination of the unit.

Ongoing During a Unit

In this case, your menu consists of a posted list of problems that relate to problems the students are already working on in the current unit of study. Children tackle the menu problems throughout the weeks of the unit after they complete whole-class, partner, or individual work. Consider asking students to complete certain menu problems by a given day so you can conduct a whole-class discussion about them.

You can post menu problems on big chart paper around the room as you introduce them. Indicate whether each problem is designed for individuals, pairs, or small groups. Include the title of the problem, the materials needed, and the instructions. You can also write the menu on an $8\frac{1}{2}$-by-11-inch sheet of paper, make photocopies, staple the copies to the inside cover of construction-paper folders, and hand out the folders to students.

Menu as Culmination of a Unit

In my classroom, I offer menu as the culmination of a unit. As mentioned above, all my students must complete the "dinner" menu problems before moving on to "dessert." I introduce one problem from the dinner menu on the first day of menu time. Then I ask that all the children complete it so they can share their problem-solving approaches at the end of the current period or the beginning of the next. On the second day, I introduce the remaining problems. Each solution has the problem title, the child's name, the answer, and a step-by-step explanation of how the child used words, numbers, and/or pictures to address the problem. At the beginning of the school year, I often present the menus in a worksheet format that I've prepared ahead of time. As the year progresses, the children set up their own problem-solving formats for each activity.

When I collect and read the students' solutions to menu problems midway through the week, I write comments such as "Your thinking makes sense to me" or "Your work is clear and convincing" on sticky notes and attach the notes to the appropriate solutions. If I spot unclear or less-than-convincing thinking, I write questions or comments such as "You have written that the difference between 56 degrees and 70 degrees is 14 degrees, but I don't see how you figured this out. Show me." I expect my students to be persistent problem solvers and to answer my questions by making their work stronger. I leave the sticky notes in place. That way, when I revisit the work, I can keep track of how the students are responding to my queries and comments. (See Figure 2–17.)

Parent Communication

Feel free to send menus home for students to share with their parents. When I do this, I often include a newsletter explaining what we've been doing in mathematics, and why. I find that parents have a clearer sense of the math-

- You do not need a partner.
- You do need a container of beans.

① When I grab a handful of beans with my right hand, I get 40 beans. Let me show you how I grouped and counted these beans.

I grouped the beans in 5's

5 10
|||| ||||
15 20   25 30 35
|||| |||| |||| |||| ||||
40
||||

① Now put skip count numbers by your tallies

|||| |||| ...
5   10

ok

② When I grab a handful of beans with my left hand, I get 35 beans. Let me show you how I grouped and counted these beans.

I grouped the beans by 10 I got 3 ten and 5 left over.

5
10   35
10   30
10

This problem ② makes sense to me.

ematics classroom when I tell them what's happening *and* the children show them their work. I also ask parents and children to sign their names to the menu to indicate that they've read it together before students bring it back. Menu work thus naturally becomes part of parent-student-teacher conferences.

Below is a sample parent letter that I wrote to accompany the addition and subtraction "dinner" menu outlined on page 59. I stapled the letter inside the front cover of the students' menu folders.

Dear Parents,

Tonight your child is bringing home the first menu of math problems he or she has done this year. We do a menu of problems at the end of each unit, and we have just completed our unit on addition and subtraction. During this unit, the children used a variety of strategies as they counted, combined, compared, and separated quantities of things—always in the context of a problem. The children also made sense of addition and subtraction by writing their own problems. The menu problems were extensions of problems we had been doing in class and for homework, so the children had a wealth of problem-solving experiences to draw from. They were expected to make sense of these problems without much adult help.

In this menu, children had six problems to choose from, and they needed to complete all six of these problems in a clear and convincing way. They chose whether to work alone or with classmates. They also decided on which problems to do first, second, and so forth. I wrote questions or suggestions on your child's work if it was not clear and convincing. I then expected students to revisit unclear solutions to make them stronger.

Measurement was a meaningful context for four of these problems. In the *Handfuls of Beans* problem, the children grouped and counted beans that they grabbed in their right hand and in their left hand. Then they combined (added) and compared the two numbers representing these quantities. Although comparison ("what is the difference") problems are considered subtraction problems, the children often "added up" as they made sense of the difference. In the *In One Minute* problem, the children continued to group and count as well as compare. The *Penny Count* problem arose from our classroom fund-raising project that followed the September 11 tragedy. Again, the children grouped and counted half the jar. Finally, in *Estimate and Measure*, students used interlocking cubes to measure the length or width of different objects in the classroom after they first estimated those dimensions.

In *Subtraction Story Problem* and *Addition Story Problem*, the children drew on their understanding of taking away one quantity from another and of combining one quantity with another. I expected correct spelling, capitalization, and punctuation in the two "telling" sentences and the one "asking" sentence in each problem.

Please take time to go over each menu problem and solution with your child and celebrate his or her persistence. Return this folder of work with your signature and your child's signature at the bottom of this letter, so I will know that the two of you had an opportunity to talk menu math together. Thank you!

Warmly,

Suzy Ronfeldt

Instead of parent letters such as the above, many teachers prefer to write a newsletter at the beginning of a unit and send that home. There are helpful examples of such newsletters in the TERC Investigations in Number, Data, and Space units published by Dale Seymour Publications and in the Teaching Arithmetic books published by Math Solutions Publications. Some of these letters can be copied and distributed as is.

Assessment: Whole Class and Partner Discussions

The idea that all U.S. teachers must use identical assessment approaches fails to honor the daily assessing that individual teachers do to meet their students' needs. This ongoing assessment constitutes a meaningful part of teaching and learning in a mathematics classroom where you're asking children to explain their thinking. You listen intently to each child's reasoning during whole-class discussions and during partner work, with an ear toward what individual children do and do not understand and how the class is making sense of the lesson as a whole.

As you listen, jot down unique understandings and critical misunderstandings on sticky notes in a file folder, as suggested in Chapter 1, or in your lesson-planning book. At the beginning of the year, you may find this form of note taking too time consuming. If so, jot down your thoughts about individual students' progress during recess or after school. Date these notes so you can track the growth of individual students' understandings over time.

On the board or on chart paper, write the strategies children are using to make sense of the math. Attach their names to their strategies. At the end of each day, review these strategies and your notes. If most students seem to understand the concept of combining in their addition problem solving, perhaps it is time to move on to more subtraction situations. If the majority seem to be struggling with combining, think of another experience or context that can help them work with this idea again the next day. Notice which children aren't participating in class; the next day, encourage them to contribute more during whole-group, partner, or one-on-one discussions.

During the first six weeks of school, think about assessment during whole-class and partner discussions only. In the next six-week period, broaden your assessment to each child's written mathematics work. The following questions might guide your active listening and note taking:

- Does the child speak up during class discussions?
- Does the child group as he or she counts?

- Can the child explain how he or she figured out the answer?
- Can the child use more than one strategy?
- Does the child reason numerically by breaking numbers into friendly or familiar parts, or by going to nearby friendly or familiar numbers?
- Does the child understand what it means to combine, compare, and separate things?

Chapter 3

October/ November

INTRODUCTION TO MULTIPLICATION

"Teachers play an important role in the development of students' problem-solving disposition by creating and maintaining classroom environments, from pre-kindergarten on, in which students are encouraged to explore, take risks, share failures and successes, and question one another."

Principles and Standards for School Mathematics
NCTM 2000, 53

Most children begin making sense of multiplication during the third grade. They bring a wealth of grouping and counting experiences to the school year. However, they continue to use everyday objects, manipulatives, and pictures to ground their reasoning. They begin by combining groups of equal size and then incorporate words and numbers to explain their sense making. ■

The Learning Environment

Give children time to construct their own understanding.

As November approaches, many teachers try to speed up their students' mathematics learning. The prospect of fall parent conferences and spring standardized testing adds to the pressure to "cover" material quickly. Try to resist this pressure. Remind yourself that with plenty of time and much support, your students will make sense of multiplication in a way that has meaning for them. Continue to listen, learn, and record the strategies your students share with you. Remind yourself that when children realize the power of their own thinking in the mathematics classroom, they bring this problem-solving disposition or "I can do it" approach to standardized tests as well.

Provide manipulatives and encourage children to draw pictures.

Most of your third graders will be exploring multiplicative situations for the first time. Thus they need to build or draw models that will help them think about how many objects they have altogether when those objects come in equal-size groups. For example, to represent rows of panes in a window, they can use colored tiles. For groups of six legs on an insect, they can draw pictures. For cookies on a tray, they can arrange pennies into rectangular arrays or draw circles on half-inch grid-paper arrays. (See Blackline Masters.) For the *Circles and Stars* game, they draw a certain number of circles with an equal number of stars in each.

All of these models help children attach meaning to the words and numbers they use as they begin working with multiplication. To foster this connection, it helps if numbers and words are included in the pictures children draw.

Support partners' problem-solving dispositions.

At this time of the school year, encourage children to work in pairs to solve problems after whole-class discussions. Circulate among the pairs, listening and supporting the students' independence. Often, partners approach the same problem using different strategies, so encourage the children to explain their thinking and to ask questions to better understand one another's approaches. You might post a list of questions that partners can use as a reference:

"How did you figure that out?"

"What did you do first, second, . . . ?"

"What does this part mean?"

"Where are your numbers or pictures?"

"How do your words connect to your numbers or pictures?"

Five or ten minutes after pairs begin a work session, interrupt the problem solving to have students explain to the whole class what is working for them and what is not. The resulting discussion can inspire struggling partners to reason, "If others can do it, so can we." At the end of the partner-work session, ask the children to describe how they worked together. Some students might point out that they work together more productively if they take turns listening to one another.

If you notice pairs of students struggling to address a problem, sit with them and ask them questions to jump-start their thinking. Here are some examples:

"What does this problem say? Tell me in your own words."

"What does this problem ask you to do?"

"Would it help to use beans or tiles to figure this out?"

"Would a drawing help you make sense of this problem?"

"What could your first step be? Show me."

"Does this problem remind you of another one we've done?"

"What question is in your mind right now?"

Of course, not all mathematics problem solving needs to be done in pairs. But the saying "Two heads are better than one" applies particularly well to mathematics classrooms in which children are encouraged to communicate their own reasoning.

Encourage writing and drawing as well as talking about mathematics.

By this time of year, your students have had practice explaining their math thinking aloud in the class. You've regularly recorded that thinking on the board. And the children have begun putting their own words, numbers, and/or pictures on paper, especially with partner help. Written communication and drawings help students sort out their thinking. They also reveal where the children are in their sense making, helping you to further support their learning. This month, start keeping a folder for each child's written and pictorial mathematics work, in which you date the work and organize it chronologically. The folders will help you assess growth over time and use your insights during upcoming report cards and parent conferences. If some of the work in the folders was done in pairs, make copies for each partner's folder.

Some children find it easier to grapple with writing or drawing tasks in pairs. Others prefer to write or draw on their own. By writing step by step what they did and using pictures with numbers to represent their thinking, many children find their "math voices." Some third graders find it valuable to explain their thinking in a letter to a younger audience, such as second graders. For others, a prompt is helpful:

"Today I (we) did _____."
"Today I (we) learned _____."
"Today _____ of us are buying lunch."
"We think that because _____."

As your students start using writing and drawing to document their thinking, meet regularly with each child or partner pair to see how they're doing. Ask questions to help the children make their work stronger or more clear and convincing:

"What does this picture show?"
"Where are your word labels, so I know what the picture shows?"
"What are these numbers about?"
"Would words help me understand your numbers better?"
"What can you add to this picture to show and tell what you did first, second, and so forth?"

You might want to have individuals or partners share their written work with the whole class at the end of that math period or at the beginning of the next day's math period. In viewing one another's work, the children could say what they think is strong about a particular example of written work, as well as ask questions. Begin listing these observations, so students gain a sense of what makes a math paper strong.

The Mathematics

Children make connections between addition and multiplication.

Help the children make connections between different strategies, such as skip-counting and multiplication. For example, when a child groups the stars he "drew in a minute" into groups of ten and has five groups, he can skip-count or "add as he goes" as he says, "Ten stars, twenty stars, thirty stars, forty stars, fifty stars." He can also multiply five groups of stars by ten stars in each group to get a total of fifty stars.

During addition, addends may or may not be equal-size groups. But when they *are* equal size, multiplying is more efficient than adding. For instance, imagine that a student has eight cookies on each of four trays. After many experiences adding ($8 + 8 + 8 + 8$) or skip-counting (8, 16, 24, 32), the child will eventually find it more efficient to multiply ($4 \times 8 = 32$).

Both multiplication and addition are commutative; that is, the sequence of the factors or addends doesn't matter. Early on, children reverse the addends to make better sense of their addition. They think of $6 + 9$ as $9 + 6$, so they can reason that $9 + 1 = 10$. Then they add 5 to get 15. Students will eventually do the same with multiplication. To illustrate, for 6×3, a child might reverse the factors to 3×6 because she finds it is easier and faster to think of three 6s (6, 12, 18) than to think of six 3s (3, 6, 9, 12, 15, 18).

Children reason as they make sense of multiplication combinations.

Children know their 2s, 5s, and 10s quite naturally because of their frequent grouping and skip-counting in these equal-size groups. When playing *Circles and Stars* over and over again, as suggested in this chapter, students acquire experiences and build pictorial models of these combinations and their reverses:

1×1

1×3 3×3

1×4 3×4 4×4

1×6 3×6 4×6 6×6

Students need to know their multiplication combinations through 10×10. There are 110 combinations in all, including the "times zero" combinations. When they understand their 0s, 1s, 2s, 5s, 10s, and the additional combinations found in *Circles and Stars* above, students will have mastered more than half of the 110 combinations. This is something to celebrate! During the *Circles and Stars* game, the children do not use zero as a factor, but they do use zero as a factor when doing *Pockets* (see pages 77–78).

When children multiply with the factors of 2, 4, 6, or 8, they have meaningful practice with everyday realities, such as the number of legs on people (2), on animals (4 legs), on insects (6), and on spiders (8).

Continue to support your students as they think about these multiplication combinations. Resist any temptation to help them merely memorize the combinations through nonsense rhymes such as "Goin' fishing, got no bait, six times eight is forty-eight" or through finger tricks. You want your students to *understand* what 6 × 8 means. Some children think in pictures when grappling with numbers; others think in numbers only. At this introductory level, encourage students to use both numerical and pictorial strategies to connect their numbers to meaningful contexts.

TEACHER-TO-TEACHER TALK Drawing pictures can help children ground their numerical work in real-world contexts. This grounding helps to develop students' *number sense* even while they're learning the combinations.

Merely reciting multiplication combinations doesn't lead to number sense—and doesn't help children solve multiplication problems. Reciting is akin to reading a list of words without making sense of stories. Children who have number sense know why multiplication makes sense in certain situations. A child who knows 3 × 8 = 24 but has no idea how that combination connects to real-world situations will have a limited ability to reason mathematically.

Below are some examples of pictorial and numerical thinking. Because most of your students are just beginning to reason using multiplication, you may see more pictorial thinking than numerical reasoning in their work.

Pictorial Thinking

■ *Things that come in groups*: "I know six octopi times eight tentacles on each equals forty-eight tentacles on all six octopi." (See Figure 3–1.)

FIGURE 3–1 ▶

Latasha drew six octopi and used skip-counting to figure the total number of tentacles.

- *Geometric arrays*: "I know that six rows with eight window panes in each row equals forty-eight window panes in the window." (See Figure 3–2.)
- Circles and Stars *game*: "I know that six circles each with eight stars inside equals forty-eight stars in all six circles." (See Figure 3–3.)

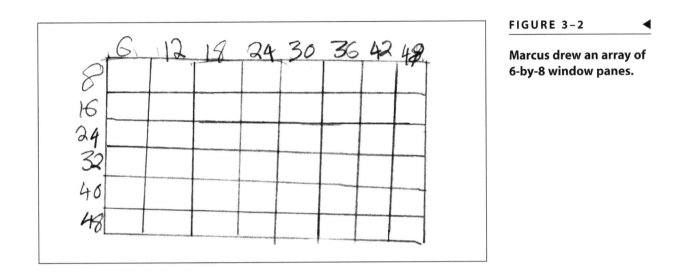

FIGURE 3–2 ◄

Marcus drew an array of 6-by-8 window panes.

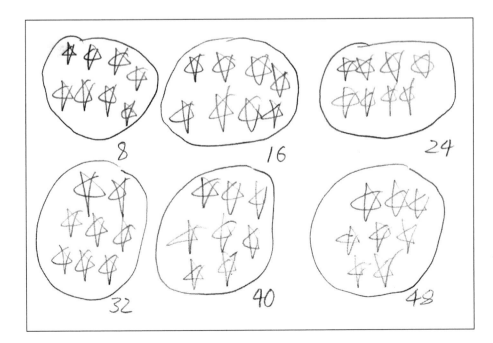

FIGURE 3–3 ◄

Nan used skip-counting to calculate the total number of stars in her circles.

Numerical Thinking

■ *Adding*

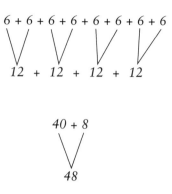

■ *Skip-counting*: "I know that six times eight is forty-eight, because I skip-counted by eights six times: eight, sixteen, twenty-four, thirty-two, forty, and forty-eight." Or, "I skip-counted by sixes eight times: six, twelve, eighteen, twenty-four, thirty, thirty-six, forty-two, and forty-eight."

■ *Going to a friendly number*: "I know that five times eight is forty, and I need one more eight to have six eights (6 × 8), so forty plus eight is forty-eight."

■ *Breaking a number into friendly parts*: "I am going to think of the six as three plus three, then multiply three times eight to get twenty-four and then do it again. Finally I'll add twenty-four and twenty-four to get forty-eight." (This strategy seems to be the least used in my third-grade classroom, though you may see it crop up more often in yours.)

Children understand that multiplication is one way to find out how many objects you have altogether when those objects come in equal-size groups.

For clear communication in your classroom, have the first factor in a multiplication equation always refer to the *number of groups* students are considering—whether they're groups of circles, rows, or insects. The second factor refers to the *number of objects within each group*—e.g., stars inside circles, window panes in a row, or legs on an insect. To help the children grasp the idea that 3 × 6 means combining three equal-size groups that each have six objects, use words and pictures. Here are some examples to go with these word/number equations.

- 3 circles × 6 stars in each = 18 stars in all 3 circles

- 3 rows × 6 window panes in each row = 18 windowpanes in all 3 rows

	3	6	9	12	15	18
6						
12						
18						

- 3 insects × 6 legs on each = 18 legs on all 3 insects

Children practice flexible thinking as they explore more than one strategy in their problem solving.

When children use several strategies to solve a problem, they show that they can think flexibly. Moreover, the differing strategies serve as a check on whether the answer is correct. Figure 3–4 shows a variety of strategies children used for making sense of the problem "There are three spiders. Each spider has eight legs. How many legs are there on all three spiders?" By putting children's names by their strategies, you can see which strategies currently make more sense to various students. By posting this record, you help the children see the range of strategies used.

FIGURE 3–4 ▶

This class used a rich array of strategies to solve the spider problem.

Variety of Strategies

There are 3 spiders.
Each spider has 8 legs.
How many legs are there on all 3 spiders?

Counting

Rebecca

16, 17, 18
19, 20, 21
22, 23, 24

Nathan

Derek

Skip Counting

Hamid
Sam
Sarah
Aaron
Deon

8 , 16 , 24

Mutiplication

Sarah
Hamid

$1 \times 8 = 8$
$2 \times 8 = 16$
$3 \times 8 = 24$

Angela   Juan
Jaime   Rebecca
Janet   Wei-Cee $3 \times 8 = 24$
Jerry   Eun-Jin

Addition

Angela   8
Sam   8
        $+ 8$
        $\overline{24}$

Jaime
Jerry $8 + 8 + 8 = 24$

Derek
Sam

$4 + 4 + 4 + 4 + 4 + 4 = 24$

Janet
Sarah
Michael $8 + 8 = 16$
Aaron $16 + 8 = 24$
Eun-Jin

Michael
Aaron

Yousif
Kihyun
Nathan $8 + 8 + 8 = 24$
Juan

TEACHER-TO-TEACHER TALK When asked to solve a problem using two different strategies, a child may get different answers from the strategies and move on as if the difference doesn't matter. Perhaps he or she views mathematics as doing the problem and getting an answer—regardless of whether the answer makes sense. Children need to understand that mathematics entails sense making. The goal is not merely to get an answer, any answer. If two answers for the same problem do not agree, encourage the child to check each strategy or to try a third strategy.

Some children may manipulate numbers on their second or third strategy to get the same answer yielded by their first strategy. In this case, the numbers will probably have little connection to the original problem. For example, suppose the problem is "How many legs altogether are there on five dogs?" A child might write $5 \times 4 = 20$ and draw pictures that make sense of the problem, but then write $5 + 5 + 5 + 5$ as his or her third strategy. (See Figure 3–5.) If you see this sort of thing happening, ask the child to show you how these 5s connect to the problem of five dogs each with four legs.

If you insist that one of the two strategies be pictorial, you may "see" how well a child understands the problem. For example, a child who has memorized $3 \times 8 = 24$ and quickly writes the appropriate number equation may have no idea how to represent those numbers through pictures. He or she might draw three sets of three spiders, each with eight legs. If this happens, ask the child to count the legs on all the spiders. Then ask him or her to read the story problem aloud. Finally, ask, "Do your pictures make sense for this problem?"

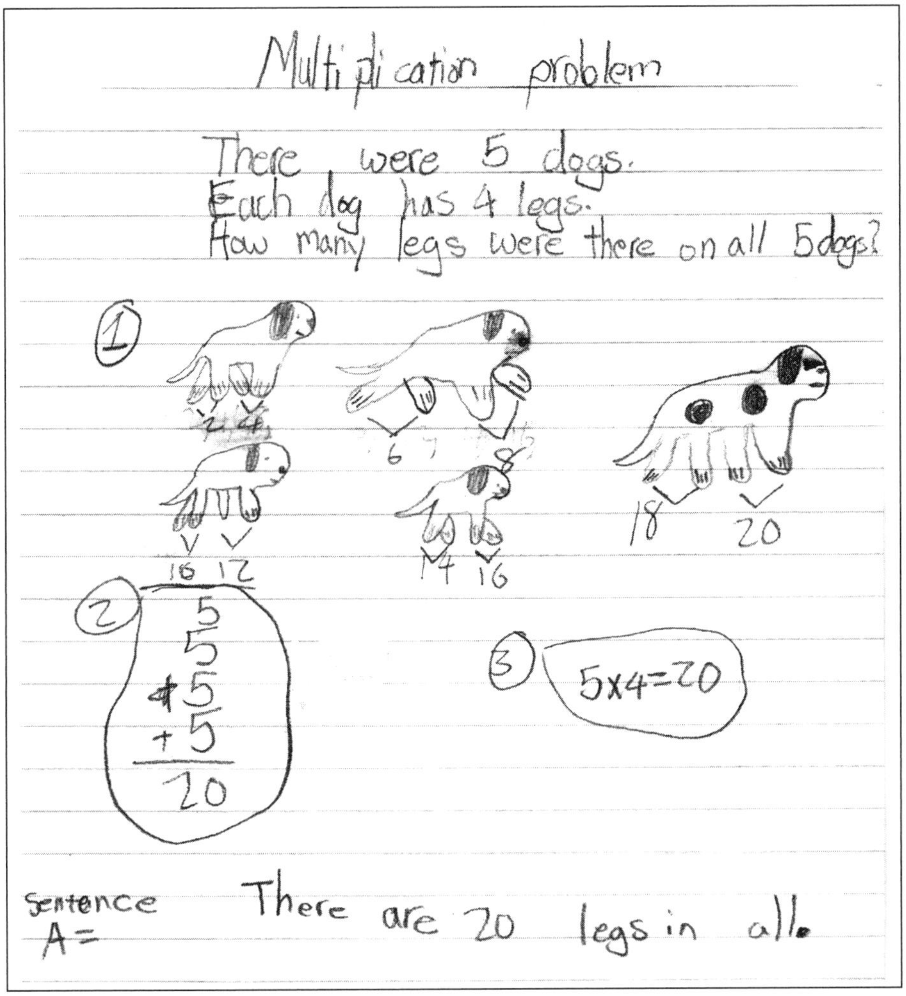

FIGURE 3–5 ◀

Though Kihyun's 5 + 5 + 5 + 5 strategy yielded the correct answer to this problem, it bears little logical connection to the problem.

Mathematics Throughout the Day

During October and November, you may wish to continue classroom-attendance and lunch-count routines, daily temperature readings, and snack-time grouping and counting. At the same time, you may want to introduce the new problem-solving activities explained below, such as *The Pocket Problem* ("How many pockets are on our clothes today?") and the number of days school has been in session. Explore multiplicative thinking when it makes sense to do so in these everyday contexts.

Snack Time

Materials

- a large box of fish crackers

Instructions

1. During recess, place an equal number of fish crackers on each napkin for four children seated at a table. Ensure that some tables have more crackers on each napkin while others have fewer. But all the children at the same table should have an equal number of crackers.

2. Ask the children at one table how many crackers there are on each napkin on their table. If they say each of them has seven crackers, ask the whole class how many crackers there are altogether at that table and how they did their figuring.

3. Record the variety of strategies the children use to figure the answer. Clarify that $4 \times 7 = 28$ is a number equation. By contrast, *4 people × 7 crackers for each person = 28 crackers altogether* could be called a word/number equation.

4. Invite the children at the remaining tables to calculate how many crackers are at their tables altogether, and to share their strategies.

5. Let the students eat the crackers.

TEACHER-TO-TEACHER TALK Some students may not be ready to reason numerically and, understand better when using word/number equations. Others may need to group beans or cubes to represent the crackers for this snack-time routine and to draw pictures. Some students might need the 1–100 chart to skip-count, for example, nine crackers four times. Make these tools readily available at each table.

Extensions

- After recording the total number of crackers at each table, have the children figure the total for the entire classroom.
- Find the difference between the table with the greatest total and the table with the least total.

The Pocket Problem

Each day, children come to school with a variety of pockets on their clothing. This situation provides an opportunity for them to gather data using two different strategies.

Table-by-Table Data

Have children figure the total number of pockets at each table group by putting an interlocking cube in each pocket, then combining the table group's cubes in ten-trains and leftovers. You might record this data as follows:

Table Totals

Table 1 = 18 pockets
Table 2 = 9 pockets
Table 3 = 14 pockets
Table 4 = 5 pockets
Table 5 = 11 pockets

Table 1 would have one ten-train plus eight separate cubes. Table 2 would have nine separate cubes. Table 3 would have one ten-train plus four separate cubes. Table 4 would have five separate cubes. Table 5 would have one ten-train plus a separate cube.

Let the children discuss and decide how to group and count the cubes from all the tables to arrive at a classroom total. They might choose to combine the 1s first and change them into ten-trains, or they might decide to group the already formed ten-trains first. If they gather the ten-trains first, prop up the trains vertically on the board tray. In this example, you would end up with three ten-trains, indicating thirty pockets so far. Record *30* on the board.

Next the children could bring up their leftover cubes. Before they combine them into ten-trains, have them look at the data recorded so far and estimate how many more ten-trains they think they'll get. Some might see that $4 + 5 + 1$ equals 10, then $8 + 9 = 17$ (or $10 + 7$), so they'll get two more ten-trains, with seven extras. Others might see $9 + 1 = 10$ then $8 + 4 = 12$ followed by $12 + 5 = 17$ or $10 + 7$.

Have the children combine the separate cubes into ten-trains to see if they do get what they expected. Listen to their suggestions on whether to record the 27 next to the 30 on the board or under the 30 on the board as they make sense of the total (57). Perhaps you will do both—adding horizontally and vertically.

People and Pocket Count

For this strategy on another day, students again put one interlocking cube into each pocket. You then record the number of students who have no pockets, the number who have one, the number who have two, and so forth. This time, show the results in the form of multiplication equations:

2 people have 0 pockets	(2 people × 0 pockets = 0 pockets)
1 person has 1 pocket	(1 person × 1 pocket = 1 pocket)
1 person has 2 pockets	(1 person × 2 pockets = 2 pockets for one person)
2 people have 3 pockets	(2 people × 3 pockets on each person = 6 pockets for 2 people)
3 people have 4 pockets	(3 people × 4 pockets on each person = 12 pockets for 3 people)
3 people have 5 pockets	(3 people × 5 pockets on each person = 15 pockets for 3 people)
2 people have 6 pockets	(2 people × 6 pockets on each person = 12 pockets for 2 people)
1 person has 7 pockets	(1 person × 7 pockets = 7 pockets)

Have the two people with no pockets come up and help you write the appropriate word/number multiplication equation. Continue with the remaining groups. As each group comes up, have each student within the group connect his or her cubes to make a tower. For example, if a group of two people each with three pockets comes up, they'll give you two towers of three cubes. Point out the factors (two groups of three), then write the corresponding word/number equation on the board.

Finally, ask the children to work in pairs to figure out the total number of pockets in the classroom. Have them record their strategies step by step and share them at the end of the current period or the beginning of the next math period.

School Days So Far

During the first six weeks of school, you may have used the *Today's Number* routine. If you've connected this routine to days of the month, your students may have written equations using numbers from 1 to as high as

TEACHER-TO-TEACHER TALK   When the children make equal-size towers of cubes representing their pockets, they create concrete models representing the idea that multiplication involves groups of equal size. When you add words to the numbers in the multiplication equations, you help the children attach additional meaning to the more abstract numbers.

Consider putting a date on each set of pocket data. That way, students can compare and combine the data from one day to the next.

You can also assign questions about *The Pocket Problem* as homework. Here's an example:

On Monday, October 14, the children in Room 33 were wearing clothing with 57 pock-ets. On Tuesday, October 15, the children were wearing clothing with 48 pockets. What is the difference between the number of pockets on these two days? If you combine the number of pockets on both of these days, what would you get?

Of course, these are addition and subtraction problems. Although multiplication is this unit's focus, other operations continue to be part of third graders' mathematics prob-lem solving. Having a robust sense of number means knowing when to add, subtract, multiply, and (eventually) divide in real-world contexts.

31. When you connect *Today's Number* to the number of days school has been in session, the possibilities expand enormously.

When you first introduce *Today's Number*, have students write equations with no constraints—then see what you get. You may be surprised at how many operations the children use to write equations that make sense. As your third graders become more comfortable with multiplication and the idea of equal-size groups, you might add the following kinds of constraints:

"Use multiplication and addition in your equation," for example, $(4 \times 10) + 2 = 42$ or $(5 \times 8) + 2 = 42$.

"Use multiplication and subtraction in your equation," for example, $(5 \times 10) - 8 = 42$.

You and your students will think of additional ideas if you adopt *Today's Number* as a routine.

Games

Games provide an enjoyable context for children's learning about multi-plication. Games also make it easier for students to communicate their growing understanding to friends and family. As with mathematical routines, encourage the youngsters to use counters, pictures, or 1–100 charts before they move on to numerical reasoning alone. As they play more and more games, children build understanding of multiplication combinations.

Circles and Stars

Before introducing *Circles and Stars*, have your students conduct the *Things That Come in Groups* investigation, described on page 101. After the children have played a few rounds of *Circles and Stars*, have them do the *Window Wall* investigation connected with the book *Amanda Bean's Amazing Dream* by Cindy Neushwander (see pages 94–98).

Circles and Stars gives children experience with the repeated-addition aspect of multiplication. It also helps them see multiplication as the combining of equal-size groups that can be represented with a multiplication equation. At the end of the game, the children use addition to figure the total number of stars they've drawn. Then they use subtraction to find the difference between their total number of stars and their partner's. The game is thus mathematically rich, and children as well as parents love to play it over and over again. (For detailed instructions of how the game works, see Blackline Masters.) Below are instructions for introducing the game and exploring specific aspects of the activity.

Materials

- 1 die per pair of students
- several pieces of $8\frac{1}{2}$-by-11-inch white paper per student

Instructions
Part 1: Introducing the Game

1. On the board, draw a large rectangle divided into two rows with four squares in each. (See below.) This is your rectangle.

2. Draw another, identical rectangle next to the first one. This is your partner's rectangle.

3. Invite a student volunteer to come up to the board. In the upper-left box of each rectangle, each of you writes the following information (using your own names, of course):

Circles and Stars

Sharon's total __
Sam's total __
Difference __

4. Roll the die and draw the corresponding number of circles at the top of the second box in your rectangle's top row. For example, if you roll a 4, draw four circles.

5. Your partner rolls the die and draws the corresponding number of circles in the second box of his or her rectangle's top row.

6. You roll the die a second time and draw the corresponding number of stars in *each* circle. For instance, if you roll a 2, you draw two stars inside each of your four circles.

7. Your partner does the same after his or her second roll.

8. You and your partner repeat these steps until you've each filled in the last two boxes in your rectangle's top row with circles and stars.

Part 2: Playing in Pairs

1. Show students how to fold an $8\frac{1}{2}$-by-11-inch sheet of plain paper into eight equal sections.

2. Have the children pair up.

3. Invite them to take turns rolling a die and drawing circles and stars in the sections across the top row of their papers—as you and your volunteer did during the demonstration. Encourage partners to check one another's work, round by round. Remind the children to leave a little room at the bottom of each section for writing.

Part 3: Multiplying

1. Later that same day, or the next day, ask the children to gather at the rug area and sit down.

2. Point to the rectangle you drew on the board, then draw students' attention to the first box in which you drew circles and stars. Write the corresponding multiplication equation below the circles and stars; e.g., $4 \times 2 = 8$.

3. Ask the children to explain what the equation means, using words and numbers. You may hear responses such as:

"Four groups of two equals eight."

"Four sets of two equals eight."

"Four twos equals eight."

"Four times two equals eight."

"Four circles with two stars in each equals eight stars in all four circles."

As the children generate the list, connect the words and numbers back to the drawing. Later, record these statements on a chart and post it in the classroom.

4. Do the same with the remaining boxes in your rectangle's top row.

5. Have the children return to their desks and generate equations for their top rows of circles and stars. Rotate through the room and check to see that the first factor indicates the number of circles and the second factor shows the number of stars in each circle.

Part 4: Adding and Subtracting

1. That same day or the next, you and your volunteer roll the die and fill in the four boxes in the bottom row of your rectangles with circles and stars. Create multiplication equations for these four boxes. (See below.)

2. Ask class members for ideas on how to add the seven products in your rectangle's boxes. Someone might suggest that you write the products vertically on the left side of the board like this:

8

6

30

12

20

15

8

Others might suggest that you group numbers that seem to go together, continuing to add on one product at a time, and cross the products off as you go:

Strategy 1

8 + 12 = 20

20 + 20 = 40

40 + 15 = 55

55 + 30 = 85

85 + 6 = 91

91 + 8 = 99

Still others might feel better grouping two products at a time and leaving the "leftover" product on its own:

Strategy 2

8 + 12 = 20   30 + 20 = 50   6 + 8 = 14   15

In this case, you may want to cross off each product in the rectangle as you use it. Then join the partial totals (20 + 50 = 70 and 14 + 15 = 29). Finally, add the partial totals (70 + 29 = 99).

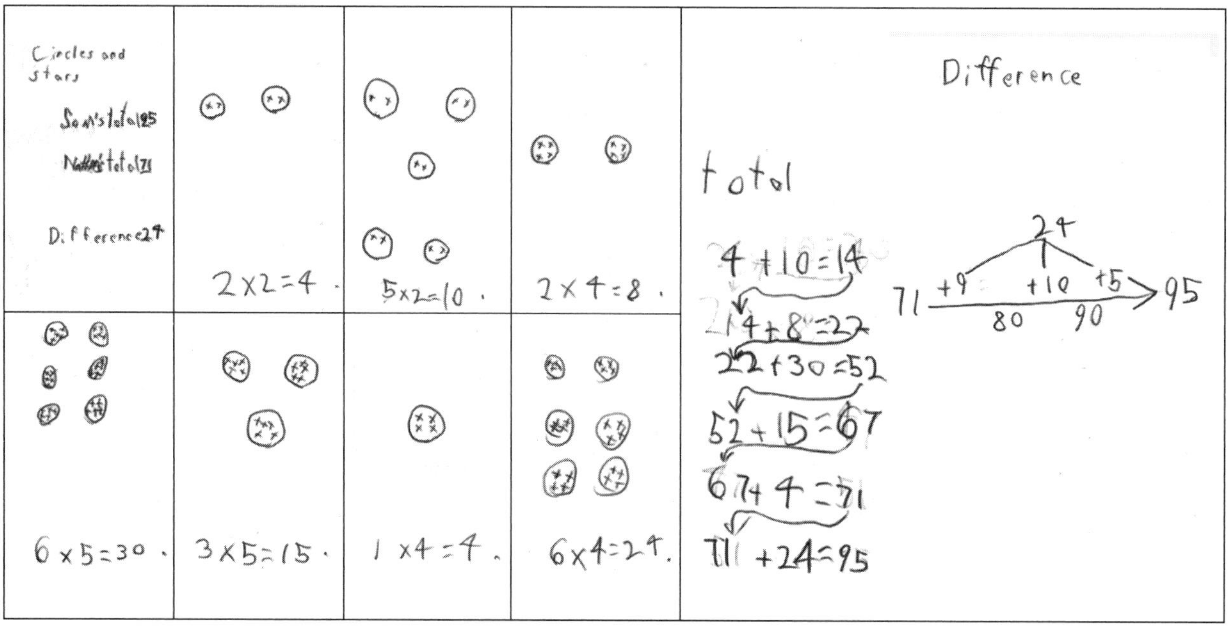

FIGURE 3–6 ▲

Sam showed how he created multiplication equations for his circles and stars, then found the total number of stars using Strategy 1. He also showed how he found the difference between his total number of stars and that of Nathan, his partner.

Your students will likely generate a number of different ideas for finding the sum of the products.

3. Now have the children find the *sum* of their own seven products. Also challenge them to find the *difference* between the total number of stars they drew and the total their partner drew. (See Figures 3–6 and 3–7 for examples.) Have partners check the accuracy of one another's work. Circulate and offer support and encouragement for children often get lost when adding seven products.

Part 5: Making Sense of Multiplication Combinations

1. Have students staple their "total" and "difference" work to their *Circles and Stars* game page and file the papers in their math folders.

2. On a later day, draw a large chart with the numbers 1 through 18 down one column and the numbers 19 through 36 down a second column. Then roll up the chart so the children cannot see it.

3. Ask the children, "What is the *smallest* product you can get when playing *Circles and Stars*?" The response may include "one," which you can get by rolling a 1 and a 1 with the die ($1 \times 1 = 1$).

4. Now ask, "What's the *largest* product you can get, and how do you get it?" Someone may respond, "You can get thirty-six by drawing six circles each with six stars inside" ($6 \times 6 = 36$).

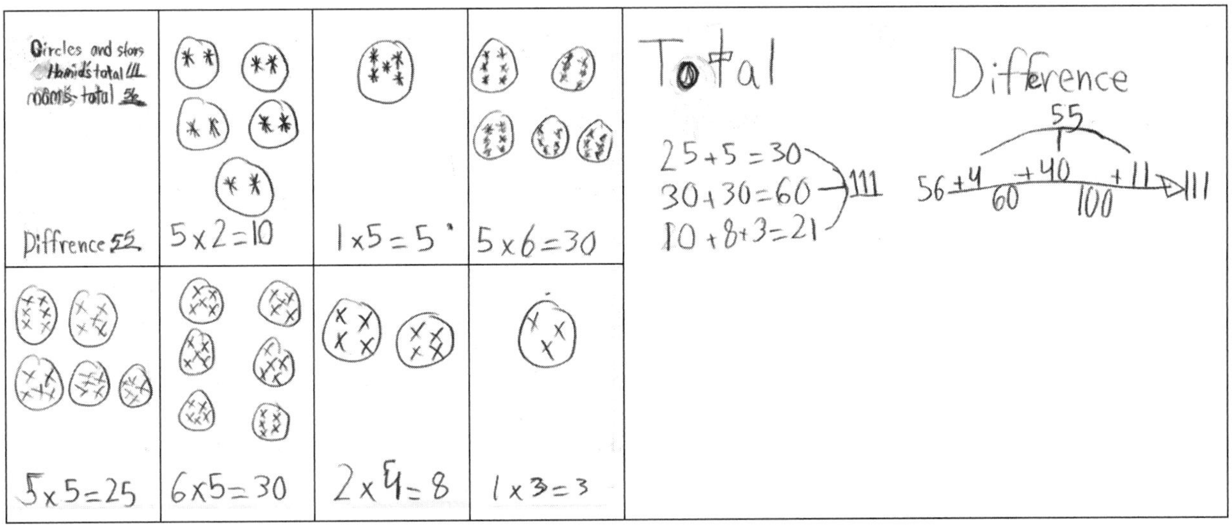

FIGURE 3–7 ▲

Hamid used Strategy 2 for getting the total number of stars.

5. Roll down the chart you created earlier.

6. Have the children get their *Circles and Stars* game sheets from their math folders. Invite a volunteer to bring up his or her *Circles and Stars* game sheet. Demonstrate using tally marks to record the seven products from the sheet on the 1–36 chart you've unrolled. That is, if the volunteer's sheet has the products 25, 20, 12, 36, 18, 6, and 2, you would put one tally mark next to each of those numbers on the class chart.

7. Have the remaining students come up to record their products on the chart. (See Figure 3–8.)

8. Discuss the recorded data. Ask why there are no tally marks next to some numbers (such as 7 and 11). Ideally, the children will realize that the die goes up to 6, and you can only get a product of 7 with these two factors—one and seven. You can only get a product of 11 with these two factors—one and eleven. These two numbers are prime numbers. (There is a discussion of prime numbers on page 97.)

9. Ask which products have more tally marks than others and why. (This line of questioning has more data support when the *Circles and Stars* products chart has tally marks recorded from two or three games per person.) You might begin with the number 12, which typically will have a lot of tally marks. Ask, "How can you get a product of twelve in this game?" Through discussion, the children will realize that they can get 12 in four different ways: three circles each with four stars, four circles each with three stars, two circles each with six stars, and six circles each with two stars.

FIGURE 3–8   ▶

Here's one class's *Circles and Stars* product chart.

Circles and Stars Products

1 ‖‖‖ ‖‖‖ ‖‖
2 ‖‖‖ ‖‖‖ ‖‖‖
3 ‖‖‖ ‖‖‖ ‖‖‖ ‖‖
4 ‖‖‖ ‖‖‖ ‖‖‖ ‖‖
5 ‖‖‖ ‖‖‖ ‖‖‖ ‖
6 ‖‖‖ ‖‖‖ ‖‖‖ ‖‖‖ ‖‖‖ ‖‖‖ ‖
7
8 ‖‖‖ ‖‖‖ ‖‖‖ ‖‖‖
9 ‖‖‖
10 ‖‖‖ ‖‖‖ ‖‖‖ ‖‖
11
12 ‖‖‖ ‖‖‖ ‖‖‖ ‖‖‖ ‖‖
13
14
15 ‖‖‖ ‖‖‖ ‖‖‖ ‖
16 ‖‖‖
17
18 ‖‖‖ ‖‖‖ ‖‖‖ ‖‖

19
20 ‖‖‖ ‖‖‖ ‖‖‖ ‖‖
21
22
23
24 ‖‖‖ ‖‖‖ ‖‖‖
25 ‖‖‖
26
27
28
29
30 ‖‖‖ ‖‖‖ ‖‖
31
32
33
34
35
36 ‖‖‖ ‖‖‖ ‖

Multiplication Bingo

This game is an apt follow-up to *Circles and Stars*. You can find detailed information and instructions for *Multiplication Bingo* in *Teaching Arithmetic: Lessons for Introducing Multiplication, Grade 3*, by Marilyn Burns, as well as in the Blackline Masters.

TEACHER-TO-TEACHER TALK *Circles and Stars* can serve as a meaningful thread tying together your students' experiences with multiplication involving equal-size groups. Continue to encourage students to play multiplication games at home. For example, *Circles and Stars* could be a weekly homework assignment. For families that don't have or don't approve of dice, you can send home a wooden cube with the numbers 1 through 6 written on each face. Or a family could use slips of paper numbered 1 through 6 that are pulled from a bowl or bag.

Before or just after winter break, the children could focus on the combinations not included in the original *Circles and Stars* game for threes, fours, and sixes:

3×7	4×7	6×7
3×8	4×8	6×8
3×9	4×9	6×9

To do this, extend the game of *Circles and Stars* by having the children use number cubes with the six faces covered with these factors: 4, 5, 6, 7, 8, and 9 or spinners with all the factors including zero (0, 1, 2, 3, 4, 5, 6, 7, 8, 9, 10). With the number cube version of the game, the totals add up to the two and three hundreds. If the children play with a number cube marked 4, 5, 6, 7, 8, and 9, or with a regular die, they will not be practicing these combinations: $3 \times 7 = 21$, $3 \times 8 = 24$, $3 \times 9 = 27$.

Materials

- 1 *Multiplication Bingo* game sheet plus instructions per child (see Blackline Masters)
- 1 die per student

Instructions

1. Give each student a *Multiplication Bingo* game sheet plus directions.

2. Ask students to fill in the products they *think* will occur when they roll a die. They must decide whether to leave some products out and whether to write some products more than once. As they fill in possible products, they might want to refer to the *Circles and Stars* products chart you've posted in the classroom. You may also want to talk with students again about the highest possible product, the lowest possible product, and products that aren't possible. Remind students which products have only one way to get them, and which (such as 12) have more than one way to get them.

3. Ask children to pair up.

4. Player 1 rolls the die once. That number stands for the number of circles. Then she rolls the die a second time. That number stands for the number of stars in her circles. She announces the resulting product and crosses it off with an *X* on her *Multiplication Bingo* game card (if she had filled it in).

5. Player 2 checks the correctness of Player 1's thinking. Then Player 2 takes his turn. Play continues until one player has Bingo: five *X*s in a row vertically, horizontally, or diagonally.

Extensions

Assign *Multiplication Bingo* as homework for children and their parents to play. Provide a copy of the *Circles and Stars* products chart and a 1–100 chart.

Measurement

At this time of year, children continue using nonstandard tools, such as interlocking cubes or paperclips, to measure objects. In the spring, they'll use standard measurement units, such as inches or centimeters.

Beans in a Jar (Volume)

Materials

- 1 one-quarter measuring cup
- 40 interlocking cubes
- 1 pint jar

Instructions

1. Ask the children if they remember how many cubes were in the pint estimation jar at the beginning of the school year. Remind them that the jar was not full.

2. Fill the measuring cup with interlocking cubes and show the children the number of cubes. (It should hold four Unifix cubes.)

3. Tell the students that you're going to use the measuring cup to scoop cubes into the pint jar.

4. Ask how many measuring cups full of cubes the students estimate it will take to fill the jar. Invite them to explain their reasoning. Ideally, some children will describe using multiplication. For example, if the measuring cup holds four cubes, and the students think that thirty-two cubes can fit in the jar, someone might explain that filling the jar will require eight cups ($8 \times 4 = 32$).

5. Record the estimates and discuss their range.

6. Then scoop one cupful at a time into the jar as the children count scoops aloud, until the jar is a little more than half full. Ask the children if anyone wants to change his or her estimate and why.

7. Finish filling the jar, then have the children help you record the findings with the appropriate multiplication equation.

Cubes in a Box (Volume)

Materials

- 1 small box (such as those used to contain bank checks) per student
- 1 bag of 2-centimeter or 1-inch wooden cubes per table

Instructions

1. Each child places one row and one column of cubes in the bottom of a box. (See below.)

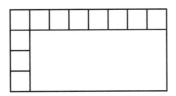

2. Drawing on their window-wall or rectangular-array experiences, students estimate how many columns and how many rows it will take to put down one layer of cubes to cover the bottom of the box. They then estimate the number of cubes it will take to fill that layer.

3. Next they actually fill in the entire layer to check their reasoning.

4. They count the cubes in the bottom of their box, then calculate the difference between their estimate and the actual count.

5. Finally, they estimate how many cubes it would take to fill the entire box, and check their estimate against the actual count. (See Figure 3–9.)

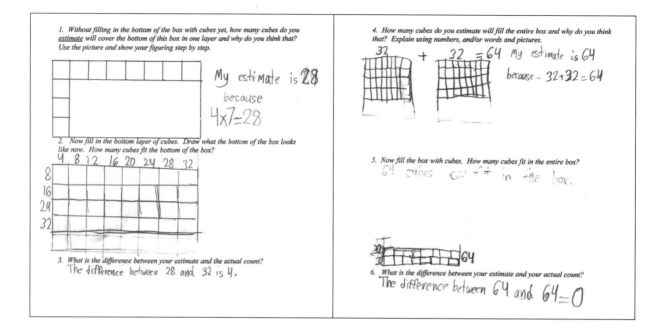

1. *Without filling in the bottom of the box with cubes yet, how many cubes do you* <u>*estimate*</u> *will cover the bottom of this box in one layer and why do you think that? Use the picture and show your figuring step by step.*

My estimate is 28 because 4x7=28

2. *Now fill in the bottom layer of cubes. Draw what the bottom of the box looks like now. How many cubes fit the bottom of the box?*

3. *What is the difference between your estimate and the actual count?*

The difference between 28 and 32 is 4.

4. *How many cubes do you estimate will fill the entire box and why do you think that? Explain using numbers, and/or words and pictures.*

32 + 32 = 64 My estimate is 64 because- 32+32=64

5. *Now fill the box with cubes. How many cubes fit in the entire box?*

64 cubes can fit in the box.

6. *What is the difference between your estimate and your actual count?*

The difference between 64 and 64 = 0

FIGURE 3–9 ▲

Jaime showed his reasoning through every step of this activity.

It is up to you whether children record their thinking by answering questions or by filling in blanks. Both of these problem sheets are fairly scripted. Here is the question option:

> *How many cubes do you estimate will cover the bottom of this box, and why do you think that? Explain your thinking using words, pictures, and numbers. Now fill in the bottom layer of cubes. How many cubes fit the bottom of the box? What is the difference between your estimate and your actual count?*

> *How many cubes do you estimate will fill the entire box, and why do you think that? Explain your thinking using words, pictures, and numbers. Now fill the box with cubes. How many cubes fit in the entire box? What is the difference between your estimate and the actual count?*

Here is the fill-in-the-blank option:

> *There are __ rows and __ columns of cubes in the bottom of my box. I estimate there will be __ cubes when one layer of the box is filled in. Here is how I did my figuring:*

> *After I filled in the layer of cubes in the box, there were __ cubes. My multiplication word/number equation shows this: __ rows of cubes × __ cubes in each row = __ cubes altogether. The difference between my estimate and the answer is __.*

I estimate that it will take __ blocks to fill the entire box. Here is how I figured out my estimate:

When I actually filled the box with cubes, I used __ cubes.

TEACHER-TO-TEACHER TALK In all honesty, I am not so sure that I am going to present this *Cubes in a Box* problem the same way next year. I feel as if I were leading the children to follow my reasoning here, and I am convinced they needed more "free exploration" time with the 2-centimeter wooden blocks and variety of boxes we had in class. They needed to get a "feel" for the idea of cubic volume by fitting the cubes into different boxes. I often rethink problem-solving activities and jot down thoughts for next year. Another thought I have jotted down is that perhaps this activity should be more open-ended. I plan to listen to what the children are thinking as they do their "free exploration." Their comments often lead to more appropriate questions or investigations.

In Half a Minute (Elapsed Time)

Materials

- wall clock

Instructions

1. Ask students to pair up.

2. Player 1 writes the letters of the alphabet from A to Z while Player 2 times thirty seconds.

3. The partners switch roles.

4. The players count their letters by grouping and multiplying. Then they write multiplication word/number equations to show their reasoning. For example:

   4 groups × 5 letters in each group = 20 letters in all 4 groups

   20 letters + the 3 leftovers = 23 letters altogether.

Extensions

- The players estimate how many letters they can write in one minute, based on their half-minute data. Then they test their estimate by writing letters in one minute.

- Players write the digits from 0 through 9 over and over again in half a minute or in one minute. They count their data by grouping and multiplying, then write equations showing their thinking.

■ Players find the difference between their half-minute or one-minute letters and digits data.

Money

When children handle money, they feel they are working with math in a way that connects to the real world. They love buying things and making change just as adults do.

Billy Wins a Shopping Spree

This activity is drawn from *Teaching Arithmetic: Lessons for Introducing Multiplication, Grade 3* by Marilyn Burns (2001). In it, Billy wins a $25.00 gift certificate to spend at the science museum store. He has lists of items that cost $3.00 (origami paper, crystal and gem magnets, furry stuffed seal pups, and a prism), $4.00 (kaleidoscope, large magnifying bug box, sun-print kit, and inflatable shark), and $5.00 (Koosh ball, glow-in-the-dark solar-system stickers, inflatable world globe, and wooden dinosaur model kit). (See Blackline Masters for Billy's Science Museum Store Price List.)

Children could work in pairs to explore two different ways Billy might spend his $25.00 and the amount of change he would receive. First they list each item they want him to buy and a quantity for each item. They work using this model:

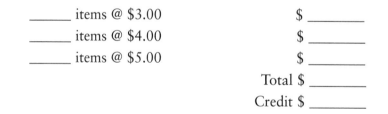

Explain that @ means "at." Ask the children to show how they do each of their "figurings." For instance, for two items that cost $3.00 each, the children would write *2 × $3.00 = $6.00*. Have students also show their strategy for adding up the total amount due and the change owed.

Classroom-Supply Shopping Revisited

Create a classroom-supply list that encourages the children to practice with specific multiplication combinations. For example, if you want students to build their knowledge of 2s, 5s, and 10s, set prices as follows: paper-clips at $.02 each, pencils at $.05 each, and erasers at $.10 each. The 5s and 10s will also give them practice grouping nickels and dimes.

If you want the children to have practice multiplying by 3s, 4s, 6s and 7s, set prices such as the following: paperclips at \$.03 each, bookmarks at \$.04 each, pencils at \$.06 each, and erasers at \$.07 each. These prices would encourage students to group pennies by 3s, 4s, 6s, and 7s before exchanging them for nickels, dimes, quarters, and so forth.

For example, if Janet bought three paperclips at \$.03 each, she should spend \$.09 (3 × \$.03 = \$.09). And if she bought four pencils at \$.06 each, the cost would be \$.24 (4 × \$.06 = \$.24). Her *total* bill would come to \$.33 (\$.24 + \$.09). She could pay her bill in a variety of ways: 33 pennies; 6 nickels, and 3 pennies; 1 quarter, 1 nickel, and 3 pennies; and so forth.

To further Janet's thinking, you could ask her to pay you with two quarters and then have her figure out the change owed to her. Next have her pay with a \$1.00 bill. This is a marvelous opportunity to build on the comparison model of subtraction in a real-world situation. Janet might figure out the difference between 33 and 100 by counting up to friendly numbers: "Here are seven pennies getting me to forty. Here is one dime getting me to fifty. Here are two quarters getting me to one hundred. The change is sixty-seven cents." Or, she might think "seven plus thirty-three is forty, and forty plus sixty is one hundred."

With this activity, you might initially act as the cashier, using a toy cash register or a money-change tray. Later, the children can take turns playing the role of cashier.

Coins in Two Pockets Revisited

Write money problems on cards; for example, *I have 6 dimes, 4 pennies, and 4 nickels in one pocket. I have exactly the same coins in my other pocket. How much money do I have altogether?* Have children pick a card and then write equations showing the solution to the problem. The solution to this card might read *6 dimes* × \$.10 = \$.60, *4 pennies* × \$.01 = \$.04, *and 4 nickels* × \$.05 = \$.20. Students can then find the total by adding: \$.60 + \$.04 + \$.20 = \$.84. *You have \$.84 in one pocket, so you have* \$.84 + \$.84 = \$1.68 *in both pockets.*

Extensions

Students write their own story-problem cards for doubling money. See *Mathematical Thinking at Grade 3* by Susan Jo Russell and Karen Economopoulos (1995) for additional ideas.

Literature-Based Activities

If the way to a child's mind is through his or her hands, heart, and imagination, children's literature provides the context for the latter two pathways. Whereas manipulatives provide work for hands, stories help children tie mathematics to the real and the pretend world.

Change for a Quarter

In *A Quarter from the Tooth Fairy* by Caren Holzman, a little boy keeps changing his mind about how to spend his quarter. When he returns each of his choices (a monster, a spaceship pencil, red swim goggles), he gets different configurations of coins equaling $.25 as change.

Read the story aloud, then encourage students to explore all the different ways to make change for a quarter by using the coins in their money bags. They could record their ideas and show their reasoning with multiplication equations. (See Figure 3–10.) Ideally, they'll identify twelve different ways to make change for a quarter.

Multiplication Connections

Amanda Bean's Amazing Dream by Cindy Neushwander ties multiplication to the real world. In the story, Amanda loves to count everything from the panes in windows to cookies on trays to sheep on bicycles. The first

FIGURE 3–10 ▶

Rebecca listed various ways of making change for a quarter.

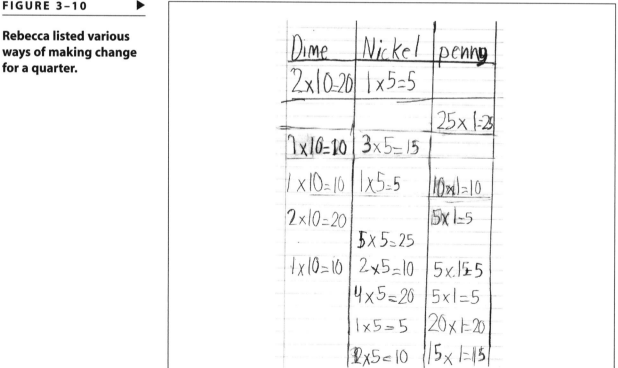

time you read the book to your class, focus on the pictures and words without pushing the mathematics. Reread the story several times, each time focusing on a different multiplication connection. Pickles in jars, books on shelves, tiles on a counter, wheels on bicycles, and many other groups of equal size are featured. At the end of the book, Amanda finally realizes that multiplication provides a short cut when you're adding equal-size groups.

First explore the pages depicting panes in windows and cookies on trays. Both of these examples provide geometric models for thinking about multiplication.

Windowpane Arrays

The first two pages of the book show windows in the purple building. The windows consist of rectangular arrays of six rows with three window panes in each row. You might have students build this array using colored tiles that represent the windowpanes. (If you do not have colored tiles, consider visiting a nearby building-supply store and getting those sheets of one-inch square tiles used on bathroom floors. Or, use one-inch squares cut from colored cardstock.)

Explain to students that a *row* is horizontal and a *column* is vertical. The word/number equation for describing the *rows* in this example is *6 rows × 3 windowpanes in each = 18 windowpanes in the window*. The number equation would be *6 × 3 = 18*. The word/number equation describing the *columns* in this example is *3 columns × 6 windowpanes in each = 18 windowpanes in the window*. The number equation would be *3 × 6 = 18*.

The next building in the story has windows consisting of two rows, each with two panes. Have the children build these windows with tiles as well, and write the corresponding word/number equation: *2 rows × 2 windowpanes in each row = 4 windowpanes in the window*.

Finally, the book shows a building in which each window has three rows, each containing two panes. The corresponding word/number equation would be *3 rows × 2 windowpanes in each = 6 windowpanes in all*.

Ask the children to use their tiles to build all the possible arrays for four windowpanes. (See below.)

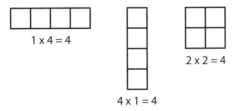

Then ask, "What are all the possible arrangements for five windowpanes? For six?" And so forth. Have the children use tiles to build them as well.

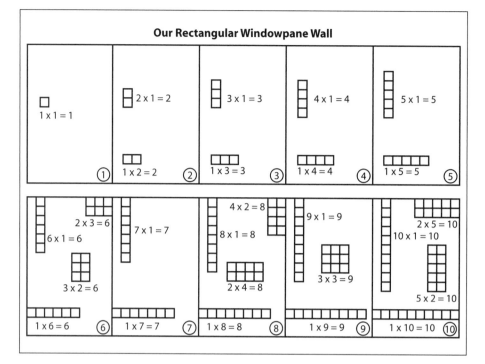

Our Rectangular Windowpane Wall

Over several days, ask class members to make arrays for windowpanes numbering 1 through 30. To do this, children can cut out half-inch grid paper to represent the windows. (See Blackline Masters.) They can then write a multiplication equation to represent each array. In my class, we posted these arrays on $8\frac{1}{2}$-by-11-inch cardstock on a "window wall" so we could refer to them over the next few months. (See Figure 3–11).

Once you've created a window wall, students can take down one of the windowpane arrays from the wall and draw designs on the board matching the different arrays. For example, arrays for six windowpanes would include a 1×6 window, a 6×1 window, a 2×3 window, and a 3×2 window. Children could use their colored tiles to create each array.

Suggest that students count the number of sides in each array; i.e., think about perimeter. Ask, "If an ant were to walk around the entire edge of the first two windows [e.g., the 1×6 and the 6×1 window], how many sides would the ant pass?" Someone might say "One plus six plus one plus six equals fourteen edges." Have the student connect this equation to the dimensions on the array. Another child might reason through the following equation: $(1 + 1) + (6 + 6) = 14$. Have that child also connect those numbers to the picture.

Ask whether anyone used multiplication in his or her figuring. For example, perhaps one child will propose these equations: $2 \times 1 = 2$ and $2 \times 6 = 12$, then $2 + 12 = 14$. Possibly another child will think of these equations: $1 + 6 = 7$ and $1 + 6 = 7$, then $2 \times 7 = 14$. Encourage these children to connect their numbers to the array as well.

TEACHER-TO-TEACHER TALK Different mathematics books approach these arrays in different ways. For instance, you might want to review Marilyn Burns's *Candy Boxes* investigations, in which children research how to package square candies in single layers in boxes (*Teaching Arithmetic: Lessons for Introducing Multiplication, Grade 3*). In the TERC Investigations book titled *Things That Come in Groups*, children are asked to arrange chairs in rectangular arrays. The important thing about arrays is that children connect this geometric model for thinking about multiplication to some real-world context.

As weeks go by, students will begin noticing square arrays on the window wall; e.g., two rows of two windowpanes (four panes), or three rows of three windowpanes (nine panes). This is an opportunity to introduce the idea of *square numbers*. The children may wish to label these special arrays with sticky notes or other signs.

Students may also eventually notice that some numbers of windowpanes have only two arrays. For example, the number 3 has just a 1 × 3 and a 3 × 1 array. Explain that these kinds of numbers are called *prime numbers*.

Eventually, you might want to begin discussing and recording the *factor pairs* represented by each windowpane array. For example, the factor pairs for a window with twelve panes would be:

1 × 12 = 12	*12 × 1 = 12*
2 × 6 = 12	*6 × 2 = 12*
3 × 4 = 12	*4 × 3 = 12*

Ask whether the 2 × 3 window and the 3 × 2 window will have the same or different perimeters. Have the children investigate. Ask the children if the 1 × 6 window and the 2 × 3 window have the same or different area. You and the children might decide to add the area (A = __) and the perimeter (P = __) next to each windowpane array on the window wall card for the number 6.

Cookies on a Tray

On the third and fourth page of *Amanda Bean's Amazing Dream*, Amanda sees cookies and brownies that are arranged in equal-size rows on trays. On one tray, there are three rows with six cookies in each row. On another tray, there are four rows with seven cookies in each row.

Draw these arrays on the board. Then ask the children how many cookies are on the second tray. Have them explain how they figured out their answer. As the children describe their thinking, record their responses on the board and encourage them to connect their numbers to the drawings of the cookie trays. For instance, if a child says that he added 7 + 7 + 7 + 7, ask him to show you the 7s in the drawing. If he points to the rows and explains that each has seven cookies, write a vertical list of four 7s to show his thinking. If he then says he combined 7 and 7 to get 14 and then another 7 and 7 to get 14 again, you could draw <. (See below.) If he ends his calculation by saying that 14 and 14 equals 28, you could use the < again.

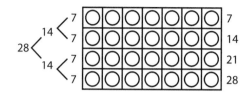

If another child says she skip-counted 7, 14, 21, 28, have her show her thinking on the drawing. List the skip-counts vertically along the other end of the array. (See above.)

Have the children help you write a word/number multiplication equation that captures this reasoning; e.g., *4 rows × 7 cookies in each row = 28 cookies in all 4 rows.*

Ask if there are any other ways to figure out how many cookies there are on the tray. Allow the children time to think. Someone might mention the columns instead of the rows and suggest adding 4 + 4 + 4 + 4 + 4 + 4 + 4 or skip-counting 4, 8, 12, 16, 20, 24, 28. Encourage students to help you write another word/number multiplication equation that expresses this thinking; e.g., *7 columns × 4 cookies in each column = 28 cookies in all 7 columns.* Have the children record both counting by rows and counting by columns. (See Figure 3–12.)

FIGURE 3–12 ▶

Sarah showed how she figured out that there are twenty-eight cookies on the tray.

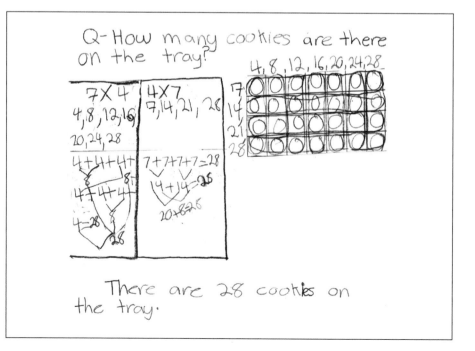

Nice Day for a Party

Through *Just Add Fun* by Joanne Rocklin, children continue to explore multiplication of groups of things, such as two cookies per person and four gumdrops per person, using repeated addition, skip-counting, and multiplication. The book also has a geometric component, revealed when Hank and Frank figure out how many cookies there are in rectangular arrays. The two friends decide to have a party at which each guest will have two gingersnap cookies, three peppermint candies, and four gumdrops. They have to keep refiguring their calculations when the guest list changes from two to four and so forth. Finally, they go shopping for the food.

Using pennies, buttons, beans, or drawings on grid paper, children can figure out "cookie riddles" such as "Which has more cookies—a tray with three rows and eight cookies in each row, or a tray with four rows and six cookies in each row?" (See Figure 3–13.)

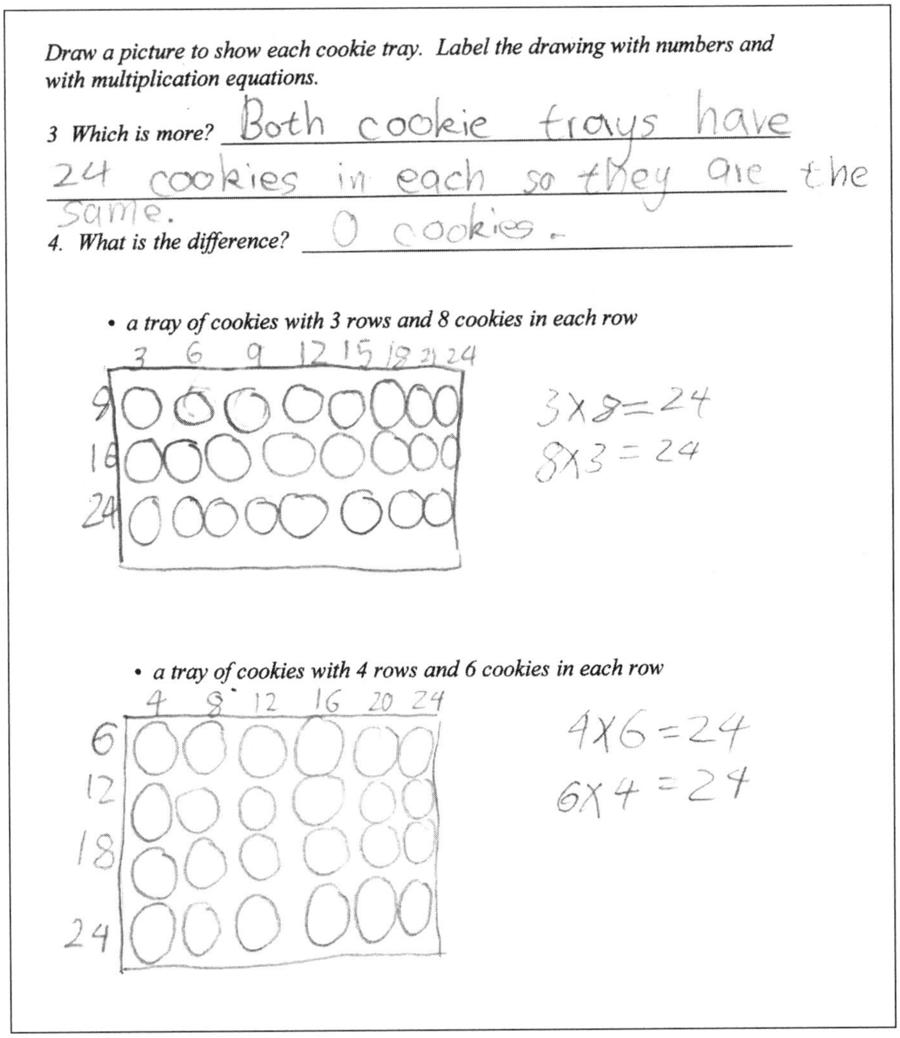

Draw a picture to show each cookie tray. Label the drawing with numbers and with multiplication equations.

3 Which is more? Both cookie trays have 24 cookies in each so they are the same.

4. What is the difference? 0 cookies.

• a tray of cookies with 3 rows and 8 cookies in each row

$$3 \times 8 = 24$$
$$8 \times 3 = 24$$

• a tray of cookies with 4 rows and 6 cookies in each row

$$4 \times 6 = 24$$
$$6 \times 4 = 24$$

FIGURE 3–13 ◀

Sasha used pictures with numbers to figure out which tray contained the most cookies.

In *Teaching Arithmetic: Lessons for Introducing Multiplication, Grade 3*, Marilyn Burns devotes an entire chapter to *Which Has More?* riddles, some of them relating to *Amanda Bean's Amazing Dream.* For example, students use words, numbers, and pictures to figure out which has more—a window with three rows of panes, each containing six panes, or a window with four rows, each containing six panes. (See Figure 3–14.)

Extensions

- Create a series of "Which has more?" problems, like those described above. Have children select and solve them.
- Create a series of "Which has more?" problems around "things that come in groups." Which has more wheels, 5 bicycles or 3 cars?

FIGURE 3–14 ▶

Janet used a similar strategy to figure out which array had more windowpanes.

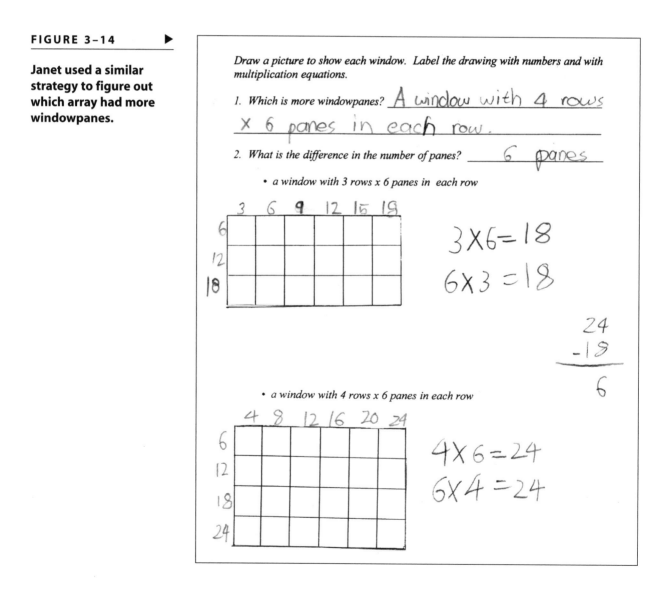

- Have the children create and solve their own "Which has more?" problems.

The Multiplication/Addition/Skip-Counting Connection

Too Many Cooks by Andrea Buckless enables students to revisit the idea that multiplication is connected to repeated addition and skip-counting (2, 4, 6, 8, 10, 12). In the story, Cara and her two brothers try to modify a soup recipe to accommodate themselves and their mother and grandparents—a total of six people. As they adjust different ingredients in the recipe using mathematics, Jay keeps slipping in his own ideas for ingredients—substituting a red rubber ball for tomatoes and two orange cars for carrots. When the children decide to eliminate the beets from the recipe, your students have an opportunity to think about why multiplying any number by 0 results in 0.

In *Teaching Arithmetic: Lessons for Introducing Multiplication, Grade 3,* Marilyn Burns describes an extensive class discussion based on Buckless's book. She has the children explore why $6 \times 0 = 0$. She puts the word *factor* and the equation's product on the board for the children's reference, then she asks students to begin writing their thoughts about why $6 \times 0 = 0$. If you introduce this activity to your students, you may see responses such as, "if you take anything times nothing you'll get nothing"; "if $6 \times 1 = 6$, then $6 \times 0 = 0$."

Story Problems

When children write their own story problems, they deepen their understanding of when to add, when to subtract, when to multiply, and when to divide in the real world. This understanding leads to a more robust sense of number. When children figure out what makes sense in story problems written by others, they also use mathematics to make sense of everyday situations. Here are some story-problem ideas for you to consider:

Things That Come In Groups

In this investigation, students think about things in the world that always come in groups of 2s (such as chopsticks), 3s (such as wheels on a tricycle), 4s (such as legs on a horse), and so on. Tie these ideas to classroom characteristics. For example, ask how many chopsticks would be needed if everyone at a team table were to have two. One child might skip-count: 2, 4, 6, 8. Another may answer "eight, because four children times two chopsticks for each child equals eight chopsticks for all four children at the table." A third child might arrive at the number 8 by reasoning through the following equations:

$$2 + 2 + 2 + 2$$
$$4 \quad + \quad 4 = 8$$

Next ask how many chopsticks would be needed for *all* the students in the class. In Figure 3–15, notice how Ted uses several numerical strategies—multiplying, adding, skip-counting, and breaking numbers into familiar parts.

FIGURE 3–15 ▶

Ted tackled the chopstick problem using several strategies.

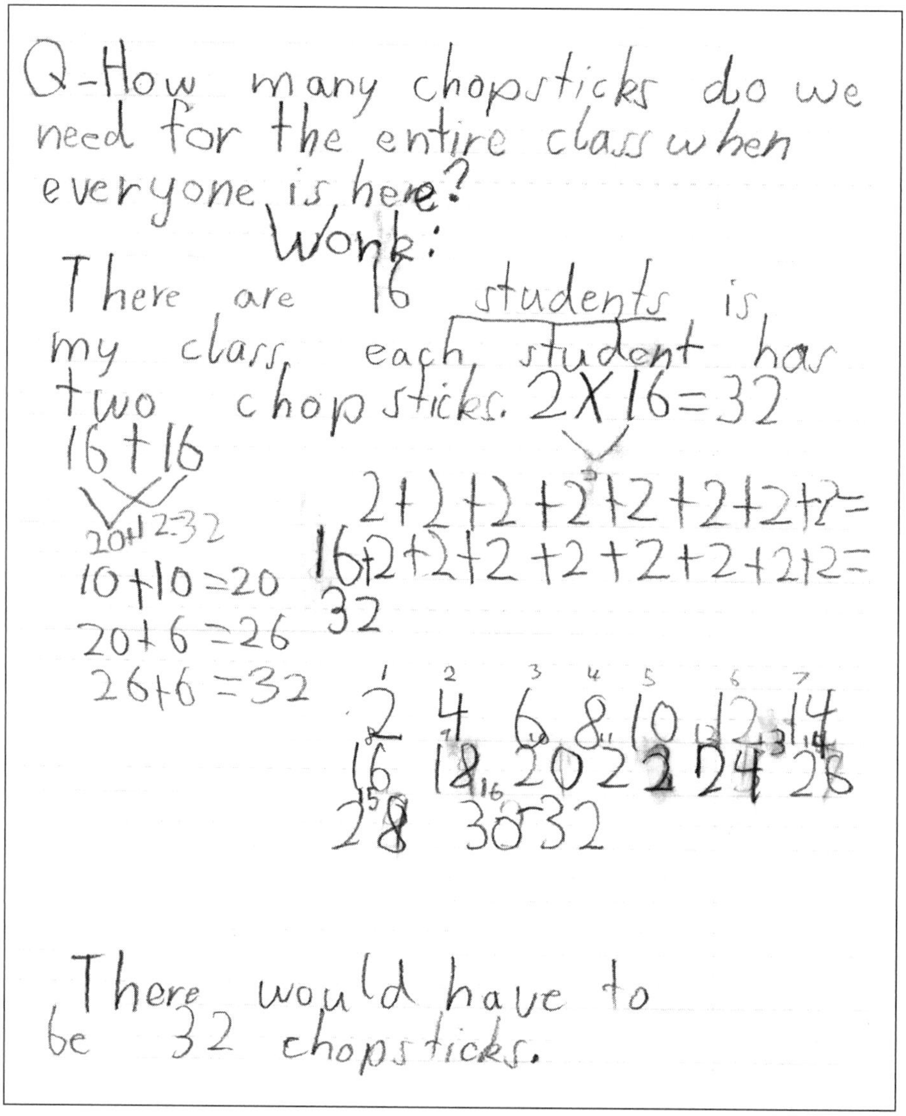

Q—How many chopsticks do we need for the entire class when everyone is here?

Work:

There are 16 students is my class, each student has two chopsticks. $2 \times 16 = 32$

16 + 16

20 + 12 = 32

10 + 10 = 20
20 + 6 = 26
26 + 6 = 32

$2+2+2+2+2+2+2+2=$
16 $2+2+2+2+2+2+2+2=$
32

2 4 6 8 10 12 14
16 18 20 22 24 26
28 30 32

There would have to be 32 chopsticks.

Then ask, "What other things always come in twos?" List students' responses on a 9-by-12-inch sheet of construction paper labeled *Things That Come in 2s* at the top. The list might include the following: legs on people, ears on a dog, shoes for a boy or girl.

Next have children work in pairs to come up with things that always come in 3s, 4s, 5s, 6s, 7s, 8s, 9s, and 10s. They can divide a piece of paper into eight equal parts and record their ideas. The final lists might look something like this:

Things That Come in 2s	*Things That Come in 3s*	*Things That Come in 4s*
shoes gloves	wheels on a tricycle	sides on a square
wheels on a bike	sides on a triangle	legs on a horse
twins	triplets	quadruples

Things That Come in 5s	*Things That Come in 6s*	*Things That Come in 7s*
sides on a pentagon	sides on a hexagon	days in a week
points on a regular star	points on the Star of David	
quintuplets	six pack of soda	
fingers on one hand	legs on an insect	

Things That Come in 8s	*Things That Come in 9s*	*Things That Come in 10s*
legs on a spider	squares on tic-tac-toe board	fingers on two hands
tentacles on an octopus		

From these lists, each child draws a picture of a set of one item on the list; for example, four triangles or three bikes. Have the children do this on a 6-by-6-inch piece of white construction paper that you've cut ahead of time. Then, on three 1-by-6-inch strips of white construction paper, the child writes sentence statements about the picture he or she has drawn. These sentences become a multiplication story problem (and, later, a division story problem). For instance, after drawing three bicycles, a child would write the following sentences, one on each strip of paper:

There are 3 bikes.

Each bike has 2 wheels.

There are 6 wheels in all.

This idea comes from *Things That Come in Groups* (Tierney, Berle-Carman, and Akers 1995). I've expanded on it in this chapter.

Students can explore the mathematics further by using a reduced 1–100 chart that has circles at the bottom. Children fill in the circles with skip-counting. With the bicycle example, a student would skip-count by 2s: 2, 4, 6. Then the student fills in a T-chart (see below). You can find a form for both T-charts and reduced 1–100 charts in the Blackline Masters.

number of bikes	number of wheels	
1	2	1 bike x 2 wheels = 2 wheels
2	4	2 bikes x 2 wheels = 4 wheels
3	6	3 bikes x 2 wheels = 6 wheels

Finally, the child takes his three strips and turns the last one over so he cannot see it. On a lined sheet of paper, he constructs a story problem that ends with a question instead of a statement. For example:

There are 3 bikes.

Each bike has 2 wheels.

How many wheels do the 3 bikes have altogether?

Students then transfer their proofread sentences onto 3-by-5-inch index cards. They glue the cards, the drawing, the T-chart, and the 1–100 chart onto a 12-by-18-inch piece of colored construction paper. (You might in turn create a class book of *Things That Come in Groups* story problems.)

Once students have written their story problems, they answer them using word/number equations, such as *3 bikes × 2 wheels on each bike = 6 wheels in all*. Or, they could write number equations only: $3 \times 2 = 6$. (See Figure 3–16.) Post the children's *Things That Come in Groups* story problem pages or bind them into the class book. Save these pages for Chapter 5 when the children will write division problems as well.

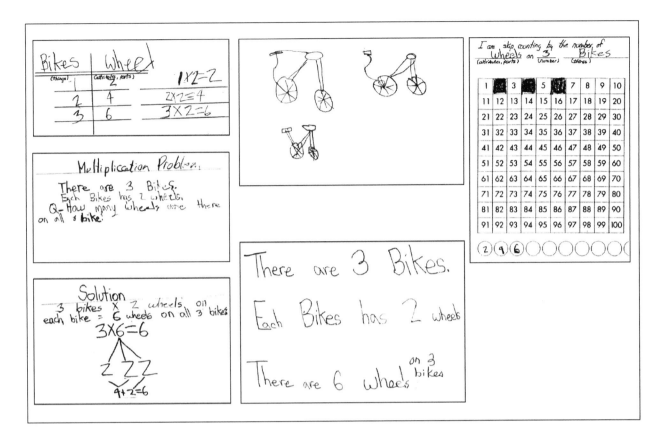

FIGURE 3–16 ▲

This is Yousif's *Things That Come in Groups* story page.

TEACHER-TO-TEACHER TALK   To ease communication about multiplication, you might want the first multiplier or factor of the multiplication equation to signify the number of groups (the number of rows, the number of columns, the number of circles, the number of insects, the number of squares, and so forth). The second factor represents the number of items in that group or characteristics of that item (panes in a window, stars in circles, legs on an insect, sides on a square, and so forth). In this situation, the × sign means *groups of*.

Since third graders have worked with addition problems for two years, they often mistake the multiplication symbol (×) for the addition symbol (+). To illustrate, if students are writing a problem involving 8 × 6, they write *There were 8 ants, then 6 more ants joined them. So how many ants are there altogether?* Point out the × symbol and discuss how that means 8 things or groups with 6 attributes or items in each. Then have the children begin by using manipulatives and pictures before writing their story problems.

But you don't want to isolate operations from one another. Many of the multiplication activities suggested in this chapter also offer opportunities to add and subtract. Knowing when to add, subtract, multiply, and (eventually) divide is a key aspect of number sense.

Extensions

If your students enjoy this activity, they might like writing a illustrated book of Halloween-related multiplication story problems; e.g., problems involving ghosts with three eyes each, vines with five pumpkins on each, haunted houses with six windows in each, and so on. If your school does not celebrate Halloween, the theme could be fall harvest, with story problems about baskets of apples, buckets of corn cobs, and so forth. (See Figure 3–17.)

Teacher-Generated Story Problems

FIGURE 3–17 ▼

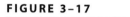

Eun-Jin figured out how many windows were in four haunted houses.

Throughout this unit, you can create your own problems as extensions of the investigations done in class (see Figures 3–5 and 3–12), or you can refer to the extensions described in this chapter. As the weeks progress, you'll begin spotting additional opportunities for multiplication problem solving throughout the school day. You'll also begin discerning what kinds of problems will most enhance your students' sense making. With the homework assignment shown in Figure 3–18, the teacher gave her students needed practice with particular multiplication combinations in a variety of contexts.

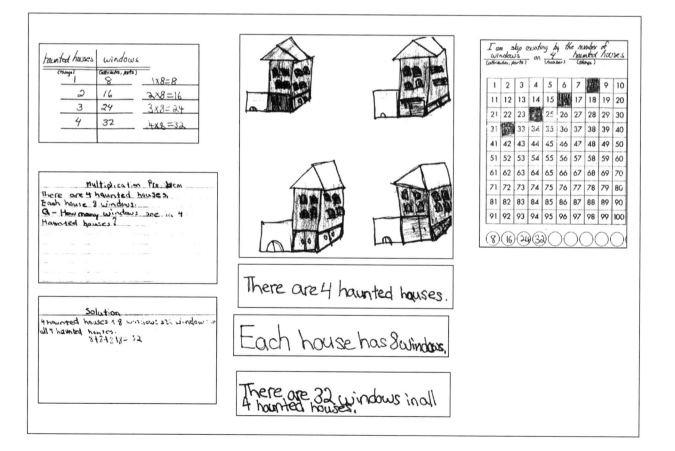

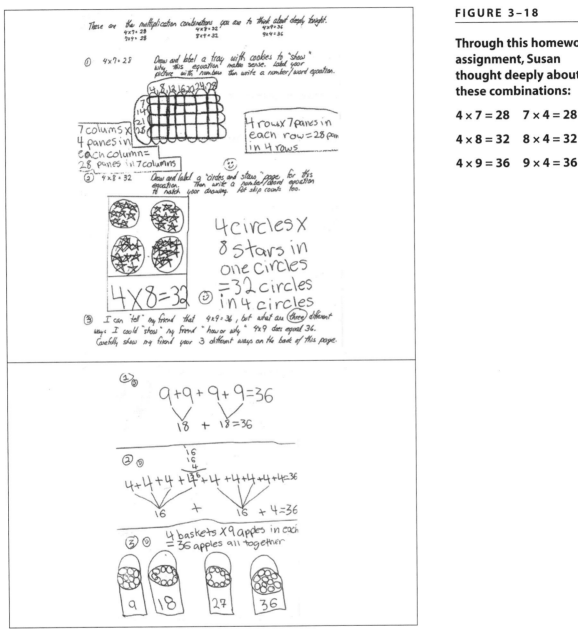

FIGURE 3–18 ◄

Through this homework assignment, Susan thought deeply about these combinations:

$4 \times 7 = 28$ $7 \times 4 = 28$

$4 \times 8 = 32$ $8 \times 4 = 32$

$4 \times 9 = 36$ $9 \times 4 = 36$

Student-Generated Story Problems

When children write their own story problems or build on equations provided by their teacher, they develop a sense of ownership of that problem. Before assigning a student-generated story problem to the rest of the class or as homework for all class members, ask the problem's author for permission to assign it. This is another way to celebrate children's voices in the mathematics classroom. (See Figure 3–19.)

FIGURE 3–19   ▶

As a homework assignment, Hamid solved story problems created by Rebecca and Juan.

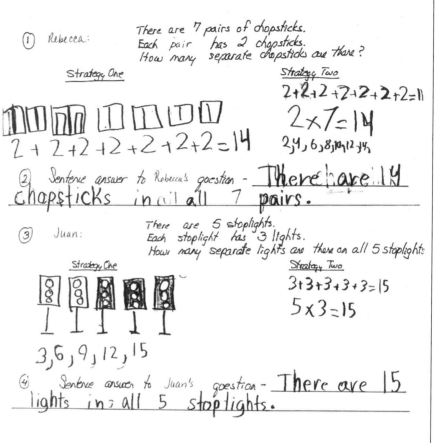

① Rebecca: There are 7 pairs of chopsticks.
Each pair has 2 chopsticks.
How many separate chopsticks are there?

Strategy One

$2 + 2 + 2 + 2 + 2 + 2 + 2 = 14$

Strategy Two
$2 + 2 + 2 + 2 + 2 + 2 + 2 = 11$
$2 \times 7 = 14$
2,4,6,8,10,12,14

② Sentence answer to Rebecca's question – There are 14 chopsticks in all 7 pairs.

③ Juan: There are 5 stoplights.
Each stoplight has 3 lights.
How many separate lights are there on all 5 stoplights?

Strategy One

Strategy Two
$3 + 3 + 3 + 3 + 3 = 15$
$5 \times 3 = 15$

3,6,9,12,15

④ Sentence answer to Juan's question – There are 15 lights in all 5 stoplights.

Station Time

At the end of Chapter 2, you were introduced to the idea of menu as a way of organizing your teaching and the children's learning. Another way to organize your curriculum is to have stations (activities) to which the children rotate in small groups. For stations, I divide my class of twenty into four groups with five students in each. At my station, I introduce a new multiplication activity or support the children in revisiting a multiplication problem that proved challenging earlier in the week. A parent volunteer introduces a new multiplication game or revisits an old game with her group of five students. The other two groups work independently on other multiplication investigations at their team tables.

Having four groups of five students allows the children to rotate through four half-hour stations in two hours on one morning or one hour one day and one hour the next. Another option is to spread thirty minutes of station time over four days. I do all four station rotations on the morning. I have a parent volunteer (whom I contact the day before), and I try to do stations a couple of times a month.

Here is a sample station schedule. Notice that I have moved an extra child to each of the tables to have four groups.

	Write a Multiplication Story Problem (with the teacher)	*Play One Round of* Circles and Stars *(with a table partner)*	*Play* Multiplication Bingo *(with parent)*	*Solve* Coins in Two Pockets *(at team table)*
8:30–9:00	Table 1 with Ray	Table 2 with Sarah	Table 3 with Latasha	Table 4 with Juan
9:00–9:30	Table 4	Table 1	Table 2	Table 3
9:30–10:00	Table 3	Table 4	Table 1	Table 2
10:00–10:30	Table 2	Table 3	Table 4	Table 1

> **TEACHER-TO-TEACHER TALK** If you and your students are not ready for this teaching approach, give yourself permission to move on. Some teachers find that the station approach helps them better connect and communicate with students. Others find it overwhelming. The key is to adopt this approach only if you can do so without becoming overburdened.

Independent Stations

At stations where students will work independently (such as working in pairs on *Circles and Stars* or working as individuals on *Coins in Two Pockets*), offer problems that build on or repeat what the children have already done in the whole-class setting. Carefully go over the instructions for those stations with the whole class before station time begins. Consider putting printed instructions, along with the required materials, at the appropriate station setting before the session begins. You and your adult volunteer or aide might also agree to occasionally check on students who are working independently and provide any needed support. During station time in my classroom, children who are working independently do so at their team table. Teacher- and volunteer-supported groups work at different tables at the back of the classroom.

For everyone's reference, post the station schedule on the board.

Adult-Facilitated Stations

For the multiplication story problem investigation in this sample station schedule, you could have students draw pictures from the *Things That Come in Groups* lists, then write three sentence statements about their pictures. If this is the first time the students in this group have done this, post the lists nearby for easy reference. Plan to meet with these same students during station time the following week—when you'll have them write multiplication story problems to go with their pictures, represent their solutions to their problems on T-charts, and show multiples on a 1–100 chart. See the "Story Problems" section in this chapter (page 101–108) to remind yourself of the details involved.

When the half-hour is over, announce that it is time for cleanup. Have the children organize their work and return to their team tables. Then, as a class, briefly discuss any problems that arose during the session—such as trouble staying on task or understanding the assigned problem, or a difficult partner interaction. During these discussions, maintain an upbeat, encouraging tone that communicates the message, "I know you can do this." Some children may not have completed the work assigned at the station they just left. If this is the case, assure these students that they'll have time to finish up during other station slots or later that day or the next. Often, the best-laid plans for a station do not work out on the first try, and you'll need to change direction based on students' input.

After this brief discussion, the students who just worked with you on multiplication story problems now do *Circles and Stars* at their team table, in pairs or small groups. Next, they spend thirty minutes at a station with your aide or volunteer, learning how to play *Multiplication Bingo*. (See pages 86–88 for instructions.)

Finally, members of this group return to their desks and work individually on one or two *Coins in Two Pockets* problem cards. (See pages 48 and 93 for instructions.) If a student finishes the work early and feels that his reasoning is complete and convincing, he can revisit other unfinished station work from earlier that day. Otherwise, the student can leave the table and go to the monthly math area, explained in Chapter 1, until the half-hour time slot is finished. Or he can work on the posted ongoing menu, as suggested in Chapter 2. The more children understand their options ahead of time, the less compelled they'll feel to interrupt other students' small-group work.

Assessment: Written Work

Written Classwork

As you continue assessing children by listening to them during whole-class and partner discussions, begin examining their written classwork to see how they're solving multiplication problems. During this unit, students clarify and document a lot of their thinking on paper, through words, numbers, and pictures. These papers give you a window into each child's understanding of multiplication. As you read each student's papers, keep the following questions in mind:

- Does the child connect multiplication to addition?
- Does he or she understand that multiplication is a way to find out how many you have altogether when things come in equal-size groups?
- Can this student connect a multiplication equation to more tangible objects or images, such as manipulatives or pictures?
- Does the child explain his or her thinking using words, numbers, and pictures?
- Can the student write multiplication story problems that make sense?

Individual Written Assessment

In addition to reviewing students' everyday problem-solving work, periodically ask children, on their own without partner input or class discussion, to explain their thinking in a variety of multiplication problems. (See Figure 3–20.) For example, at the beginning of the multiplication unit, have

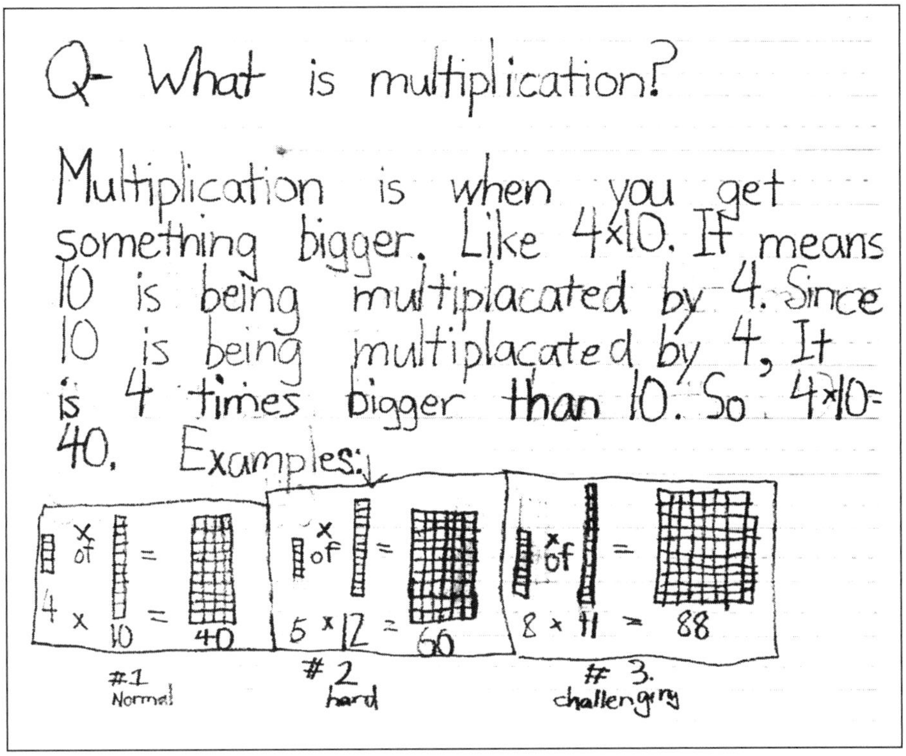

FIGURE 3–20 ◀

Kihyun provided his thoughts about what multiplication is.

each child respond to the question, "Pretend a second grader asked you, 'What is multiplication?' How would you explain multiplication to this second grader?"

As students write their thoughts about these sorts of questions, they begin seeing for themselves what they do and do not understand. This kind of assessment both contributes to the child's learning and informs your teaching. After reading a class set of these papers, you will have a better sense of your students' general understandings and misunderstandings and will be able to fine-tune your next teaching steps accordingly. The Teaching Arithmetic and Math By All Means series of books published by Math Solutions Publications have further suggestions for assessment problems.

If you ask students to respond to the "What is multiplication?" question at the beginning *and* end of the unit, you can assess an individual's

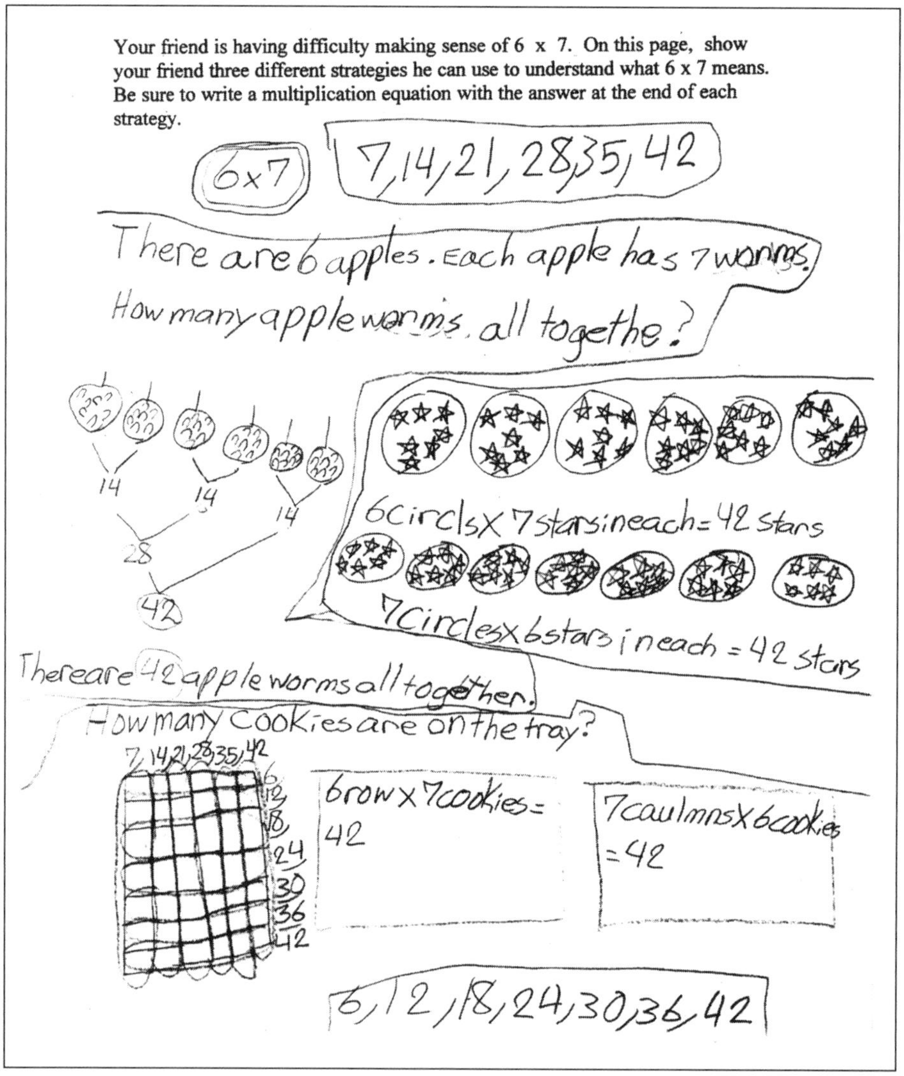

FIGURE 3–21   ▶

Angela offered these strategies for understanding 6 × 7.

Your friend is having difficulty making sense of 6 x 7. On this page, show your friend three different strategies he can use to understand what 6 x 7 means. Be sure to write a multiplication equation with the answer at the end of each strategy.

growth in making sense of multiplication and can share your observations during parent conferences.

During the course of the unit, try asking different questions, such as: "Your friend is having difficulty making sense of six times seven. Show your friend three different strategies he can use to understand what six times seven means." (See Figure 3–21.) Or ask students to write and solve their own multiplication story problem using words, numbers, and pictures. (See Figures 3–22 and 3–23.)

Keep these individual written assessments in chronological order, with samples of the child's written classwork problem solving. That way, you can follow each child's journey toward making sense of multiplication and can show these steps during parent conferences.

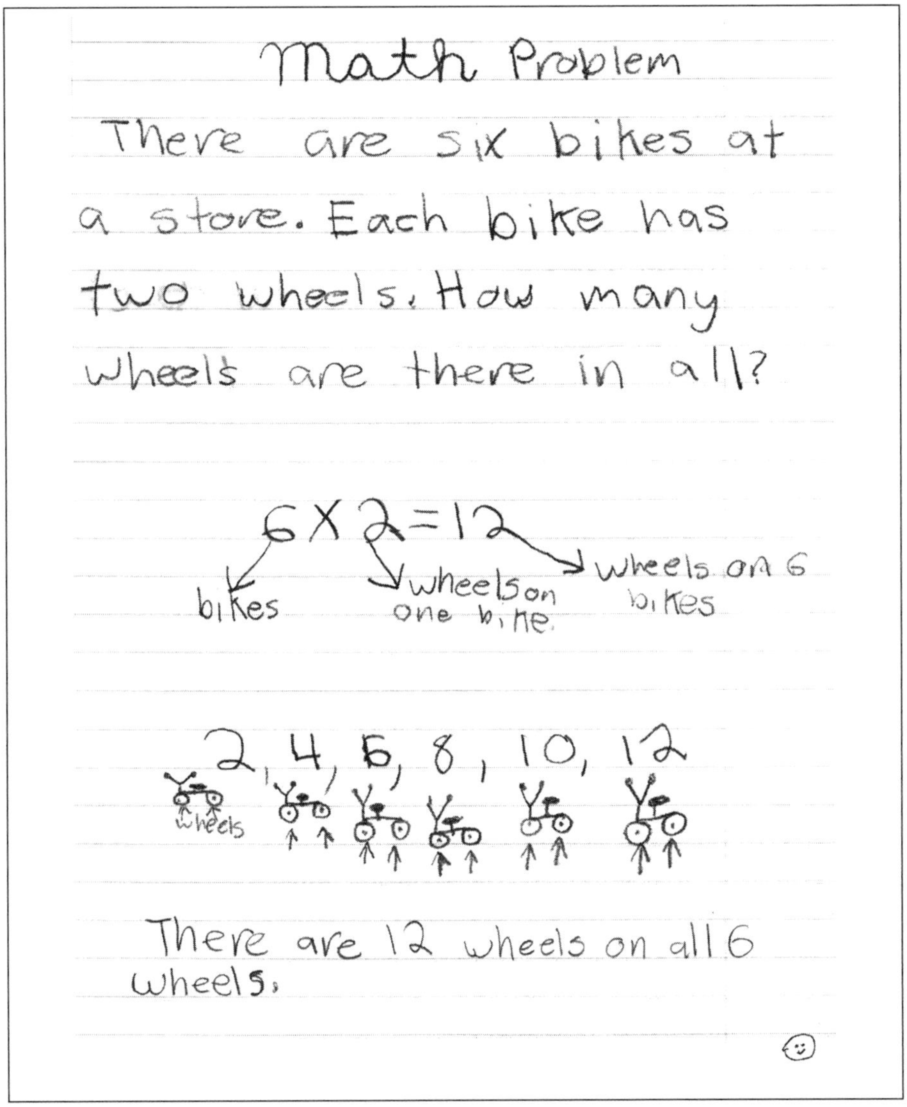

FIGURE 3–22 ◄

Sasha solved a multiplication story problem she created about the number of wheels on six bikes.

FIGURE 3–23 ▶

Marcus wrote this story problem about the number of legs on eight flies.

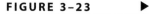

See *Teaching Arithmetic: Lessons for Introducing Multiplication, Grade 3* (Burns 2001) and *About Teaching Mathematics* (Burns 2000) for additional assessment ideas.

Chapter 4

December

TWO-DIMENSIONAL GEOMETRY

"Geometry is more than definitions; it is about describing relationships and reasoning."

Principles and Standards for School Mathematics
NCTM 2000, 41

Throughout the school year, you'll encourage your students to make sense of arithmetic problems using geometric models—number lines for addition and subtraction; rectangular arrays for multiplication and division; and pattern blocks for fractions. In December, students will study geometry as a separate area of mathematics, not as a tool for making sense of their numerical thinking.

A note about this chapter and Chapter 9 (which also explores geometry): Unlike the other chapters in this book, which have problem solving activities in the context of mathematics throughout the day—games, measurement, money, children's literature, and story problems—Chapters 4 and 9 are organized around geometric problem-solving activities. For example, children use triangles to form a variety of polygons, build different shapes with tangram pieces, and design paper quilts from construction-paper squares.

Both geometry chapters provide a change of pace for you and your students. You might want to use some of the activities in Chapter 9 during December, or some of Chapter 4's lessons during May and June. Or, you may decide to substitute two- and three-dimensional geometry activities of your own for the ideas described in these chapters. ■

The Learning Environment

Encourage children to take a break from reasoning numerically by reasoning spatially.

Some children find it easier to think in terms of shapes than to think arithmetically. Geometry gives these students an opportunity to shine as mathematicians. They happily construct two-dimensional shapes from four triangles, then rotate and flip their shapes to see which are congruent (have the same shape and size). These same children not only "see" shapes, but they also make shapes from other shapes with ease (for example, form four triangles into a parallelogram).

Have students work in groups of four as they problem solve.

Up to this point, your students have probably worked in pairs during collaborative problem solving. By December, you may well have built a caring community of learners who can cooperate in groups of four. You will want to discuss rules for working in groups of four, discussed more fully in Marilyn Burns's *About Teaching Mathematics: A K–8 Resource, Second Edition* (2000):

1. Children are responsible for their own work and behavior.

2. Children must be willing to help any group member *who asks*.

3. Children may ask the teacher for help *only* when everyone in the group has the same question.

Read many picture books.

There are many picture books that capture children's interest and imagination as they make sense of polygons and learn the language of two-dimensional geometry. Find these books ahead of time in your school library, city library, or a colleague's classroom and have them available when December begins:

Eight Hands Round: A Patchwork Alphabet by Ann Whitford Paul
Grandfather Tang's Story by Ann Tompert
The Greedy Triangle by Marilyn Burns
The Josefina Story Quilt by Eleanor Coerr
The Keeping Quilt by Patricia Polacco
The Patchwork Quilt by Valerie Flournoy
Selina and the Bear Paw Quilt by Barbara Smucker
The Tangram Magician by Lisa Campbell Ernst and Lee Ernst
Three Pigs, One Wolf, Seven Magic Shapes by Grace Maccarone

Make geometric puzzles and decorations for gift-giving.

By encouraging students to bring two-dimensional geometry projects home as gifts, you help them connect mathematics learning with home. Tangram puzzle pieces and student-made puzzle designs challenge adults and children alike. Paper-quilt designs make colorful cards. Children can also make decorative hangings from polygon rotating designs.

The Mathematics

Children understand that polygons have specific attributes.

Polygons are closed-plane shapes with sides that are straight-line segments. Their names correspond to their number of sides:

3 sides = triangle   8 sides = octagon

4 sides = quadrilateral   9 sides = nonagon

5 sides = pentagon   10 sides = decagon

6 sides = hexagon   11 sides = undecagon

7 sides = heptagon   12 sides = dodecagon

If your students have played with pattern blocks, they've become used to seeing equilateral triangles and hexagons with equal sides. In this unit, your students will discover that not all triangles, pentagons, and hexagons look the same. For example, a triangle formed from four smaller triangles is a right triangle. The six different hexagon shapes formed from four smaller triangles are all irregular, meaning they have six sides of different lengths. There are five quadrilaterals, or four-sided shapes, formed from the four smaller triangles. (See Figure 4–1 on page 123.) Four of the five are parallelograms—that is, they have opposite sides which are parallel and equal in length. For instance, the *rectangle* has four 90-degree angles. The *rhombus* has four equal sides and unequal angles. The *square* is a rhombus with equal angles. The *trapezoid* has one set of opposite sides that are parallel.

Children realize that geometric figures can be composed of or broken down into other geometric figures.

By cutting two square pieces of paper on the diagonal, students create four triangles. They can tape these triangles together in different ways to form fourteen different polygon shapes. In the tangram investigation described later in this chapter, children first make two-dimensional animal and people shapes using their tangram pieces. Next they form geometric shapes (squares, right triangles, rectangles, trapezoids, and parallelograms) with their tangram pieces.

Children relate geometric ideas to the world around them.

Buildings and other human-made structures feature many polygon shapes. When students look around your classroom, the school, or their neighborhoods, they'll find polygons everywhere.

Children explore shapes to see how they fit together and fill up space.

As children create their own quilt patterns and play with pattern blocks, they learn to fit shapes together in a repetitive pattern that leaves no gaps. In geometry, this is referred to as a *tessellation*.

The Four-Triangle Problem

You will find extensive discussions of this activity in Marilyn Burns's *About Teaching Mathematics* (2000) and Cheryl Rectanus's *Math By All Means: Geometry, Grade 3* (1994).

Materials

- 200 3-by-3-inch construction-paper squares of two contrasting colors (e.g., green and blue)
- 1 9-by-12-inch envelope per table group of four students
- 1 roll of Scotch tape per table group
- 1 pair of scissors per student
- 1 27-by-32-inch piece of chart paper ruled into four blank horizontal sections

Instructions

Part 1: Searching for Two-Triangle Shapes

1. Place the following materials at each table group of four students: at least twenty blue and twenty green construction-paper squares, one 9-by-12-inch envelope, one roll of Scotch tape, four pairs of scissors.

2. Refer the children to the rectangular window arrays they created in the previous unit. Encourage them to discuss the fact that each array is formed from squares.

3. Draw a square on the board and ask what makes it a square—four equal sides and four square corners, or right angles. Write the word *square* on the chart of *Geometry Words*. Throughout this unit, introduce geometry words in the context of the class discussion.

4. Tell the children that this time they will be making different kinds of shapes, using the blue and green squares on their tables.

5. Show students how to fold one square on the diagonal then cut along the fold to create two triangles. Ask the children what two shapes you have now—two triangles.

6. Draw a triangle on the board to match the shape of the ones you just created. Write the word *triangle* on the chart of *Geometry Words*.

7. Draw a square with a diagonal line from corner to corner, and ask what we call this line. Then write the word *diagonal* on the poster.

8. Invite each student to fold a paper square on the diagonal and cut along the fold to make two triangles. Then have them experiment to

see how many shapes they can make with their two triangles. The shapes must follow these two rules: Two sides of the same length must touch, and these sides must match in length exactly. Students cannot form a shape by having the two triangles "kiss" corners. (See below.)

This shape follows the rules.   These shapes do not follow the rules.

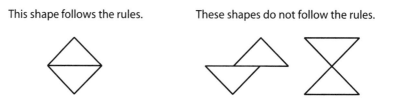

9. Ask the children to tape their shapes' triangles together, so they can hold them up without having them fall apart.

10. Have the four children in each table group examine all the shapes to identify *congruent* ones (shapes that fit exactly on top of one another). They'll need to rotate and flip their shapes to determine congruency. Write the word *congruent* on the chart of *Geometry Words*.

11. Have a volunteer come up and tape to the board a shape that he or she has created. Ask what the children think the shape is called. Then introduce and define the name of the shape. For example, if the shape looks like the one shown below, it is a parallelogram. Define *parallelogram* and add the term to the chart of *Geometry Words*.

Parallellogram

12. Ask if anyone made a shape that matches the one taped to the board. Students may need to come up one at a time to rotate and perhaps flip their shapes to see if they fit directly on top of the posted shape.

13. Ask a new volunteer to come up and post a different shape. Suppose the new shape is a triangle. Again, allow other children to come up and see if their shapes are congruent to the posted one. To help students understand that a "triangle is a triangle" no matter how you turn it, post the new shape in a different position. (See below.)

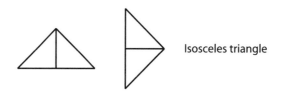

Isosceles triangle

14. Again, invite someone to bring a new shape up. If the new shape is a square made of two small triangles, show that a square is a square no matter how you position it. (See below.)

Square

Part 2: Searching for Four-Triangle Shapes

Now that the children have made other polygons from two triangles and understand the concept of matching sides, raise the level of difficulty a bit.

1. Review the rules for working in groups of four. Have a short class discussion about what helps students work together well, and what doesn't help.

2. Invite each child to cut one blue square on the diagonal and one green square on the diagonal—and then to use the resulting four triangles to form new shapes. As they work, they must check with their table partners to see if they are making congruent or unique shapes.

    The children will need this class period and perhaps the next class period to generate all the possible arrangements that can be made from four triangles taped together (following the two rules mentioned on the previous page). As they're working, they'll likely ask you if they have all the shapes yet. If they haven't generated all the shapes, reply that they are almost there, or that they have a ways to go, depending on what you're seeing. Don't reveal that there are fourteen possible shapes. As you wander around the class and listen to the children's thinking, comment aloud to a group when you notice two congruent shapes. Let the children discover which two shapes are congruent.

3. Have the children keep exploring arrangements until they feel they cannot explore any longer. Then ask each table group to place all their shapes into the envelope provided, and to label the envelope with their table number.

    For those groups that find all fourteen possible polygons early, have them begin one of the following extensions.

Extensions

- The students sort and group their fourteen shapes in some way that makes sense to all of them. Then they call you over to explain the groupings. This takes real cooperation among the four table members. If they are "cooperation fatigued," consider moving to the next extension.

■ Individual students cut groups of three squares of the same color into six triangles. Then they see what kinds of shapes they get when they put sides of the same length together.

Part 3: Sorting the Four-Triangle Shapes

By the third day, most of the table groups will have decided that there are fourteen possible noncongruent shapes to be made from four triangles. Those groups who have not yet found all fourteen shapes will have a chance to do so during this next section.

1. Post the 27-by-32-inch chart paper (with four blank horizontal sections) on the board. The chart will ultimately be filled with the various four-triangle polygons created by the students—and sorted into triangular, quadrilateral, pentagonal, and hexagonal categories.

2. Have each table group take out their set of four-triangle shapes and spread them over their desks for easy viewing.

3. Select a table. Call on a volunteer from one table at a time to bring one of the table's four-triangle shapes up to the board. Tape the shape onto one of the four sections of the chart, without telling the children your rule for sorting. (Remember: The four sections are not yet labeled.)

4. As you tape shapes onto the four horizontal sections of the chart, invite the children to be "math detectives"—to watch and think about possible rules for sorting the shapes. As each child brings up a shape, have him or her determine whether the shape is congruent with another shape already posted. The students will find that many of their shapes, when flipped or rotated, are indeed congruent.

5. After you have placed about ten different shapes on the chart, have the children indicate which area of the chart the next shape needs to be placed. When the children sense that you are sorting shapes by number of sides, ask for their thoughts. A child might reply, "I think that all the shapes with four sides go in the second space."

6. When you have finished posting shapes into the four sections of the chart, write the word *Polygons* at the top. (See Figure 4–1.)

7. Explain that all of the shapes on the chart are called polygons. All polygons have three or more straight lines that enclose a space, like a fence around a yard.

8. Explain that this chart shows four kinds of polygons. Point to the first section and ask for words to describe the triangle. Then ask what we call a polygon that has three sides and three corners. Label that section *Triangle*.

9. Continue until the children have described the number of sides, number of corners, and the name of the shapes in the chart's remaining

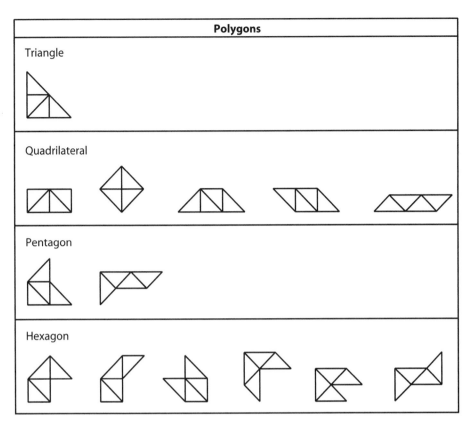

FIGURE 4-1 ◀

This is how your class's polygon chart will look once you've posted the fourteen shapes that can be made from four triangles.

sections. Some children may express surprise that none of the hexagons look like the hexagon in their pattern-block set. Have them explain again the rule for a hexagon: six sides and six corners. Check to ensure that each hexagon on the chart fits this rule.

10. Then check whether you've posted all fourteen possible polygons on the chart. You may well have left one out. If so, don't panic. This is a learning opportunity for the students. Turn the problem over to them: Tell them that there's a missing shape and that it has five sides. Ask them to check their four-triangle shapes for another pentagon (or other missing polygon). Or hand out two more squares to each child and ask students to create another four triangles and use them to form another five-sided shape.

Part 4: Guess My Rule

On future days, you can borrow a complete set of the fourteen polygons and play *Guess My Rule* again. (But first let students make doubles of all the shapes.) As the children sit on the rug with you, place shapes one at a time on the board, sorting them into two groups according to a rule you've made up but haven't yet revealed. Examples of rules include:

- quadrilaterals that are rectangles (including the square) and quadrilaterals that are not rectangles.
- hexagons that have one right angle (a corner that is square; i.e., consisting of a 90-degree angle) and hexagons that have more than one right angle.
- shapes with right angles and shapes without right angles.
- shapes with one line of symmetry (it's identical on both sides of the line) and shapes without one line of symmetry.

If you use these sorting rules, be sure to explain right angles and lines of symmetry. To identify the later, students can hold a ruler on edge, along the center of the shape, and see that the shape looks the same on both sides of the ruler. Or, they can hold a mirror along the line and see that what's in the mirror matches the other half of the design.

Part 5: Rotating Designs

1. Each child picks one of the four-triangle shapes. Then he or she traces that shape onto a piece of tagboard or cardstock, using a ruler to make straight lines.

2. The child cuts out the shape, then draws a dot in the center of a piece of 12-by-18-inch drawing paper. The child places a corner of the shape on this dot and traces. Then the child rotates the shape and traces again.

3. The child continues with at least eight rotations, until he or she returns to the starting point. Then the child colors this rotating design and writes his or her name on the back. Students can cut their shapes out and post them around the room, or attach strings to their designs and take them home to use as hanging decorations. (See below.)

Part 6: Same and Different

1. Borrow two four-triangle shapes from one table's envelope.

2. Trace each of these shapes on the board.

3. Then make a chart with columns labeled *Same* and *Different*.

4. Ask the class to help you take notes on how these two shapes are the same and how they are different. Encourage the class to look at the chart of *Geometry Words*. Write down their comments on the board. Figure 4–2 shows an example of possible responses.

5. Ask children to pair up or work in groups of four. First they take two different four-triangle shapes from their table envelope. They trace them onto a 12-by-18-inch sheet of paper and label each shape. Next they draw a chart such as the one you modeled on the board. Finally, they write down the ways the shapes are the same and different. (See Figure 4–3.) As an alternative, you could have students work on a smaller activity sheet that you copy for them. (See Blackline Masters.)

Same	Different
each can be made with four triangles	one has 4 corners one has 3 corners
both are polygons	one has 4 square corners one has 1 square corner
sides are not equal	one is a rectangle one is a triangle

FIGURE 4–2 ◀

This class generated numerous ideas for describing similarities and differences between a triangle and a rectangle.

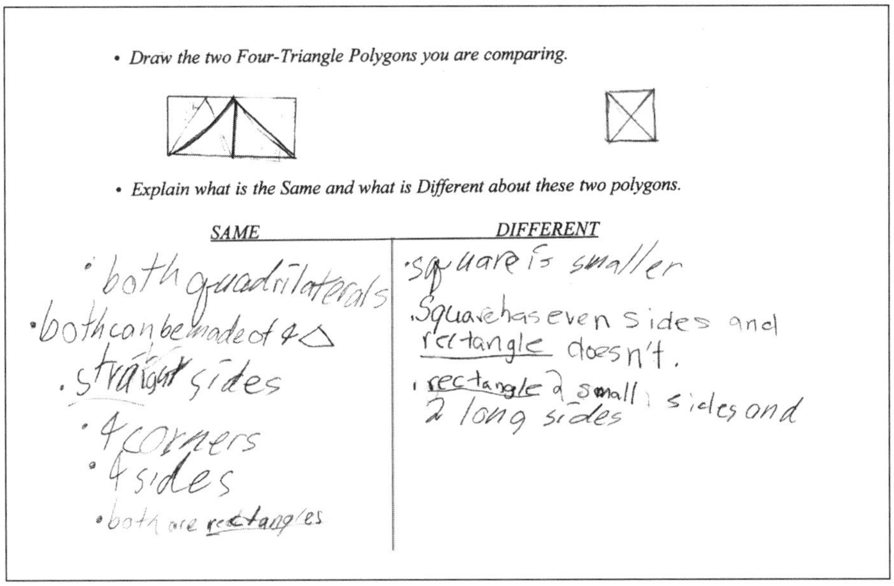

• Draw the two Four-Triangle Polygons you are comparing.

• Explain what is the Same and what is Different about these two polygons.

SAME	DIFFERENT
• both quadrilaterals • both can be made of 4 △ • straight sides • 4 corners • 4 sides • both are rectangles	• square is smaller Square has even sides and rectangle doesn't. • rectangle 2 small sides and 2 long sides

FIGURE 4–3 ◀

Rebecca and Eun-Jin noted several similarities and differences between their two polygons.

The Greedy Triangle

Now that your students have created different polygon shapes from four triangles, they may enjoy Marilyn Burns's *The Greedy Triangle*. In this engaging story, a busy little triangle spends his time holding up roofs, supporting bridges, being slices of pie, and serving many other purposes. Eventually, he begins to feel dissatisfied with his life. He goes to a "shape shifter," who changes him into a quadrilateral. In his new form, he has many different jobs, from being a computer screen to serving as a book page. The triangle-turned-quadrilateral soon tires of his new role and goes to the shape shifter again—who changes him into a pentagon. And so the story goes.

After reading the story to the class, take your class on a walk around the school. Give students clipboards and invite them to be "shape detectives," recording the various shapes they see and the places where they found them. Once back in the classroom, have the children describe all the places where they saw circles (such as on car wheels or a store clock), all the places where they saw rectangles (e.g., fence, window), and so forth.

Extensions

- Refer back to Rebecca and Eun-Jin's paper in Figure 4–3. Have students compare the size (area) of their four-triangle rectangle and their four-triangle square. Are they the same size? Are they different?

- The children find various polygons in the classroom or at home.

- The children draw a scene filled with different shapes, using rulers to create the line segments. (See Figure 4–4.)

FIGURE 4–4 ▶

Janet drew several engaging shapes featuring polygons.

Tangrams

Tangrams are ancient Chinese puzzles. If you have many Chinese-American students in your class, tangram puzzles honor their heritage. A tangram consists of a square that's cut into seven specific shapes, each of them called a *tan*. The shapes include:

- two large congruent triangles,
- one medium-size triangle,
- two small congruent triangles,
- a square,
- and a parallelogram.

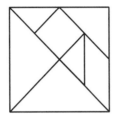

The five triangles are all right triangles. Children can use these seven pieces (tans) to form shapes found in the real or pretend world.

Part 1: Tangram Picture Books

You may want to read the following three books over several days as your students are conducting their four-triangle investigations. That way, the children develop a sense of what tangrams are and an eagerness to use the puzzle pieces.

Grandfather Tang's Story by Ann Tompert In this story, Grandfather Tang and his granddaughter, Little Soo, each have a tangram set. Together they make up a story about two fox fairy friends, Chou and Wu Ling, who change into the shapes of different animals as they try to outdo one another. The animals formed with the tangram pieces are as follows: rabbit, dog, squirrel, hawk, turtle, crocodile, goldfish, goose, and lion. As you read the book for the first time, the children will delight in the illustrations and the story.

The Tangram Magician by Lisa Campbell Ernst and Lee Ernst As you read the story, encourage students to focus on each shape that the magician changes into. Many of the shapes are animals—bird, fish, mountain goat, swan, camel, dog, cat, rabbit, lion. Others include a sailing boat, house, tree, and tea set. The magician strikes a variety of poses, from running to lying down, as he shifts shape.

***Three Pigs, One Wolf, Seven Magic Shapes* by Grace Maccarone** In this engaging story, three little pigs go off to seek their fortunes. As they journey, magic animals (duck, rabbit, swan) give each of them seven magic shapes (tangram pieces). These animals advise the pigs to use their shapes wisely.

The first little pig makes a cat for companionship, but a wolf eats both the pig and the cat. The second little pig makes a candle so he can see in the dark, but the wolf blows out the candle and eats the pig. The third little pig makes a house, which the wolf tries to blow down but fails. Then this third little pig marries the pig who made a house of bricks in the original story *The Three Little Pigs*. Together, they build a beautiful sailboat and sail off on their honeymoon.

In this story, children see tangram pieces formed into a duck, cat, rabbit, candle, swan, house, and sailing boat. In the back of the book, there are a tangram dog, a cat, a running man, a whale, a bear, a seal, a bridge, a seven, and a T.

Part 2: Making Tangram Sets
Materials

- several 6-by-6-inch pieces of colored construction paper per student; a different color for each student at a table
- 1 pair of scissors per student
- 1 business-size envelope per student

Instructions

1. Make your own tangram puzzle pieces, using the instructions shown in Figure 4–5.

   Through a whole-group lesson or station-time sessions consisting of four to six children at a time (see Chapter 2), teach students how to make tangram puzzle pieces. Use a larger square to demonstrate each fold and cut step by step.

2. Give each child a regular business-size envelope. Have them write their names on the outside.

3. After the children cut their own tangram pieces following the above instructions, have them label the back of each piece with their first and last names. Then ask them to put their pieces in their envelopes.

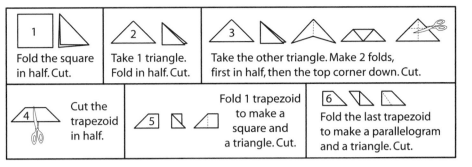

FIGURE 4–5 ◀

Instructions for making tangram pieces.

Part 3: Making Tangram Puzzle Cards

Have each child make shapes using all seven of their tans. They can refer to the tangram shapes shown in the books you've read aloud, or they can come up with their own designs. After they have arranged a shape or puzzle that pleases them, they use drawing paper or cardstock to trace the outline of their shape (employing a ruler to make straight lines). If you have plastic tangram sets in your classroom, consider letting the children use them to trace the outline of their design.

Students place their names on their puzzle's outline and label it with a title. Collect the outlines, mix them up, and hand them out during a math period. Children can then try arranging their tangram pieces to create the shape shown on the outline. As children solve one another's puzzles, they sign their names on the front of an outline, under the title. If a child feels that the puzzle does not make sense, he can go to the puzzle maker and discuss his or her concerns.

Extensions

Send each child's puzzle, along with a set of cut-out tangram pieces made from cardstock, home as a gift.

Part 4: Making Geometric Shapes Using Tangram Pieces

Allow your students plenty of time to try making squares, right triangles, rectangles, trapezoids, and parallelograms with the three small triangles in their tangram set. Give each group of four students a large piece of butcher paper (56-by-36 inches) with sample polygons drawn across the top. (See page 130 for an example.) Have the children draw on the chart the various polygons they created with their tangram pieces. Then have them make similar polygons with their five smallest tangram pieces. Finally, have them use all seven pieces. This investigation gives children added practice in using the language of polygons.

	□	◺	▭	⬭	▱
3 small triangles	◳				
5 small pieces					
all 7 pieces					

The children work together in groups of four to see how many of the chart's sections they can fill in. When they find a polygon that fits, they trace the exterior *and* interior lines so anyone looking at the diagram can see which tangram pieces the students used and how they fit them together. Reassure the children that they don't need to fill in all the chart's sections—it's more important to have fun seeing which sections they *can* fill in.

As an alternative, you could post one large chart for the entire class to fill in.

Paper Quilts

In this investigation, each child first uses squares made of two colors of construction paper to create his or her own design for a nine-patch quilt block. Children then work in groups of four to first make four nine-patch quilt blocks following a traditional design; they then join their four blocks into a four-by-four square paper quilt. Finally, each child uses his or her own original nine-patch design and makes a four-block paper quilt.

See Chris Confer's *Math By All Means: Geometry, Grade 2* (1994) for extensive class discussions about about these quilting activities. Many of the ideas below also come from my colleague and friend, Nancy Litton, author of *Second-Grade Math: A Month-to-Month Guide* (2003).

Part 1: Reading Quilting Picture Books

These following five books explore quilts and the stories they tell, which are often family stories. Since holiday time frequently entails extended family time, these books are especially appropriate reading at this time of year.

Eight Hands Round: A Patchwork Alphabet by Ann Whitford Paul This book describes twenty-six different traditional quilt patterns, one for each letter in the alphabet. Each page has a picture followed by a story explaining the pattern's history. The patchwork design that connects with each story (e.g., log cabin or maple leaf) is colorfully displayed at the bottom of the page as a separate block and as a quilt made up of several blocks of that design. Many of the designs are nine-patches.

Selina and the Bear Paw Quilt by Barbara Smucker Selina and her Mennonite family travel all the way from Pennsylvania to Canada to escape the U.S. Civil War. They do not believe in war as a way to solve problems. Selina's grandmother is too old to travel, so she stays in Pennsylvania. She gives Selina a precious quilt in which she has used the Bear Paw pattern. In the quilt are dark green patches from Grandmother's wedding dress and flowered daisies from Selina's baby clothes. Throughout the book, Smucker mixes traditional quilt-pattern borders with more modern patterns. At the back of the book, you can find the pattern names.

The Josefina Story Quilt by Eleanor Coerr As Faith and her family travel to California by covered wagon in 1850, they have happy and not-so-happy experiences. Along the way, Faith makes a patchwork quilt that will help her remember the various events of the journey. At first, Faith's father doesn't want her to bring her beloved hen, Josefina, on the trip. But finally he relents. Josefina has many adventures on the journey, too. Most of the chapters begin with a geometric patchwork design.

The Keeping Quilt by Patricia Polacco The author's great-grandmother came to America from Russia when she was a child. She wore a colorful blue dress and a red babushka. As she outgrew the dress, her mother used it—along with other family members' discarded clothing—to make a quilt of animals and flowers so that Patricia's great-grandmother would always remember her Russian home. The babushka became the quilt's border. This quilt has been passed down from generation to generation. It has served as a huppa during weddings, as a tablecloth during the Sabbath, and as a blanket to welcome each new child born into the family. The book reveals that quilts, and their stories, can provide a meaningful thread throughout a family's history. The designs on this quilt are not polygons.

The Patchwork Quilt by Valerie Flournoy Grandma, who lives with her daughter's family, is making a quilt out of scraps of material from the family's discarded clothes. Mama frets about the mess of quilt scraps and suggests buying a quilt at the store. Tanya, the granddaughter, understands that her grandmother must make this quilt to feel needed. So, she decides to help her grandmother make the quilt. Soon Mama realizes that quilts do tell life stories, and she helps, too. When Grandma falls ill, Papa and Tanya's brothers help cut quilt squares so that Tanya can work on the quilt. Grandma completes the quilt covered with colorful squares when she is well again. The last square reads, "For Tanya from your Mama and Grandma."

Part 2: Making Individual Nine-Patch Blocks
Materials

- 1 6-by-6-inch piece of newsprint, prefolded into nine squares, per student—or 1 6-by-6-inch piece of cardstock, block marked into a nine-square grid, per student (see below)

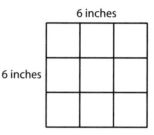

- 2-by-2-inch squares, cut from construction paper of four to six different colors; at least 9 squares per student
- 1 scissors per student
- 1 glue per table

Instructions

1. Decide whether to do this activity with the whole class at the same time or during a station-time session with five children at a time.

2. Give each student a newsprint block folded into nine squares or a piece of cardstock block marked into a nine-square grid.

3. Allow each student to select *nine* 2-by-2-inch squares in *two* different colors from four to six different colors (for example, three blue squares and six green).

4. Allow each child to decide whether he or she wants to cut all, none, or some of the squares into triangles on the diagonal fold.

5. Have students experiment with making different designs by arranging their squares and triangles. (See below.)

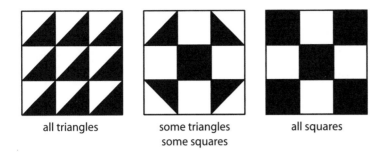

all triangles   some triangles   all squares
                 some squares

6. Ask students to glue their construction paper designs to their piece of newsprint or cardstock.

7. Post around the room.

Part 3: Making a Traditional Nine-Block Quilt as a Team

In this part, students make several traditional nine-patch quilt patterns found in Ann Whitford Paul's *Eight Hands Round: A Patchwork Alphabet*. The patterns the children explore from this book are Churn Dash, Jacob's Ladder, Letter X, Maple Leaf, Storm at Sea, and Variable Star. (See below.)

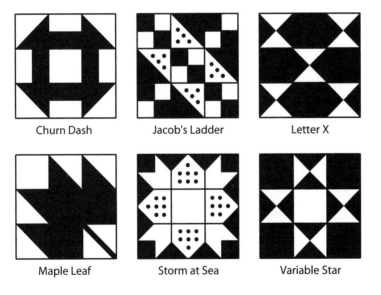

Churn Dash   Jacob's Ladder   Letter X

Maple Leaf   Storm at Sea   Variable Star

Materials

- a copy of the book *Eight Hands Round: A Patchwork Alphabet*
- 9 6-by-6-inch pieces of newsprint, prefolded into nine squares, per student—or 1 6-by-6-inch piece of cardstock, block marked into a nine-square grid, per table or group of four

- 2-by-2-inch squares, cut from construction paper of four to six different colors; 20 per student
- large 18-by-18-inch sheets of butcher paper for gluing final quilts, 1 per team

Instructions

1. Read the book with your students. For each of the six design patterns, discuss how the original nine-patch block has been positioned in the quilt. Have some blocks been rotated? Are the colors the same in each nine-patch block?

2. Give children the 2-by-2-inch construction-paper squares and the 6-by-6-inch newsprint or cardstock backing pieces, and encourage them to practice re-creating each of the six designs in the book. They do not do any gluing during this exploration time.

   If you think that providing a set of 6-by-6-inch sample blocks of each pattern ahead of time to each table will help students better understand how the squares are subdivided, do so. Rather than showing the children how to do each nine-patch block pattern, encourage them to notice the different shapes in each design. Students should do their own geometric problem solving as they try to copy the different blocks. They will make mistakes, so be sure to emphasize that "mistakes are opportunities to learn." Also provide extra colored squares.

3. As you and the class look at the six different patterns, also notice the color choices. Churn Dash has two colors; one is mostly background, while the other is design. In Jacob's Ladder, a third color is introduced in the middle patch. Variable Star uses the same three colors throughout this book. Maple Leaf has a background color, a leaf color, and a stem color. Storm at Sea involves four colors. The Letter X can have five blocks with one background color and four blocks with another.

4. After giving the children time to explore the traditional designs, have teams decide which one pattern they wish to follow for their team quilt. Then they decide whether they are going to follow the colors shown in the book or implement other color ideas.

5. When a group of four completes nine blocks of their nine-patch design, they lay the blocks out on a table or the floor to see how they want to arrange the blocks. They try different arrangements before deciding on one and gluing it onto a large (at least 18-by-18 inches) sheet of butcher paper.

6. Hang the paper quilts in the classroom or in more public places in your school.

Part 4: Making Individual Nine-Patch Mini-Quilts

1. Have individual students retrieve their original practice nine-patch quilt blocks, which they constructed with 2-by-2-inch squares in Part 2 of this activity.

2. Provide each child with three more 6-by-6-inch pieces of newsprint, prefolded into nine sections, or three more 6-by-6-inch pieces of cardstock marked with grid lines for nine squares.

3. Ask each child to make three more blocks of his or her practice design, and then to arrange the blocks on a 12-by-12-inch sheet of construction paper to make a four-block mini-quilt. Nancy Litton points out that this activity can have surprising results. For example, an asymmetrical design suddenly takes on symmetry when each block is turned a quarter turn around a central point. (See below.)

The same four nine-patch blocks can make different quilts.

Extensions

Instead of providing 2-by-2-inch squares cut from colored construction paper, you could give students pieces of festive wrapping paper. For example, you could use metallic gold, red, green, blue, magenta, and silver paper that has paper backing for gluing. You might also find patterns of holly or snowflakes to complement solid colors. Whichever design you select, choose papers that are not specific to any particular belief system.

If you use patterned wrapping paper in addition to solid-color construction paper, each child will need to make four new blocks of their original design instead of three. Moreover, each will have to pick either three patterned squares and six solid-color squares or vice versa (six patterned squares and three solid-color squares).

If your students want their mini-quilts to look more like fabric, select wrapping papers that feature small, repetitive patterns resembling those on bolts of cloth you might find in quilting stores.

The resulting mini-quilts of four blocks can go home as gift cards or gift hangings.

Pattern Blocks

Children love fitting pattern blocks together into colorful symmetrical and asymmetrical designs. Marilyn Burns's *About Teaching Mathematics: A K–8 Resource, Second Edition,* contains numerous pattern-block explorations.

Symmetrical and Asymmetrical Designs

Invite students to use pattern blocks to make symmetrical designs that radiate out from a center. These designs have *rotational symmetry* if they continue to look the same even after being rotated. Also encourage them to build shapes of animals, people, and other asymmetrical objects using the blocks.

Roads

Have the children figure out which blocks can be fit together without gaps, to make a straight road. Then invite them to build roads that can turn a corner.

Pattern-Block Puzzles

Have students build a shape with pattern blocks, then trace the outline of their shape onto cardstock. They put their name and the name of the shape at the top of the paper, as they did with their tangram puzzles. This time they also indicate how many pattern-block pieces they used to make the design. For their own reference, children can also make an extra copy of their puzzle that shows the internal lines of each pattern block used.

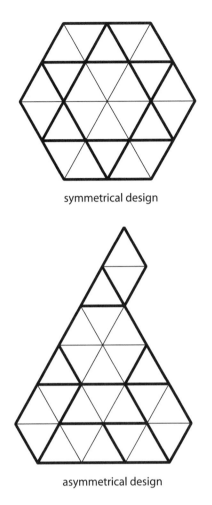

symmetrical design

asymmetrical design

Congruent Hexagons

Suggest that your students use only green triangles to build a shape exactly the same as a yellow hexagon. Then they use only red trapezoids, then only blue rhombi to build a yellow hexagon shape. Have them try to cover the yellow hexagon with only white-diamond or orange-square shapes.

Area

Have students use the green triangle from the pattern-block set to find the area (in green-triangle units!) of the blue, red, and yellow pieces from the set.

Hexagon Fill-In Puzzles

Give each student several copies of a large hexagon shape. (See Blackline Masters.) Have the children use the shape to solve the following pattern-block investigations

- Use three yellow pattern-block hexagons and three blue parallelograms to fill in the entire hexagon shape. (This is the fewest blocks needed to cover the shape.)
- Use twenty-four green triangles to cover the hexagon. This is the most blocks needed to fill in the space without leaving any gaps.
- Try filling the hexagon with seven different pattern-blocks, eight different blocks, nine different blocks—and so on, up to twenty-three.

Menu Possibilities

After your students have completed the four-triangle, tangram, quilt-making, and pattern-block activities, you could develop a menu of problems from the extensions to those activities, or from the suggestions below, depending on your students' needs.

Same and Different

With your partner, take two four-triangle polygon shapes from your table envelope and trace these two shapes at the top of an 18-by-24-inch newsprint sheet. Label one half of your paper *Same*. Label the other half *Different*. Under the appropriate labels, explain what is the same and what is different about the two shapes you took from the envelope. Look at the chart of *Geometry Words* as you do this problem.

Polygon Search

Look around you in the classroom for polygon shapes. List them on a recording sheet, including the name of the shape and the object in which you've seen the shape. Feel free to draw pictures to go with your words.

Tangram Puzzles

With your own tangram pieces, fill in at least four puzzles that your class-mates have made. Record the puzzles you have completed by naming each puzzle and each puzzle maker.

Hexagon Fill-In Puzzle

Look at what your class has completed of the Hexagon Fill-In Puzzle suggestions on the previous page. Write a menu problem that addresses what the children have not yet done.

Chapter 5

January

INTRODUCTION TO DIVISION

"The ability to read, write, listen, think, and communicate about problems will develop and deepen students' understanding of mathematics . . . In grades 3–5 classrooms, communication should include sharing thinking, asking questions, and explaining and justifying ideas."

Principles and Standards for School Mathematics
NCTM 2000, 194

After winter break, many third graders return to school transformed from wiggly students focused primarily on their own needs into patient learners who listen better, stay on task longer, and cooperate with their teammates. These changes enable you to introduce units that are three to four weeks in length instead of six weeks.

Enjoy the fact that the children are both "doing" and "talking" mathematics. Even though standardized tests are more imminent, stay the course. Give your students time to make sense of mathematics and to communicate their sense making. Continue to support students' problem-solving dispositions by providing opportunities to share equal groups of things or group things into equal-size groups. Help the students connect division experiences to the multiplication problem solving they did earlier. ■

The Learning Environment

Encourage the grouping and sharing of everyday objects or manipulatives.

Although third graders have been adding and subtracting for a couple of years, they will likely have their first school experience with division during January. As in any introductory work in mathematics, children need to begin at a concrete level—using models while thinking and reasoning. The most concrete models are everyday objects that can be shared or grouped, such as sheets of paper, pencils, books, and raisins. Eventually, children can represent these items through drawing pictures or using manipulatives. Numbers and words, which explain the operation, are used in conjunction with the models.

Connect division to experiences children have already had at school and at home.

At school, children make sense of multiplication by playing *Circles and Stars*. This same game gives children experience with division as they share and group images. If a child rolls a 4, she draws four circles. If she next rolls a 5, she draws five stars in each circle. The equation $4 \times 5 = 20$ can be stated in these words: Four circles with five stars in each equals twenty stars altogether.

The related division question would be, "You have twenty stars in all, and you want to *group* five stars equally into circles. How many circles would you need?" Or, "You have twenty stars, and you want to *share* these stars equally among four circles. How many stars would be in each circle?" The idea that there are two types of division problems (grouping and sorting) is explained further in "The Mathematics" section.

Your students have also multiplied by arranging windowpanes into arrays. For example, three rows times five windowpanes in each row equals fifteen windowpanes. This arrangement could become a division situation as well: Fifteen windowpanes *grouped* so there are five panes in each row equals three rows. Fifteen windowpanes *shared* so that there are three equal-size rows means that there are five panes in each row.

At home, children often share food, especially desserts. At school, they can share snacks such as raisins or crackers or group them into equal-size groups. These real-life food experiences provide valuable opportunities to practice division.

Encourage children to problem solve in groups of four.

The idea of fair shares is integral to division. At their table groups, children have a ready-made situation for sharing things among four people. Take advantage of this.

Four children cooperating together is a bit more complex than students' working in pairs—because each child needs to be heard, and each voice needs to be respected. Many third graders find this sort of cooperation challenging. With practice and frequent whole-class discussions about what worked and what didn't work when groups of four worked together, students can begin to do some powerful problem solving. Remind the children to be fair and friendly to one another and to look at and listen to each speaker. Point out the rules for working in groups of four. (See Chapter 4, pages 116–17.)

Encourage children to take turns being responsible for tasks such as recording the steps in the group's problem solving and offering ideas and suggestions. You could also have the children rotate the recording round-robin style; i.e., each fills in a small part of the whole recording sheet for the entire group.

Have children use more writing to explain their thinking.

Now that the second half of the third grade is approaching, you may wish to provide fewer preformatted worksheets. Gradually, give students more responsibility for deciding how to organize and explain their thinking on their math papers. Ask the children what they think makes a paper strong, or clear and convincing. Then you and the class develop these thoughts into a list of ideas to which the children can refer as they work. The list might look something like this:

A Strong Math Paper Has

- the date, the time, and your name
- the question or the problem

- the steps you used to figure out the answer to the problem (including words, numbers, and/or labeled drawings)
- the answer to the question or problem

Express enthusiasm as your students use all four operations in their problem solving.

By this time of the school year, your students are adding, subtracting, multiplying, and beginning to divide. Thus they should feel more comfortable dealing with problems in which they have to decide which operation applies. Provide a variety of story problems that give children experiences with all four operations. Children who have this robust sense of number will be ahead of the game when grappling with standardized-test story problems that feature a mix of operations.

When children feel they are powerful math learners, they relish the opportunity to figure things out in a way that makes sense to them. They recognize multiplication and division when they see it, but they also understand they can use a number of operations to make sense of a situation. They can use addition to make sense of subtraction problems, and now they can use multiplication to understand division.

The Mathematics

Children experience both types of division problems.

When children subtract, they experience both take-away and comparison problems. When children divide things equally, they are either grouping or sharing these things. If one child at a table has twenty-four sheets of paper that she *shares* equally with her other three tablemates, each person gets six sheets of paper.

On the other hand, if this same child grabs a handful of twenty-six sheets of paper and *groups* the paper in stacks of two sheets, she will end up with thirteen stacks, or groups.

In either case, the resulting groups are of equal size, just as they are in multiplication.

Children use addition, subtraction, and multiplication as they make sense of division situations.

When children compare two temperatures, they often add up from the lower temperature to the larger to find the difference, even though this is technically a subtraction problem. The same is true in division situations. Students often use multiplication to make sense of division. For example, the child with the twenty-four sheets of paper might reason, "I know that four times six equals twenty-four; therefore, four children times six sheets of paper each equals twenty-four pieces of paper altogether." Sometimes in a division situation, children add or subtract instead of multiply. For instance, a child might "count up," thinking "Six plus six equals twelve. Twelve plus six equals eighteen. Eighteen plus six equals twenty-four." Or the child might "count down," thinking "Twenty-four sheets take away six equals eighteen. Eighteen minus six equals twelve. Twelve take away six equals six. Then six minus six equals zero."

Remind yourself that each child makes sense of a division situation in his or her own way by adding, subtracting, or multiplying. Celebrate the fact that your students are making sense of what they are doing instead of blindly following memorized procedures that make no sense to them.

Children represent division using three different kinds of notation.

By encouraging your students to represent division horizontally, you help them reason and to avoid rotely following the traditional "divide, multiply, subtract, and bring down" procedure. You also help them feel more comfortable grounding the numbers in written words. The words *share* and *group* are pivotal in making sense of both kinds of division situations. For example, $15 \div 3 = 5$ can represent "Fifteen candies shared fairly among three children equals five candies for each child." In this *sharing* situation, the total amount is known, and the number of shares (or groups) is known (3). The *size* of each share or the number of candies in each group is the unknown (5).

The equation $15 \div 3 = 5$ can also represent fifteen children grouped so that each group has three children, which requires five groups. In this *grouping* situation, the total amount is known, and the size of each group is known (3). The number of groups is the unknown (5).

Both of these division situations can be represented by two additional forms of notation:

$$3\overline{)15}^{\,5} \quad and \quad \frac{15}{3} = 5$$

At this point in their introduction to division, have the children group or share everyday objects or manipulatives that represent the quantities they're working with. You want them to build their understanding of division on a firm foundation.

Children understand "leftovers" (remainders).

When your students grouped and counted stars during the *Stars in a Minute* activity, they had some stars left over. This happens often in real life. But some leftover objects can't be broken apart for equal sharing. For example, though students can break leftover cookies or candy bars into fraction pieces for more sharing, they can't do the same with leftover balloons. By having children explain what they are doing with their leftovers as wholes or as parts, they must make sense of the context or the situation in the problem. Mathematics becomes more real to them, and they begin to understand fractions.

> **TEACHER-TO-TEACHER TALK**   The idea that you can use the words *remainders* and *leftovers* interchangeably can confuse young children, especially if English is not their first language. When you share or group real items and there are leftovers, take time to show what did not fit into the equal-size groups. Talk about these items as being "leftovers" or "remainders," and put the words on the board. Then explain that mathematicians use an R to mean remainders. But they do not use an L for leftovers.

Mathematics Throughout the Day

You may want your students to revisit doing daily temperature readings, *Today's Number*, and *The Pocket Problem*. Certainly, you will want to take advantage of situations that lead to division, such as sharing supplies and snacks or grouping classmates.

Grouping and Sharing Supplies

During January, you can provide various items on each table of four, and ask students to divide the objects into fair shares. For example, place sixteen pieces of paper at each table and ask how many sheets of paper each of the four children at a table will get. Have the children share the paper, then have them write down their solution in words and numbers. You might also ask them to use the three kinds of division notation. But the important thing is that they use the word *shared*. Their responses might include the following:

16 pieces of paper shared among 4 of us equals 4 pieces of paper each

16 pieces of paper ÷ 4 children = 4 pieces of paper each

$$16 ÷ 4 = 4$$

$$4\overline{)16}^{\,4}$$

$$\frac{16}{4} = 4$$

Eventually, you could provide each table with eighteen pieces of paper and prompt a discussion about what to do with leftovers—and how to record them. Eighteen pieces of paper shared among four children equals four pieces of paper per child, with two pieces leftover. Have the children indicate what they are going to do with the leftovers. For example, the children might decide to put the remaining two pieces of paper back on the shelf. Then ask them to explain this in writing. The three notations show remainders as follows:

$$18 \div 4 = 4 \; R2 \qquad \frac{18}{4} = 4 \; R2 \qquad 4\overline{)18}^{\,4\,R2}$$

You can hand out erasers, books, and bottles of glue to groups of four to present similar sharing problems. If you want the children to work with a different divisor, hand out the classroom supplies to pairs of children.

Also write problems that require grouping instead of sharing. For example:

There are 10 books. If each person at your table gets 3 books, how many people will get books? How many books will be left over? What should be done with them?

Have the children talk first with their table partners about the problem and then share their thinking with the rest of the class. Encourage them to use counters or drawings as they make models to help themselves think. Finally, have a volunteer hand out three books at a time to a table group, then record what happened on the board.

Here's another grouping problem:

I have 38 erasers. I am grouping the erasers so each person in the class gets 2 erasers. How many of you will get erasers?

Help the children understand that, in these kinds of problems, they know the number of fair shares or things being shared. What they have to find out is how many *groups* of these shares they will end up with.

Extensions

- When you feel students are ready, have pairs or groups of four set up their own division situation for the rest of class, using objects in the room. They could write their story problems using two declarative sentences and one interrogative sentence, as in the problems described above. On the back of their paper, they show how they found the answer to their own question, including the word *share* or *group*.

- Write up some additional sharing and grouping problems that require students to divide classroom supplies.

Classroom Groups

In *Classroom Groups*, children experience division as grouping. You can find this activity and many others described in this chapter in *Teaching Arithmetic: Lessons for Introducing Division, Grades 3–4* by Maryann Wickett, Susan Ohanian, and Marilyn Burns (2002).

Instructions

1. Ask the children what kinds of real-life situations would cause the class members to be organized into groups of 2, 3, 4, 5, 6, 7, 8, 9, and 10. Responses might include, "We get into groups of two when we work in pairs," "We get into groups of four at our tables," and "We get into groups of three on field trips."

2. Ask how many groups there would be if the class members were grouped in pairs. Have the children explain how they know the answer. Some students may use skip-counting to count the number of youngsters in the room, then figure out how many counts they did. For example, 2, 4, 6, 8, 10, 12, 14, 16, 18, 20 requires ten skip-counts. So, there would be ten groups if the class members were grouped in pairs. Other students may take out twenty counters and group them by 2s, then figure out the answer. Still others might start with the number 20, then subtract out 2 at a time until arriving at 0, then count the number of times they subtracted 2. Some might draw lines or other shapes, each representing a child, then circle pairs of shapes to arrive at a solution. A few might count by using numbers in groups:

   1, 2

   3, 4

   5, 6 and so forth up to 20

3. Ask if anyone can use multiplication to make sense of this problem. Someone may say, "I know that two times ten equals twenty, so there must be ten groups." If someone does respond with a solution involving multiplication, include this strategy as you list the various ways students have expressed their solutions to the problem. If no one replies, wait. For example:

20 children grouped so there are 2 children in each group equals 10 groups

20 children ÷ 2 children in each group = 10 groups

$$20 ÷ 2 = 10$$

$$2)\overline{20}^{\,10}$$

$$\frac{20}{2} = 10$$

10 groups × 2 children in each group equals 20 children (10 × 2 = 20)

4. Have the children group themselves into pairs to see if all their numerical reasoning makes sense.

TEACHER-TO-TEACHER TALK Watch for children who confuse *grouping* children so there are two children in each group with *sharing* children into two groups. Both situations are represented by the same division notation or number equations (20 ÷ 2 = 10), but they have different meanings in the real world. You want your students to understand this difference just as they understand the difference between take-away and comparison subtraction. Here are some word/number equations that may help clarify things:

- 20 children *grouped* so that there are 2 children in each group = 10 groups with 2 children in each.

- 20 children *shared* equally between 2 groups = 10 children in each group.

---

5. Have the children pair up and figure out how many groups there would be if the class members were organized into groups of *three*. If some pairs finish early, ask them to figure out another way to do the problem to see if they get the same answer. When everyone is done coming up with their first strategy, have pairs share their thinking with the rest of the class. See how they handle leftovers. For example, "20 children grouped so that there are 3 children in each group = 6 groups with 3 children in each and 2 children leftover (20 ÷ 3 = 6 R2)."

6. Have class members organize themselves into groups of three to see if their calculations are correct.

7. Finally, have pairs figure out, on their own, how many groups there would if class members were organized into groups of four, five, six, seven, eight, nine, and ten people. Encourage the use of manipulatives or pictures to solve these problems.

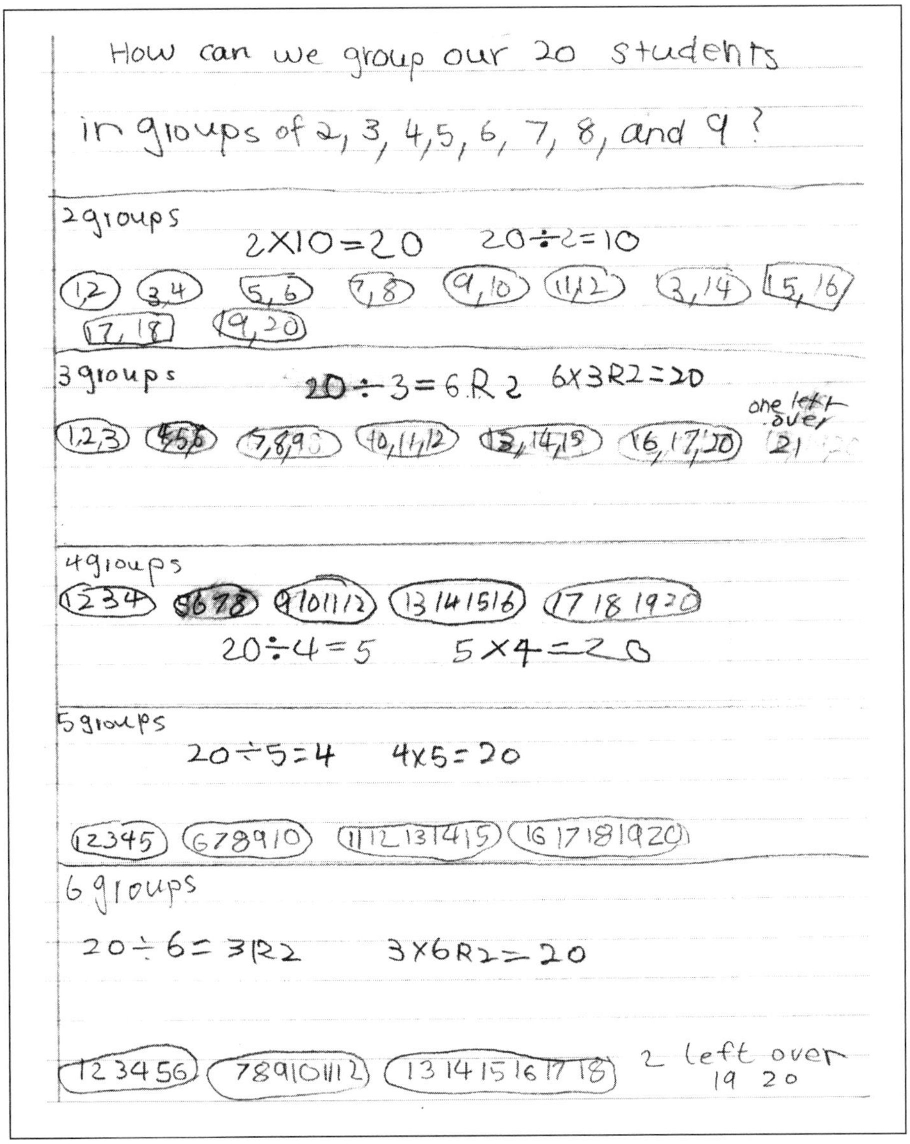

FIGURE 5–1   ◀

Nan used multiplication and division notations to represent her groupings. She confused her counting when grouping by threes.

8. That day or the next, have a class discussion about the children's strategies. Look at what students are doing to make sense of these grouping problems, then ask pairs to share their solutions. Some children may have organized their thinking in remarkably creative ways. (See Figures 5–1 and 5–2.)

Some children may notice that certain groups have remainders and others do not. For examples, in a class of twenty students, groups of two have no remainders, groups of three have two remainders, groups of four have no remainders, groups of five have no remainders, and groups of

FIGURE 5–2 ▶

Deon used multiplication notation to represent each grouping. For remainders, he wrote an addition equation.

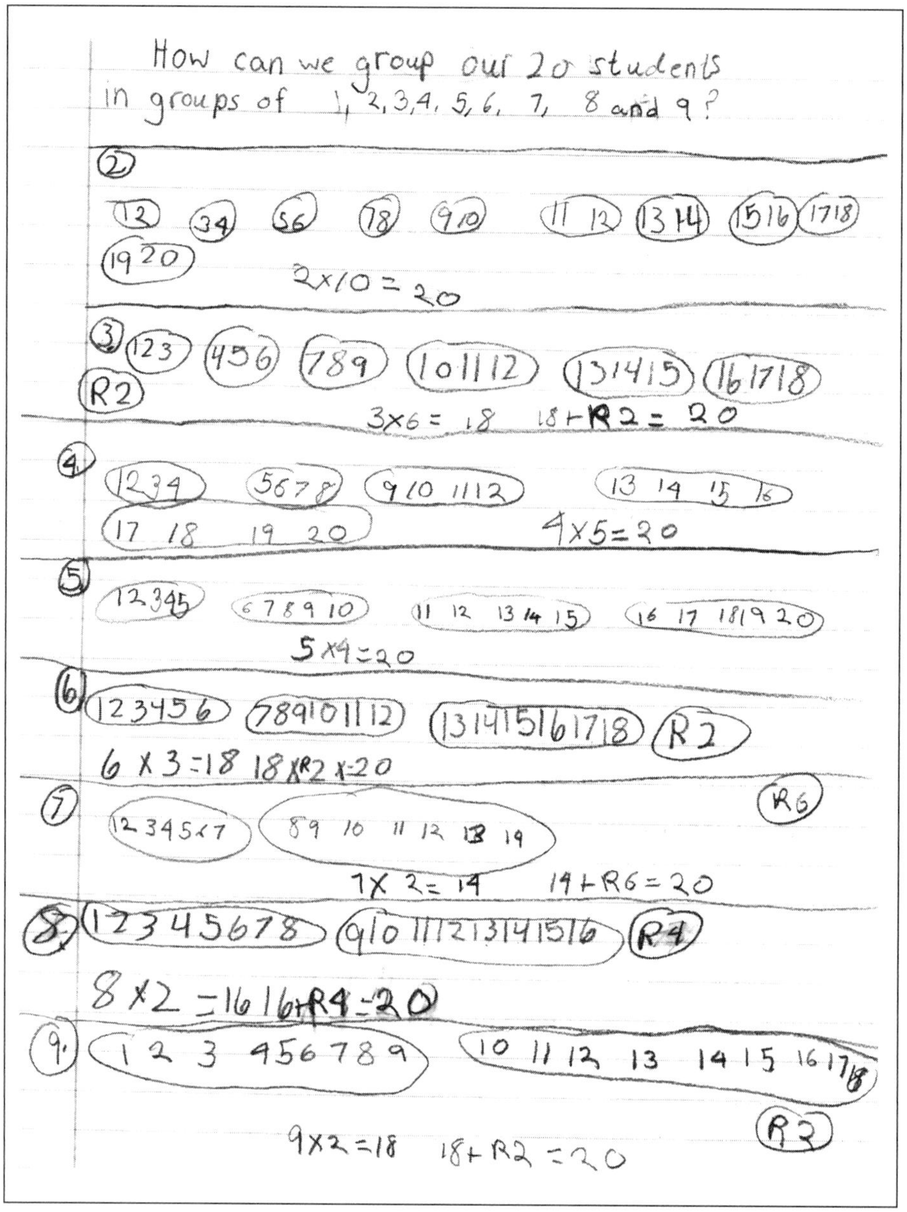

six have two remainders. If someone brings this up, ask why some groupings have no remainders.

Sharing Raisins Revisited

You know how much children love having classroom snacks. From a teacher's perspective, a snack that coincides with some meaningful mathematics is a worthy snack indeed! When your students began working with multiplication in October and November, they shared crackers without remainders. This time around, they will be sharing raisins with remainders. (As always, have children wash their hands before working with and eating food.) At the beginning of this lengthy investigation, the children group as they divide. At the end, they share as they divide.

Materials

- $1\frac{1}{2}$-ounce box of raisins per student
- 1 large piece of paper per student, for sorting raisins
- 1 $8\frac{1}{2}$-by-11-inch piece of paper per student, for recording counts
- overhead projector

Instructions

Part 1: Grouping and Counting Raisins

1. Give each child a box of raisins.

2. Ask them to guess how many raisins are in the box—without opening the box.

3. Record the guesses, from smallest to largest, on the board.

4. Determine the range of the guesses. For example, if the largest guess is 65 and the smallest is 20, the range is $65 - 20 = 45$. (Third graders love to estimate high, because they view big numbers as the best numbers.)

5. Invite the children to open the boxes.

6. Explain that now that the boxes are open, the children can estimate the number of raisins—whereas they were only able to guess when the boxes were closed.

7. Ask for and record estimates, identifying the range. Ideally, the range of estimates will be less than the range of guesses.

8. Open a box of raisins on the overhead, and group your raisins to count them. If you group by 5s, circle each group of 5s. If you have three remainders, leave them in a group without a circle.

9. Suppose you ended up with seven groups of raisins circled. Ask the children how you can figure out the total number of raisins. One child might suggest that you write skip-counts below each circle: *5, 10, 15, 20, 25, 30, 35.* Then below that, you would write *35 + R3 = 38.* Another might suggest that this activity seems a little like *Circles and Stars.* Perhaps you could write *7 circles × 5 raisins in each equals 35 raisins,* then *35 raisins plus 3 leftovers equals 38 raisins. 7 × 5 = 35.* Then, underneath, *35 + R3 = 38.*

10. Ask for volunteers to help you write division grouping statements, such as:

38 raisins grouped so there are 5 raisins in each group equals 7 groups with 3 leftovers.

38 raisins ÷ 5 raisins in each group = 7 groups with R3

$$38 \div 5 = 7 \ R3$$

$$5\overline{)38}^{\,7\,R3}$$

$$\frac{38}{5} = 7 \ R3$$

11. Have the children group their own box of raisins, but don't permit them to eat any yet. Assure them that they will be able to eat the raisins when the investigation is finished.

12. Ask students to record their multiplication and division sentences. Also have them place drawings or numbers inside each circle so classmates will know what they grouped by. (See Figures 5–3 and 5–4.)

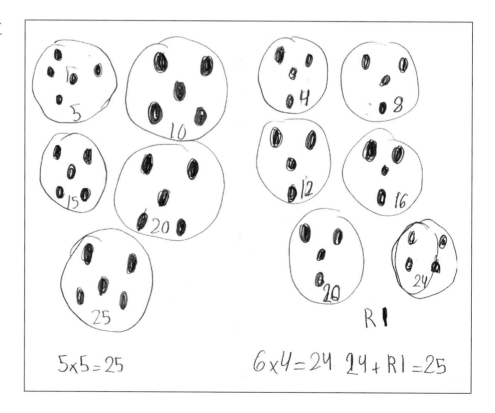

FIGURE 5–4 ◀

**Jaime grouped his
raisins by 10s.**

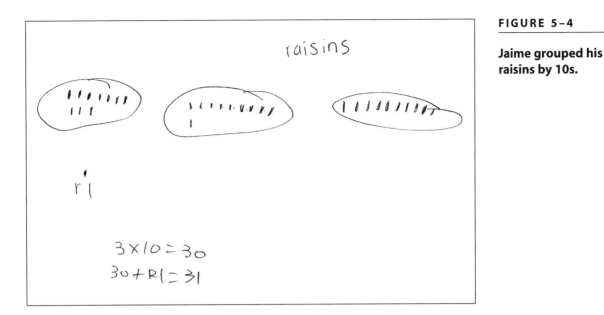

13. As children finish, check their work. Ask them to group their raisins in a different way on a new sheet of paper and see whether they get the same total count.

14. When everyone has finished counting and recording their number of raisins, ask the students at each table who had the *fewest* raisins at their table. Then find out who had the fewest raisins in the entire class.

15. Ask who had the *most* raisins in each team and the most raisins in the entire class.

16. Draw a line graph on the board whose *x*-axis starts with the lowest number of raisins and ends with the highest. Have each child say his or her total, and record the numbers as *x*s on the graph. (See Figure 5–5.)

17. Once all the data are recorded on the graph, discuss the range (the difference between the smallest number of raisins in a box and the largest number) and the mode (the number that occurred most frequently).

18. Ask the children who grouped their raisins a second way whether they got the same counts the second time that they got the first time. Have them show their work to their classmates. (This sharing is easier if everyone gathers on the rug to view one another's recording sheets. You might stay in the background and let the children share their work without any interpretation or recording.)

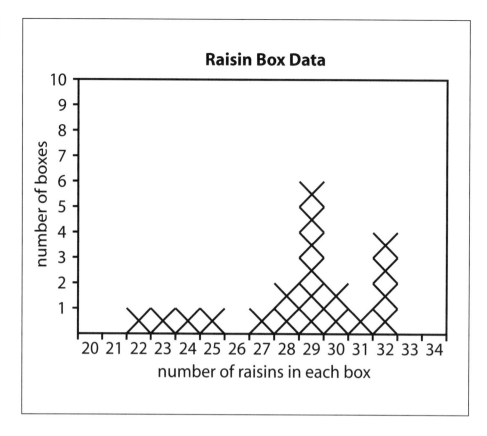

Part 2: Sharing Raisins in Groups of Four

1. Now that each child has counted his or her raisins, have all four students at a table calculate the total number of raisins at their table
   and record the result on a separate sheet of paper. Ask them to also
   explain how they are going to share those raisins equally among themselves. (See Figures 5–6 and 5–7.)

2. When the students have explained their figuring, invite them to eat
   their raisins.

Extensions

Look at the children's grouping raisin papers and write or pose problems
such as these:

*Margo grouped her raisins in groups of 4. She had 8 groups of raisins with 3
leftovers. How many raisins did she have altogether? How did you figure this
out?*

*Do you get the same total when you group Margo's raisins into groups of 10?
Show me how you figured this out. Write words and numbers to go with your
pictures as you solve the problem.*

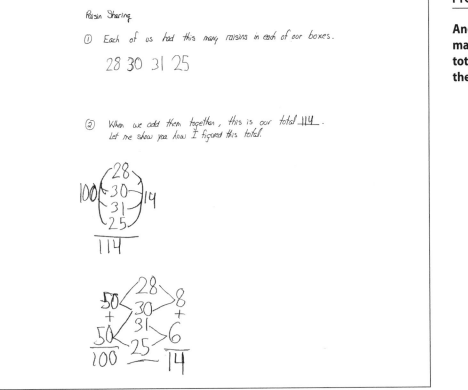

FIGURE 5–6 ◄

Angela and her table-mates showed how they totaled the raisins at their table.

FIGURE 5–7 ◄

Angela and her table-mates showed how they would share the raisins equally.

Games

As children continue to play counting games, they can begin connecting division to multiplication. The games described below provide meaningful mathematics links between home and school. In all these activities, the ability to communicate one's thinking is an important ingredient.

Circles and Stars Revisited

Materials

- number cubes with the following factors on the faces: 4, 5, 6, 7, 8, and 9; 1 cube per student. (These multipliers give children practice with the larger multiplication combinations.)

Instructions

1. Model *Circles and Stars* with a volunteer from the class. For example, if you roll a 6, draw six circles. Roll the number cube again. If you get a 5, draw five stars in each of your six circles.

2. Write the resulting multiplication sentence, using numbers and words. For instance, write *6 × 5 = 30* and *6 circles times 5 stars in each equals 30 stars in all*. Also write the reverse: *30 stars shared so that there are 5 stars in a group equals 6 circles, or groups. 30 ÷ 5 = 6*. (See Figure 5–8.)

TEACHER-TO-TEACHER TALK By using division hand in hand with multiplication, children realize the deep connection between the two operations. When I was a child, I was taught to check my division problems by multiplying, but I never understood the connection. You will find that your students often use multiplication to make sense of division, just as they use addition to make sense of subtraction.

This is true in their story-problem work as well. For example, suppose a child writes this multiplication story problem:

There are 3 bikes. Each bike has 2 wheels. How many wheels are there?

In this case, the multiplication equation 3 × 2 = 6 represents the problem. But the problem also offers two opportunities to think in terms of division:

6 wheels shared among 3 bikes equals 2 wheels per bike (6 ÷ 3 = 2)

6 wheels grouped so there are 2 wheels on each bike equals 3 bikes (6 ÷ 2 = 3)

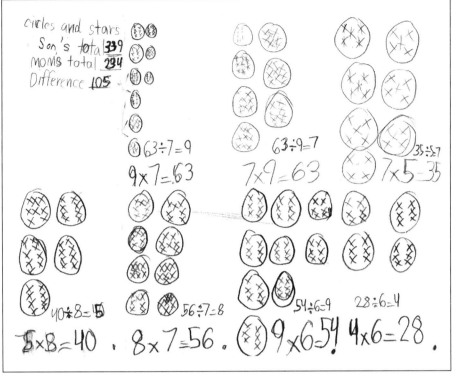

FIGURE 5–8   ◀

Sam played *Circles and Stars* with his mom, and showed his results. He needed to rethink 4 × 6 = 28.

Leftovers

This game gives students additional experience with the sharing kind of division and with leftovers.

Materials

- 1 plastic half-pint-sized container, filled with 15 colored tiles, per pair of students
- 6 small paper plates per pair of students
- 1 die per pair of students
- 1 plastic bowl per pair of students
- 1 recording sheet per pair of students

TEACHER-TO-TEACHER TALK Consider having one pair of students play this game with another pair. The pairs can talk about what is happening during the game and reinforce one another's understanding. *Leftovers* involves doing division with remainders and recording the resulting equations—a new experience for third graders. Thus two heads may be better than one.

Instructions

1. Put fifteen colored tiles in each of the plastic containers.

2. Give each pair of students a tile-filled container, six paper plates, and a die.

3. Player 1 rolls the die and places that many plates on the table. He rolls the die again, placing that many *tiles* on *each plate*. Any leftover tiles go in a reject bowl, not to be used again until the start of a new game.

4. Player 1 writes a division equation representing his arrangement of plates and tiles. For example, if the player rolled a 3 and then a 4, he should have put four tiles on each of three plates. The corresponding division equation would be 15 ÷ 3 = 4 R3. After writing the equation, the player places his initials on the recording sheet and puts the tiles from the plates back into the container—leaving the leftovers in the bowl.

5. Player 2 takes a turn, starting with twelve tiles since the three leftovers have been removed. If she rolls a 4, she puts out four plates. Next, if she rolls a 3, she places three tiles on each plate. In this case, there are no leftovers.

6. Player 2 writes her division equation on the recording sheet under Player 1's equation, and initials the equation: 12 ÷ 4 = 3R0.

7. The children keep playing until there are no possible moves left.

In the first few rounds of this game, you might have the children work on recording sheets that have words and blank spaces that the students can fill in. (See Blackline Masters and Figures 5–9 and 5–10.)

As partners play *Leftovers*, rotate among the pairs to ensure that they're removing the leftovers on each round. If you want to add the idea of a winner to this game, have each player add up his or her remainders at the bottom of the recording page. The player with the most leftovers wins the game.

Most classrooms keep a running chart of all the *Leftovers* division equations that have no remainders. This chart leads to interesting discussions about why there are no remainders. For 12 divided by 4 equals 3 R0, the children ideally will realize that you can multiply 3 × 4 and get 12 or you can skip-count by 3s or by 4s and land on 12.

You may also want to have students play *Leftovers* with a family member as a homework assignment. If you do this, be sure to send home the *Leftovers* homework rules. (See Blackline Masters.)

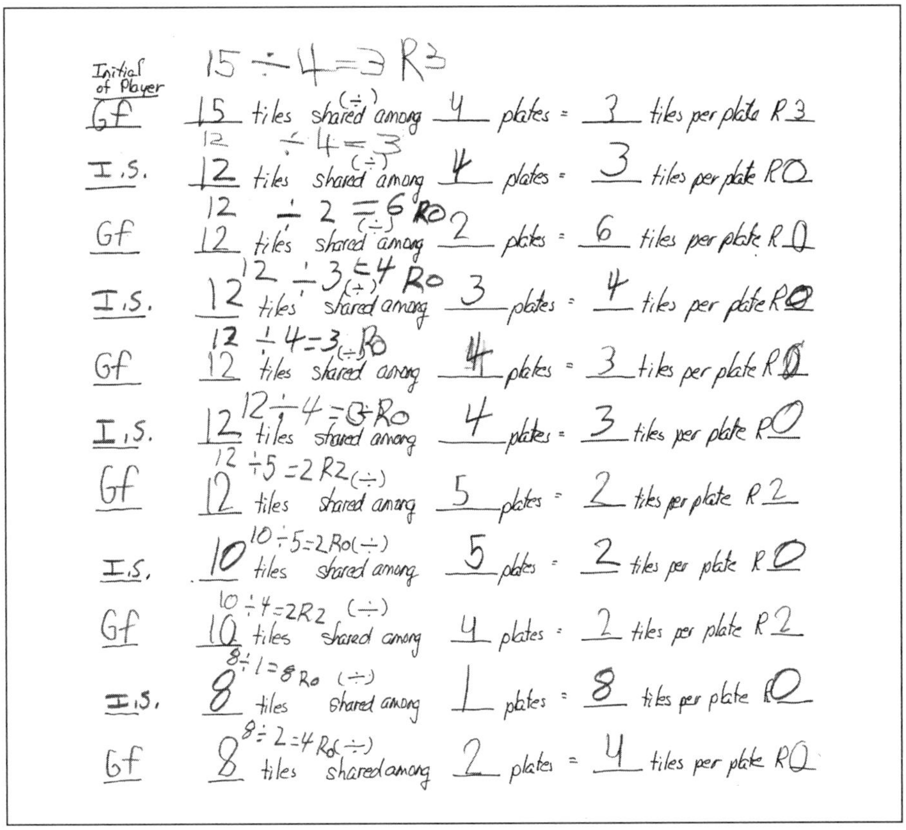

Initial of Player				
Gf	15 ÷ 4 = 3 R3 — 15 tiles shared (÷) among	4 plates =	3 tiles per plate	R 3
I.S.	12 ÷ 4 = 3 — 12 tiles shared (÷) among	4 plates =	3 tiles per plate	R 0
Gf	12 ÷ 2 = 6 R0 — 12 tiles shared (÷) among	2 plates =	6 tiles per plate	R 0
I.S.	12 ÷ 3 = 4 R0 — 12 tiles shared (÷) among	3 plates =	4 tiles per plate	R 0
Gf	12 ÷ 4 = 3 R0 — 12 tiles shared (÷) among	4 plates =	3 tiles per plate	R 0
I.S.	12 ÷ 4 = 3 R0 — 12 tiles shared among	4 plates =	3 tiles per plate	R 0
Gf	12 ÷ 5 = 2 R2 (÷) — 12 tiles shared among	5 plates =	2 tiles per plate	R 2
I.S.	10 ÷ 5 = 2 R0 (÷) — 10 tiles shared among	5 plates =	2 tiles per plate	R 0
Gf	10 ÷ 4 = 2 R2 (÷) — 10 tiles shared among	4 plates =	2 tiles per plate	R 2
I.S.	8 ÷ 1 = 8 R0 (÷) — 8 tiles shared among	1 plates =	8 tiles per plate	R 0
Gf	8 ÷ 2 = 4 R0 (÷) — 8 tiles shared among	2 plates =	4 tiles per plate	R 0

FIGURE 5–9

Gary and Isa used the Blackline Master to record their division equations.

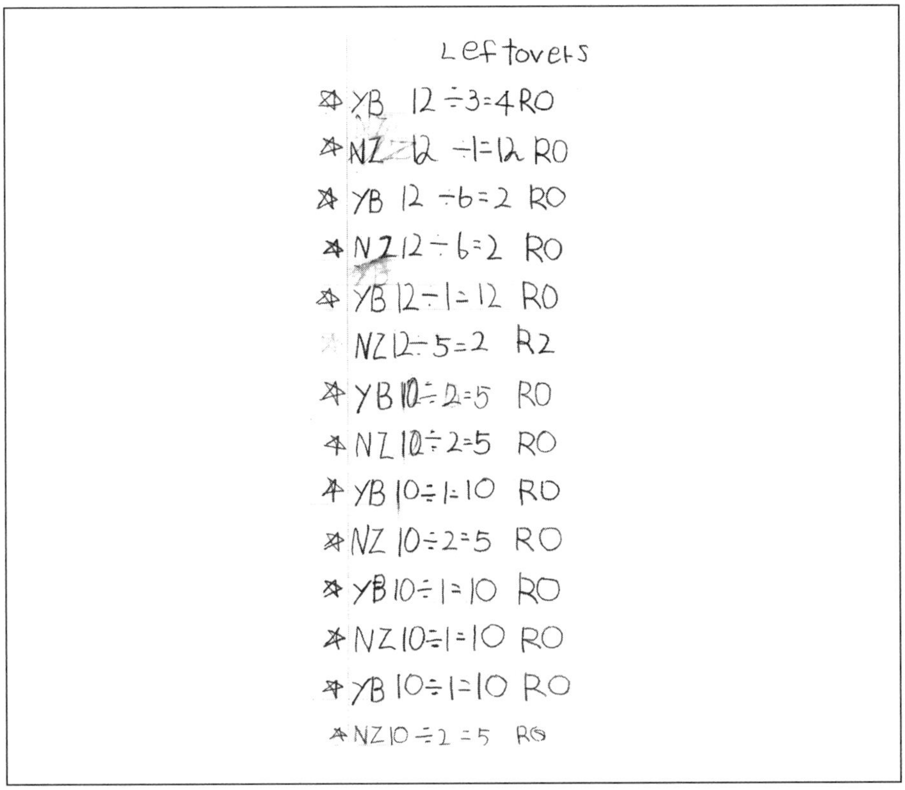

Leftovers

YB 12 ÷ 3 = 4 R0
NZ 12 ÷ 1 = 12 R0
YB 12 ÷ 6 = 2 R0
NZ 12 ÷ 6 = 2 R0
YB 12 ÷ 1 = 12 R0
NZ 12 ÷ 5 = 2 R2
YB 10 ÷ 2 = 5 R0
NZ 10 ÷ 2 = 5 R0
YB 10 ÷ 1 = 10 R0
NZ 10 ÷ 2 = 5 R0
YB 10 ÷ 1 = 10 R0
NZ 10 ÷ 1 = 10 R0
YB 10 ÷ 1 = 10 R0
NZ 10 ÷ 2 = 5 R0

FIGURE 5–10

Yang and Nan listed their division equations on a blank recording sheet.

> **TEACHER-TO-TEACHER TALK**   When it seems appropriate, help your students connect their division thinking by looking at the windowpane wall for arrays that have a specific number. For example, if the number is 12, they could look for arrays that have three rows of four windowpanes each or four rows with three panes each. Point out that the factors for the number 12 are 3 and 4. When children skip-count by 3s *or* 4s, they land on 12. Explain that 12 divided by 4 equals 3 R0 because 3 times 4 equals 12—and 3 and 4 make up a *factor pair* for 12.
>
> The big idea here is that when the *divisor* (the number you are dividing by) is a factor of the *dividend* (the number being divided), the *quotient* (the result of the division) is the factor partner of the divisor and there is no remainder. Children might make this same factor-pair connection while doing the *Classroom Groups* activity.

Measurement

Many children love measurement activities. Rather than devise new measurement investigations every month, you can revisit previous problems and think of applicable sharing or grouping situations. Often students will have ideas of their own. One year, my students decided to measure the length and height of the classroom with interlocking cubes. It was difficult to count each cube. So, they made different-colored ten-trains, hooked them together, then counted the trains. *Estimate and Measure Revisited*, described below, expands on this idea.

Stars in a Minute Revisited

Whether your children use stars, dollar signs, the alphabet, or digits, they can play some version of *Stars in a Minute* and record their results with a multiplication word/number equation or number equation followed by a related division word/number equation (or number equation). In *Stars in a Minute*, if a child grouped thirty-five stars into seven groups of five stars each, he or she could write this multiplication equation: *7 groups times 5 stars in each equals 35 stars in all 7 groups (7 × 5 = 35)*. For a division equation, the student could write *35 stars* shared *equally among 7 groups equals 5 stars in each group (35 ÷ 7 = 5)*. He or she could also write *35 stars* grouped *so there are 5 stars in each group equals 7 groups (35 ÷ 5 = 7)*.

Estimate and Measure Revisited (Linear)

Have the children again measure things in the room with interlocking cubes made into different-color ten-trains and then represent their results with division equations. For example, if a bookcase is 42 cubes high, students could write *42 cubes grouped into ten-trains equals 4 ten-trains plus 2 leftovers (42 ÷ 10 = 4 R2)*.

Consider having the children think of two things in the classroom they would like to compare, to see which is longer, wider, or higher. They can also compare length to width, height to length, and so forth. They record what they are measuring and then measure using ten-trains. They represent their grouping work with division and then compare the two measurements.

Money

Divvying up money fairly is another frequent experience children have in their everyday lives. You will want to take advantage of this real-world connection.

Sharing Five Dollars

Materials

- 1 money bag per table group of four students

Instructions

1. Have the children gather in groups of four at their work tables.

2. Put a money bag on each table.

3. Ask the children to figure out how they can share five dollars equally among the four of them, and to record step by step how they arrived at their solution. Remind students to include words and number labels on any drawings to ensure clarity. Show the children again how to write the symbols for dollars and cents. To provide additional decimal practice, ask the children to write twenty-five cents as *$.25* instead of *25 cents*. (See Figures 5–11 and 5–12.)

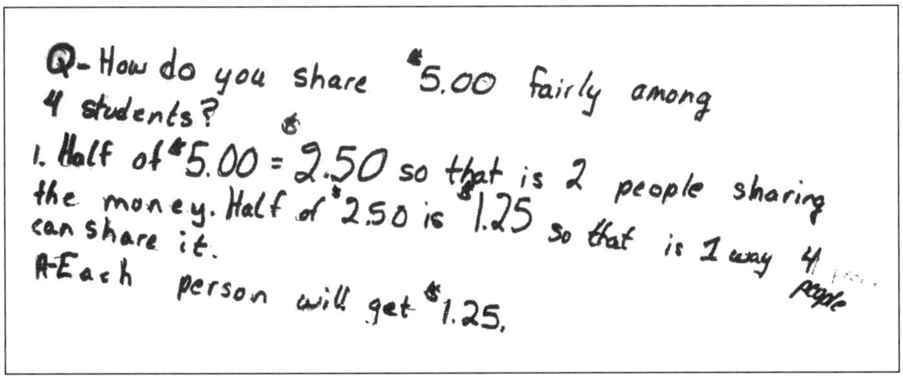

Q- How do you share $5.00 fairly among 4 students?
1. Half of $5.00 = 2.50 so that is 2 people sharing the money. Half of $2.50 is 1.25 so that is 1 way 4 people can share it.
A-Each person will get $1.25.

FIGURE 5–11 ◀

Wei-Cee used words and numbers to show her table's thinking about the same problem.

FIGURE 5–12 ▶

Marcus used words, numbers, and drawings to show his table thinking about how four people might share five dollars.

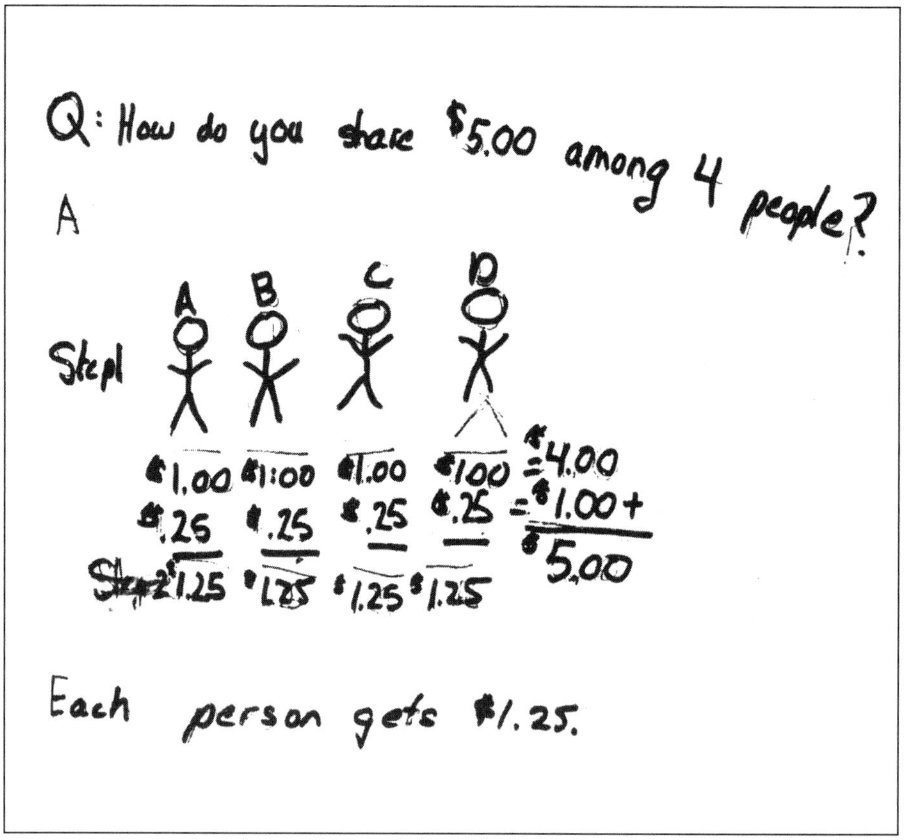

For groups that finish early, check their work and ask questions if you think the written solutions need additional information to be clear and convincing. If time permits, early finishers may also figure out another way to share five dollars.

As always, have the children share their various strategies with the class. Start making overhead transparencies of the children's work for them to share. This way, you help them move into the foreground as their own recorders.

Extensions

- The children figure out how to share fifty cents equally among four people and what to do with the remainder.
- The children figure out how to share ten dollars equally among four people.

Coins in Two Pockets Revisited

Write problem cards for the children to solve using real or pretend coins. For example, one card might read:

I have $.28. I want to put half of the money in one pocket and half of the money in the other pocket. How much money do I put in one pocket?

Have students record the reasoning they used to figure out the answer. On some cards have uneven numbers such as $.45 to see what the children decide to do with the leftovers. For other ideas, you might wish to look in *Mathematical Thinking at Grade 3* (Russell and Economopoulos 1995).

Literature-Based Activities

Watch for "math moments" in books you're reading aloud in class. The selections below offer many opportunities to explore various math concepts.

Buying Jawbreakers

One such moment is in the chapter titled "Two Heads Are Better Than One" in *Judy Moody was in a mood. Not a good mood. Not a bad mood,* by Megan McDonald. In the story, Rocky and his friend, Judy, each has one dollar. Judy's little bother, Stink, has six cents. If each jawbreaker costs twenty-five cents, how many jawbreakers can the three children buy by pooling their money?

Sharing Cookies

In *The Doorbell Rang* by Pat Hutchins, Mom gives each of her two children six cookies to eat. Before they have a chance to gobble the treats, two of their friends arrive. Now they must share the twelve cookies fairly among four children. The doorbell rings a few more times before the youngsters can eat the cookies, so the original twelve treats must be shared with more and more friends. Eventually, twelve children are hankering after the cookies—with the prospect of getting only one each. Fortunately, Grandma arrives on the scene with more cookies. (**Note:** You may want to do the *Dividing Cookies* problems found in the "Story Problems" section of this chapter before you do the series of problems below.)

Materials

- 1 12-by-18-inch sheet of paper per student

Instructions

1. Before you read the story, ask if anyone is already familiar with the book. If so, ask them to explain what the story is about.

2. As you read, stop at each place in the story where the characters must figure out how many cookies each child will get. Ask your students to do the figuring. For example, for twelve cookies being shared by four children, one student might use addition: *3 cookies + 3 cookies + 3 cookies + 3 cookies = 12 cookies.* Another might subtract: *12 cookies − 3 cookies for one child = 9 cookies. Then you take away 3 more cookies for the next child, and you get 6 cookies left. Then you give 3 cookies to each of the other two children.* If no one offers a solution, ask about using multiplication to figure out the answer. Ideally, a student will suggest that *4 children times 3 cookies each equals 12 cookies.*

3. As you discuss each cookie-sharing situation in the book, write each problem on the board. Then write the three ways to represent that problem. Here are some examples:

Sharing Problem #1

12 cookies shared equally between 2 children equals 6 cookies for each child

12 cookies ÷ 2 children = 6 cookies for each

$$12 ÷ 2 = 6$$

$$2\overline{)12}\ \ \text{(6)}$$

$$\frac{12}{2} = 6$$

Sharing Problem #2

12 cookies shared equally among 4 children equals 3 cookies for each child

12 cookies ÷ 4 children = 3 cookies for each

$$12 ÷ 4 = 3$$

$$4\overline{)12}\ \ \text{(3)}$$

$$\frac{12}{4} = 3$$

Sharing Problem #3

12 cookies shared equally among 6 children equals 2 cookies for each child

12 cookies ÷ 6 children = 2 cookies for each

$$12 ÷ 6 = 2$$

$$2\overline{)12}^{\,6}$$

$$\frac{12}{6} = 6$$

Sharing Problem #4

12 cookies shared equally among 12 children equals 1 cookie for each child

12 cookies ÷ 12 children = 1 cookie for each

$$12 ÷ 12 = 1$$

$$12\overline{)12}^{\,1}$$

$$\frac{12}{12} = 1$$

4. Have the children fold a 12-by-18-inch piece of paper into eight sections, as they did for their *Used to Be Rich* stories (Chapter 2). In the first box, each child writes his or her name and the label *The Doorbell Rang*. In each of the next four boxes, the children write a word/number equation and one division notation to represent each of the four cookie-sharing problems. Then they draw pictures to illustrate their equations.

   Rotate among the children and ask questions if you find any illustrations or equations confusing. Don't be surprised if you see children writing equations with divisors and dividends reversed. Ask them to explain in words what their notations show, and have them refer to the equations you've written on the board.

5. When many children have completed their equations and illustrations, have class members examine the picture in the story that shows an array of cookies on Grandma's tray. The picture shows six rows with thirteen cookies in each row. Because adding these seventy-eight cookies to the original twelve would produce a very large number, pose a simpler problem. Suggest that Grandma brought only eighteen cookies, then ask what eighteen plus twelve cookies equals.

6. Once students agree that 18 + 12 = 30, ask whether they can share thirty cookies equally among four children.

7. Refer the children to the following directions for the remaining cookie-sharing problems in the story.

Sharing Problem #5

30 cookies shared equally among 12 children = ___ cookies for each child

Sharing Problems #6 and #7

Create a cookie-sharing problem of your own. Decide if more people arrive to share thirty cookies fairly, or if more cookies arrive that twelve children will share. Or, change both the number of people and the number of cookies. Write two division equations showing how you solved your problem. Illustrate your solutions.

Notice that with Sharing Problem #5, there will be leftovers. Thus students will need "noodle-around time" to decide how they would handle the leftovers. Some would leave them on a plate or in the refrigerator. Others would divide each leftover in half and hand out the halves fairly. In either case, they may not know how to write the corresponding notation. When many children have worked through their thinking on this problem, you could have them share their thinking so far and provide notation help. For example, for six leftover cookies, the notation could be *2 with 6 leftovers*, or *2 R6*.

The notation for one-half is $\frac{1}{2}$ (see page 168). Because the answer to Sharing Problem #5 is two and one-half cookies, the children need to understand how numbers involving fractions are usually written (in this case $2\frac{1}{2}$). But if students make more sense of the situation by including the word *and* (2 and $\frac{1}{2}$ cookies) in their notation, let them. Be sure to ask if they have any other questions before they return to their problem solving at their desks.

See Figure 5–13 for an example of how one student illustrated the cookie-sharing problems from the story.

8. Have students share with classmates the cookie-sharing problems they created.

> **TEACHER-TO-TEACHER TALK** Sharing Problem #5, with its leftovers, presents one of those opportunities to let your children feel some confusion. When children experience disequilibrium, they often take big steps in their learning. I call these teachable moments. However, you don't want students to become overly frustrated by the idea of leftovers, so judge your "stop and share" time with care. Know when to step aside and when to step back in with moral or more concrete support.

Extensions

The children brainstorm other things (besides cookies) that can be shared. Then each child writes his or her own sharing story in the eight sections

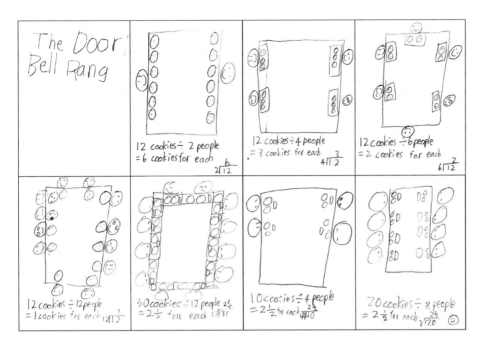

FIGURE 5–13 ◀

Salina drew pictures of friends sitting at tables to show how she solved various cookie-sharing problems.

of a new sheet of paper. (See *Teaching Arithmetic: Lessons for Introducing Division, Grades 3–4* [Wickett, Ohanian, and Burns 2002], for more ideas regarding this extension.)

Changing Numbers of Cookies

One Hungry Cat by Joanne Rocklin is an interesting follow-up to *The Doorbell Rang*. In this book, Tom the cat bakes a dozen cookies for himself and two friends. He figures out how to share the cookies in equal-size groups of four on three plates. Then he eats his plate of cookies. Now he has to share eight cookies equally on three plates. Unlike in *The Doorbell Rang*, the number of cookies changes, while the number of characters and plates does not.

One thing leads to another as Tom eats all the cookies then bakes a square lemon cake to share. Finally he bakes two blueberry muffins for his guests, who in turn want to fairly share the nine blueberries in their muffins. By exploring the situations in the book, your children have experiences with division involving leftovers. The section on sharing the lemon cake leads to thinking about fractions, but you might want your students to explore this topic more thoroughly through the activities in the next chapter.

Materials

- 12 round disks or interlocking cubes per pair of students
- 3 paper plates per pair of students

Instructions

1   Give each pair of students twelve "cookies" (disks or interlocking cubes) and three paper plates.

2   Have the students act out the beginning of the story, in which Tom shares twelve cookies among three people.

3. Have them act out the part where Tom must share eight cookies among three people. Be sure to discuss what to do with the two leftovers. Some student might suggest giving them to the guests only. Others might suggest cutting the cookies up and sharing them. This is a great jumping-off place for a discussion in which you explain that fractions are equal-size parts of a whole. Draw two round cookies on the white board and invite suggestions for how this equal sharing of *parts* of cookies can solve the problem in the story. See Figure 5–14 for several possibilities.

TEACHER-TO-TEACHER TALK Most children find it difficult to divide drawings of cookies into thirds, even when they have circular paper cookies to cut out and fold. Take their suggestions, but remind them that each fractional part must be equal in size to the others. Show what works and what does not. (See below.)

This works.   This does not work.

Be aware that this might be your students' first formal experience with fractions, so introduce correct notations and explain their meaning with a light touch. The notation $\frac{1}{3}$ means that the whole cookie has been divided into three equal-size pieces, and one of those pieces is being talked about. If the answer to a cookie-sharing problem is "two one-thirds," the notation might be $\frac{1}{3} + \frac{1}{3}$, or $\frac{2}{3}$. Your students will many opportunities to explore fraction notation further through the activities in the next chapter.

But to get them started, sketch on the board what happens if you first divide the two leftover cookies into halves. On each half, write $\frac{1}{2}$. This notation means that the whole has been divided into two equal-size pieces, and that you are referring to *one* of these pieces. Then point out that there's still a half a cookie remaining to hand out. The children may suggest that you divide this remaining half into three equal parts and refer to each of those parts as one-third. Explain that for each piece of cookie to be one-third, it must be one-third of the *whole* cookie. One-third of a half a cookie is one-sixth of a whole cookie. (See below.)

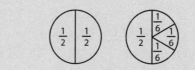

Children will see that Tom and his two friends get two whole cookies when sharing eight cookies. If they decide to share the two whole cookie remainders, there are several strategies.

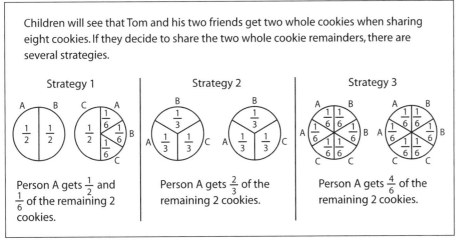

Strategy 1	Strategy 2	Strategy 3
Person A gets $\frac{1}{2}$ and $\frac{1}{6}$ of the remaining 2 cookies.	Person A gets $\frac{2}{3}$ of the remaining 2 cookies.	Person A gets $\frac{4}{6}$ of the remaining 2 cookies.

Arrays of Ants

In *One Hundred Hungry Ants* by Elinor J. Pinczes the ants are trying to line themselves up in ways that will get them to a picnic as quickly as possible.

Materials

■ a set of counting cubes or other manipulatives for each group of four students

Instructions

1. On the board, write *100 ants put into one line equal 100 ants in one line.*

2. Write the three notations:

$$100 \div 1 = 100$$

$$1\overline{)100}^{\,1}$$

$$\frac{100}{1} = 100$$

3. Read the story one part at a time, without revealing how many ants are in each line. Invite the children to figure out the answers by putting manipulatives into different-size lines. First the ants share themselves evenly into two lines. Have each group of four students count out 100 counters and line them up into two equal lines. Ask how many counters are in each line.

4. Have the children write word/number equations for this answer, followed by the three corresponding division notations.

5. Next the ants group themselves into four equal-size lines. Give students time to estimate the number of ants in each line. Listen to their reasoning. Then give them time to do this grouping. At this point in their thinking about division, children find it helpful to have lots of experiences putting tangible objects into equal-size groups.

6. Continue until the students have addressed all the division problems in the story.

Extensions

Students explore what happens when twelve ants try to group themselves into two rows, three rows, four rows, and so on, up to twelve rows.

Sharing Amusement-Park Tickets

In *Two Tickets to Ride* by Teddy Slater, Amy has fifty tickets for rides at an amusement park. She is trying to decide how many friends to invite to her birthday party, which will be held at the park. When she thinks of inviting her classmates plus herself, she comes up with twenty-five children. She has to figure out how many amusement-ride tickets each child will get if she shares the tickets fairly. Then she thinks about having three friends and herself share the tickets—four people. She adds her brother, bringing the number to five. The number of tickets stays the same, but the number of children sharing them changes.

After Amy, Sam, Max, and two other friends have been at the amusement park for a while, Max wins thirteen free tickets. He figures out how to share them and what to do with the extra ones. At the end of the story, Amy and her guests must decide how to share eleven tickets and what to do with the one leftover. As you can see, this book provides a meaningful context for decisions about leftovers.

Story Problems

Dividing Cookies

See *Teaching Arithmetic: Lessons for Introducing Division, Grades 3–4* (Wickett, Ohanian, and Burns 2002) for more details on this activity.

Materials

■ 1 sheet of blank cookie drawings (see Blackline Masters)

- several recording sheets per group of four students (see Blackline Masters)

Instructions

1. Copy the cookies Blackline Master onto colored copy paper and the recording sheet Blackline Master onto white copy paper.

2. Cut out the colored cookies.

3. Explain to your students that for each cookie problem they'll be working on today, the "cookies" are to be shared among four students at a table—even if someone is absent from a table.

4. Hold up four paper cookies. Ask the children how many cookies each child will get at a table of four.

5. Glue the one cookie onto each of the four sections on the recording sheet. Label each cookie *1 whole.*

6. For the question *How much did each person get?* decide whether you want the children to write a sentence, a word/number equation, a number equation, or all or some of the above. (Notations could include *4 cookies shared among 4 children equals 1 cookie for each child, 4 cookies ÷ 4 children = 1 cookie for each,* or *4 ÷ 4 = 1.*)

7. Have the groups of four work on sharing six cookies among four people and show you their recording sheet when they finish. Check that their one-half pieces of cookies are equal, and see how the children label these fractional parts. Be sure the children also label their whole cookies. (See Figure 5–15.)

8. Give students the following four problems and have them show their solutions on their recording sheets:

Cookies	*People*
5	4
3	4
2	4
1	4

9. As the children work, circulate among them and listen to how they are sharing the problem solving and making sense of the division and fractions. If groups finish early, have them divide seven cookies among four people. (See Figures 5–16 and 5–17.)

10. Have a class discussion about the activity: Ask how the children shared one cookie equally among four people, and check whether the children understand that the fraction $\frac{1}{4}$ means one piece out of the

FIGURE 5–15 ▶

Susan and Peter showed
how they would share
six cookies equally
among four people.

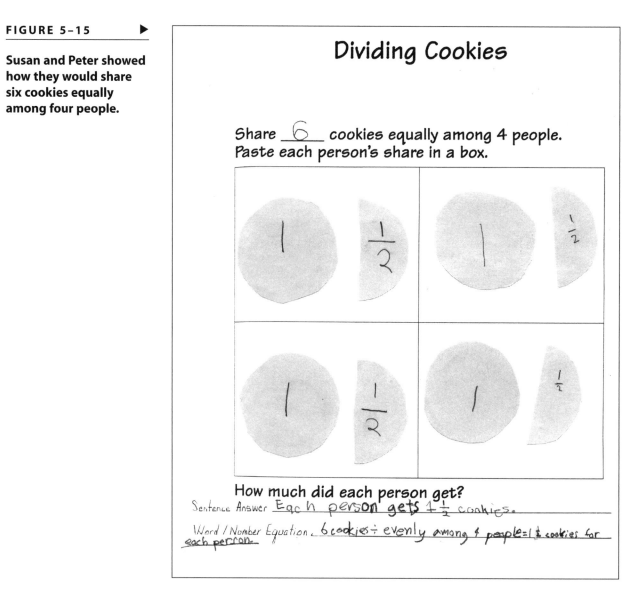

Dividing Cookies

Share ___6___ cookies equally among 4 people.
Paste each person's share in a box.

How much did each person get?

Sentence Answer Each person gets 1½ cookies.

Word / Number Equation 6 cookies ÷ evenly among 4 people = 1½ cookies for each person.

four equal-size pieces the whole has been divided into. This is a valuable opportunity for children to learn about fractions in a meaningful context.

In figuring out how to share two cookies equally among four people, some students will have divided their two cookies into halves. Others will have divided into fourths. These differences give you a chance to ask whether half of a cookie is the same as two-fourths of a cookie.

In sharing three cookies equally among four people, some students will have given each person one-half and one-fourth of a cookie. Others will have given each person three-fourths of a cookie.

FIGURE 5–16   ◀

**Salina and Ray showed
how they would share
five cookies among four
people.**

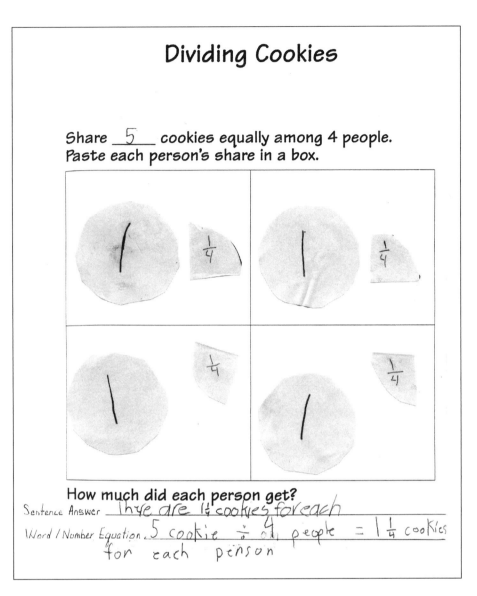

Dividing Cookies

Share __5__ cookies equally among 4 people.
Paste each person's share in a box.

How much did each person get?

Sentence Answer _thye are 1¼ cookies for each_

Word / Number Equation _5 cookie ÷ 4 people = 1¼ cookies
for each person_

See what most of your students do about sharing five cookies among
four people.

Extensions

Teaching Arithmetic: Lessons for Introducing Division, Grades 3–4 (Wickett, Ohanian, and Burns 2002) describes the following extensions. These
activities will be especially appropriate if your class has already had many
discussions about factors and has played *Leftovers* with equations that have
no remainders, or if your class has discussed how the factor-pairs on the
window pane arrays connect with these *Leftover* equations.

FIGURE 5–17 ▶

Yousif and Eun-Jin fig-
ured out how to share
three cookies among
four people.

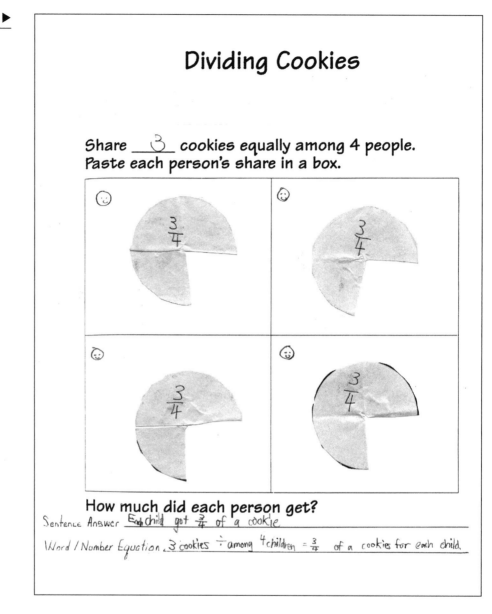

- Students explore how many cookies can they share equally in their group of four and have no cookies left over. Point out to them that when they shared four cookies among four people, there were no left-overs. Ask, "For what other numbers of cookies will this be true? How do you know?"

- Students figure out which numbers of people could share twelve cookies equally with no leftovers, and explain how they know.

- Students figure out how to share specific numbers of cookies among six or eight people instead of four.

Things That Come in Groups Revisited: Adding Division Problems

Chapter 3 (page 101) contained an activity in the "Story Problems" section called *Things That Come in Groups*. The investigation required students to write three sentence strips to go with their drawings; for example:

There are 3 bikes.

Each bike has 2 wheels.

There are 6 wheels in all.

To write multiplication word problems, students removed their last strip and added this question instead:

How many wheels do all 3 bikes have?

They then answered the new question with a word/number equation and a number equation:

3 bikes × 2 wheels on each bike = 6 wheels in all

$$3 \times 2 = 6$$

Hand out these 12-by-18 story problem sheets once again. If you have them in a bound class book, you will have to remove them from the book.

Now your students can write a sharing division story problem and a grouping division story problem on these story problem sheets by keeping the bottom strip (or the total number) as the first sentence in their problem and removing one of the others. For example, if a student removes the top strip in the above problem (*There are 3 bikes*), he or she can write a *grouping problem* that starts with the bottom strip and moves up:

There are 6 wheels in all.

Each bike has 2 wheels.

How many bikes are there?

The child can express the answer as follows: By placing the division sign above or next to the word *grouped* and the word *shared*, my students tell me it helps them make more sense of division situations.

6 wheels grouped (÷) so there are 2 wheels on each bike = 3 bikes

$$6 \div 2 = 3$$

The connected multiplication equation is:

$$3 \times 2 = 6$$

When the student puts the top strip back in and removes the middle strip, he can write a *sharing problem* that starts with the bottom strip and moves up:

There are 6 wheels in all.

There are 3 bikes.

How many wheels are there on each bike?

The child can express the answer as follows:

6 wheels shared (÷) among 3 bikes = 2 wheels on each bike

$$6 \div 3 = 2$$

The connected multiplication equation is:

$$2 \times 3 = 6$$

This activity brings home the idea that multiplication and division are connected. Decide whether you want your students to write one or both division story problems based on the work they did in *Things That Come in Groups*. (If you bind the colorful pages into a class book or into two class books, the resulting volumes can provide meaningful math reading for students and their parents. [See Figures 5–18 and 5–19.])

TEACHER-TO-TEACHER TALK Writing the division problems can be a bit tricky for students. They need to decide whether a problem involves grouping or sharing. Thinking about what is known and what is unknown helps. In the first division problem, the number of wheels and the number of wheels per bike are known. The number of bikes (or groups) is the unknown. Thus this is a *grouping* problem. In the second division problem, the number of wheels and the number of bikes are known. The number of wheels shared equally between the bikes is the unknown. Thus this is a *sharing* problem.

If you offer this activity during station time, help the students work through these reasoning steps.

Extensions

- Children create another multiplication/division word problem with things that come in groups. Examples might include:

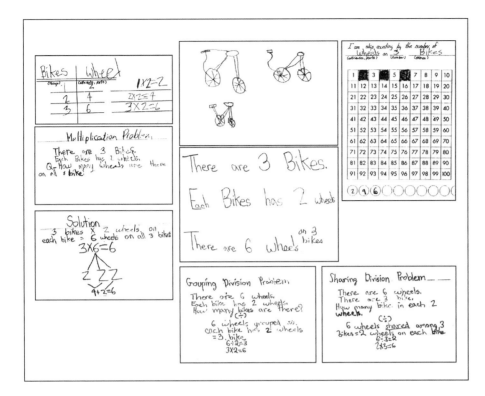

FIGURE 5–18 ◄

Yousif provided pictures and equations to show his division thinking about the bike problem he had begun in November. (See page 105.)

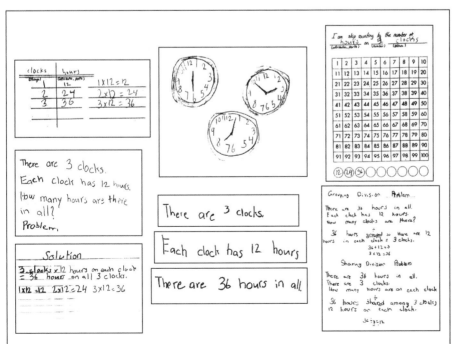

FIGURE 5–19 ◄

Latasha dealt with the factors of 3 and 12 on her *Things That Come In Groups* story problem page.

apples in a basket
books on a shelf

Ask the children to use 7, 8, or 9 as a factor in their multiplication problem, to give them practice with more multiplication combinations. If you assign this extension as homework, children could take home their original *Things That Come In Groups* story problem page and use it as a model, as well as show it to their parents.

- You type up one problem (multiplication or division) from each child and write his or her name next to the problem. Be sure to include some of each type of division problem. The students decide whether they should multiply or divide in each situation. Remember: Many children will multiply to make sense of a division situation, but their word/number equation will represent the problem as division. (See Figure 5–20.)

Mastering Multiplication Combinations

By now, your students have been using multiplication combinations in different groupings. They began by connecting 2s, 5s, and 10s to their innate sense of counting by these numbers. Then they focused on the combinations used again and again with a die in *Circles and Stars*. These combinations extended from 1×1 through 6×6. Around winter break, the children began to make sense of new combinations as they played *Circles and Stars* with a number cube with the factors 4, 5, 6, 7, 8, and 9. These combinations consisted of:

$$4 \times 7 \qquad 6 \times 7$$

$$4 \times 8 \qquad 6 \times 8$$

$$4 \times 9 \qquad 6 \times 9$$

(To become familiar with 3×7, 3×8, and 3×9, students will need other game or story-problem experiences.) Now some of your students may be ready to master the "super six" combinations:

$$7 \times 7$$

$$7 \times 8 \qquad 8 \times 8$$

$$7 \times 9 \qquad 8 \times 9 \qquad 9 \times 9$$

By breaking combinations into these groupings, students find mastering them less daunting. Moreover, they can focus on certain combinations over a particular time frame.

Sarah

1. Ted - There are 7 people. Each person has 8 apples. How many apples are there if each person collects 8 apples?

word/number equation - *7 people x 8 apples per person = 56 apples in all.*

There are _56_ apples. (look at answer above) There are 7 people. How many apples does each person get?

word/number equation - *56 apples ÷ evenly among 7 people = 8 apples per person.*

(This is a sharing division problem.)

2. Nan - There were 9 buckets. Each bucket had 8 apples in them. How many apples are there in all?

word/number equation - *9 buckets x 8 apples per bucket = 72 apples in all 9 buckets*

Scott had to pick _72_ apples. (look at answer above) He only had buckets which held 8 apples in each. How many buckets did Scott need?

word/number equation - *72 apples ÷ evenly so each bucket gets 8 apples = 9 buckets.*

(This is a grouping division problem.)

3. Jaime - There are 7 fruits. Each fruit has 9 seeds in it. How many seeds are there in all?

word/number equation - *7 fruits x 9 seeds per fruit = 63 seeds in all 9 fruits.*

There are _63_ seeds. (look at answer above) Each apple has 9 seeds in it. How many ~~apples~~ are there? (grouping division problem)

word/number equation - *63 seeds ÷ so that each fruit gets 9 seeds = 7 fruits.*

You and the students can create story problems connecting these new combinations to both multiplication and division situations. (See Figure 5–21.)

And you can play games such *Circles and Stars* and, later, *Multiplication Bingo* with the number cube mentioned on the previous page. In Chapter 8, there is a game called *Multiplication Tic-Tac-Toe,* which gives the children further practice with these combinations.

At this time, continue to support the children's use of manipulatives or drawings as pictorial models when learning the combinations. Later on, some children may use numerical reasoning to make sense of these facts. Remember, the most important thing is for students to understand when and how to use the combinations to make sense of problems.

FIGURE 5–21 ▶

Latasha wrote a multiplication and a grouping division story problem for 9 × 9 = 81.

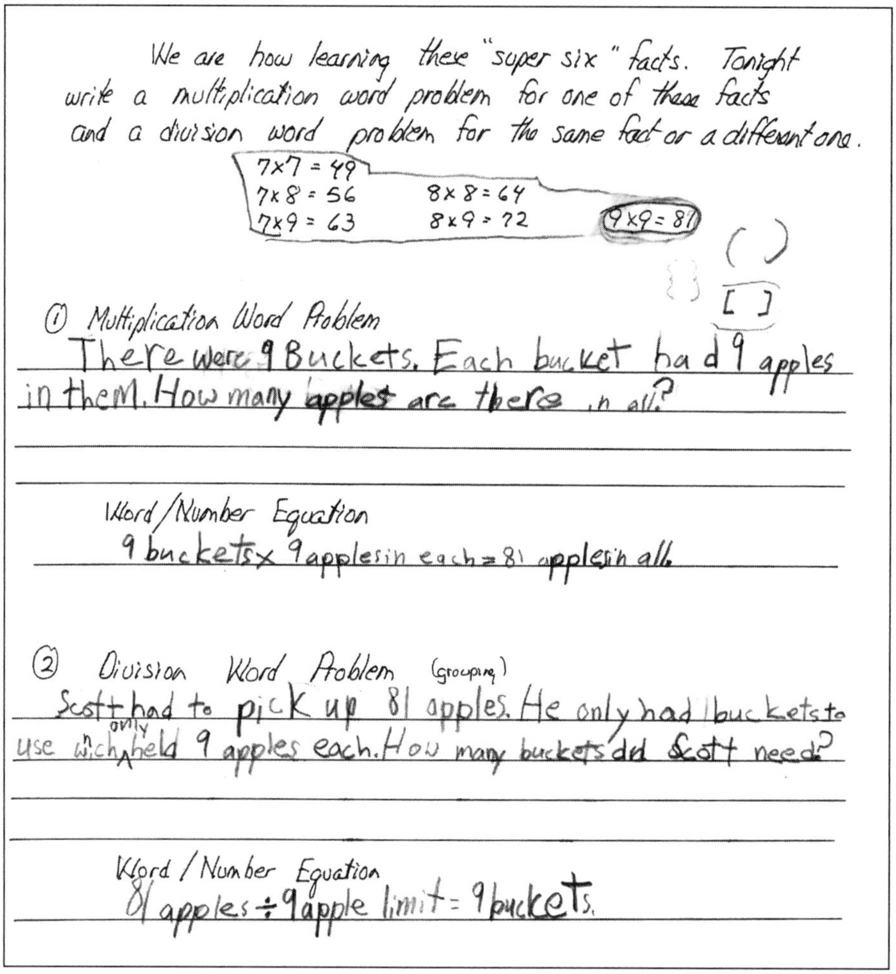

We are how learning these "super six" facts. Tonight write a multiplication word problem for one of these facts and a division word problem for the same fact or a different one.

7×7 = 49
7×8 = 56   8×8 = 64
7×9 = 63   8×9 = 72   9×9 = 81

① Multiplication Word Problem
There were 9 Buckets. Each bucket had 9 apples in them. How many apples are there in all?

Word/Number Equation
9 buckets × 9 apples in each = 81 apples in all.

② Division Word Problem (grouping)
Scott had to pick up 81 apples. He only had 1 buckets to use which only held 9 apples each. How many buckets did Scott need?

Word / Number Equation
81 apples ÷ 9 apple limit = 9 buckets.

Parent Newsletter

You may wish to send home a letter now and then that informs parents about what their children are doing in mathematics, how they're doing it, and why. I've offered a sample letter below that you could send at the beginning of or midway through your division unit. You may want to write your own letter instead or adapt one from the Teaching Arithmetic books (Math Solutions Publications) or the Investigations in Number, Data, and Space series (Dale Seymour Publications).

Dear Parents,

I hope this letter helps you better understand what your children are doing in mathematics these days. In October and November, they got the product or answer in a multiplication problem by combining several groups of equal size. They connected multiplication to addition. For example, if there were three baskets of apples and each basket had nine apples, they added 9 + 9 + 9 = 27, skip-counted 9, 18, 27, and multiplied 3 × 9 = 27.

Division Thinking: Now your youngsters are connecting their division thinking to their multiplication reasoning. In both operations, they are dealing with several equal-size groups. For example, if there are three circles and each has four stars inside during a round of *Circles and Stars*, there are twelve stars altogether: *3 circles × 4 stars in each = 12 stars in all.* Now the children use division as they think about each round of *Circles and Stars*.

The children make sense by using both types of division—grouping and sharing. Here's an example of *grouping* division: *There are 12 stars. We want to place 4 stars in each circle. How many circles (groups) do we need?* Here, the number of groups is the unknown. Twelve stars grouped so that there are four stars in a circle equals three circles.

The *sharing* division problem would be: *There are 12 stars. We want to share the stars evenly among 3 circles. How many stars go into each circle?* Here, the number of items in the equal-size groups is the unknown.

Your child does not need to identify each type of division problem, but he or she needs many experiences solving both forms of division.

Learning a New Concept Concretely: As children build an understanding of the operation of division, they begin dividing real, everyday objects, such as sixteen papers among four students (sharing) or eighteen pencils grouped so that each child gets three (grouping). You and your child can do these same operations together when setting the table, buying groceries, or sharing food.

In our classroom, the students are also doing problems featuring "leftovers," or remainders. For example, when eighteen papers are shared among four children, each child gets four papers. There are two leftover papers. They might be put back on the shelf or torn in half so each child gets a half sheet plus four sheets. When children share paper cookies, they divide the remainders into fractional parts.

Besides sharing or grouping real things in class or in a game like *Leftovers*, which you can play with your child at home, the students draw pictures or use paper models to make sense of division. With these models, they use words and numbers to explain their thinking. Eventually, they represent their problem-solving steps with these abstract notations:

$$18 \div 3 = 6$$

$$\frac{18}{3} = 6$$

$$3\overline{)18}^{\,6}$$

Thank you for your continued support as you and your child play *Circles and Stars* and *Leftovers* on a regular basis.

Warmly,
Suzy Ronfeldt

Assessment: Student Interviews

In the "Assessment" section at the end of Chapter 2, you focused on hearing and seeing each child's understanding of addition and subtraction during whole-class discussions and partner work. At the end of Chapter 3, you assessed children's understanding of multiplication by reading their classwork and their individual written assessment work. You'll want to continue all of these forms of assessments and you might also consider interviewing some students one-on-one to get a better sense of their thinking in sharing and grouping division situations. Suggestions for one-on-one student interviews follow ideas for individual written assessments presented here.

FIGURE 5–22   ▼

Sarah explained her understanding of division over two pages.

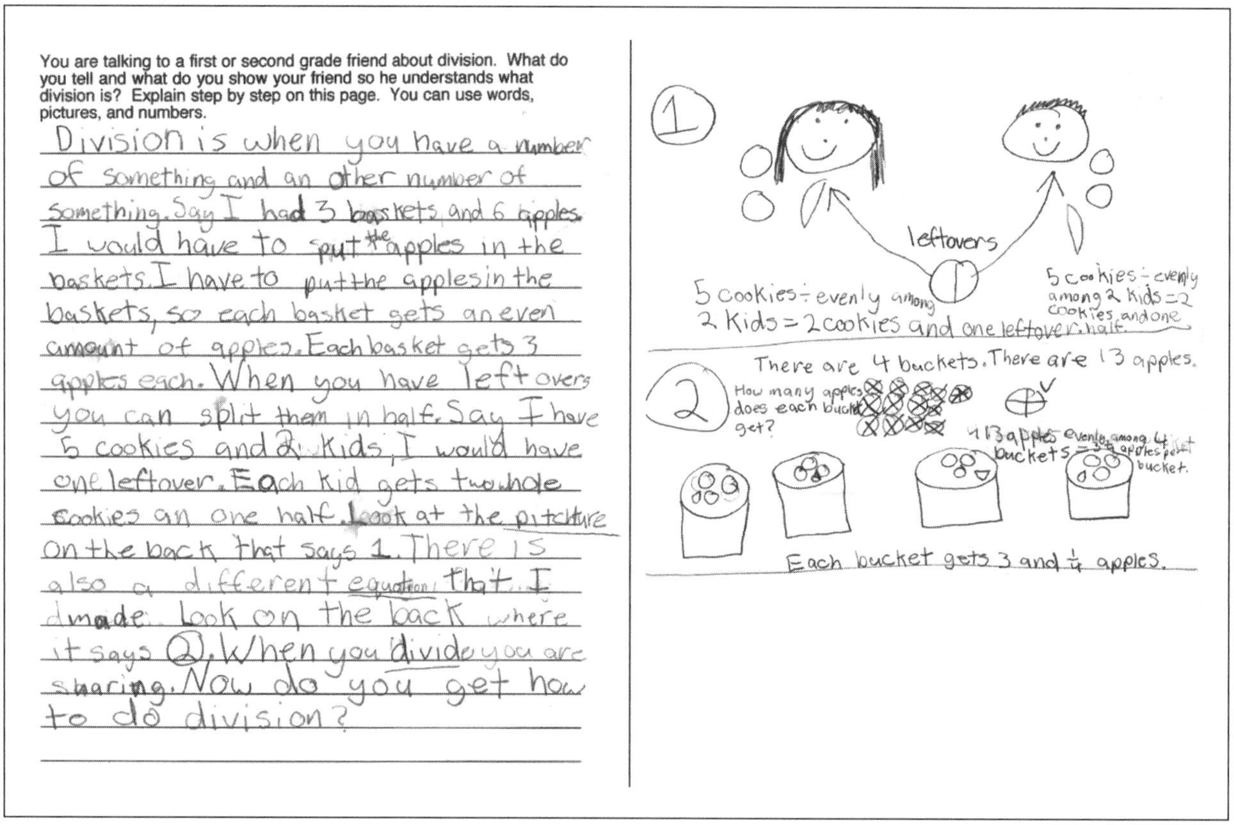

Individual Written Assessments

For individual written assessments during this unit, you could ask:

- *What is division?* (at the beginning and again at the end). (See Figure 5–22.)

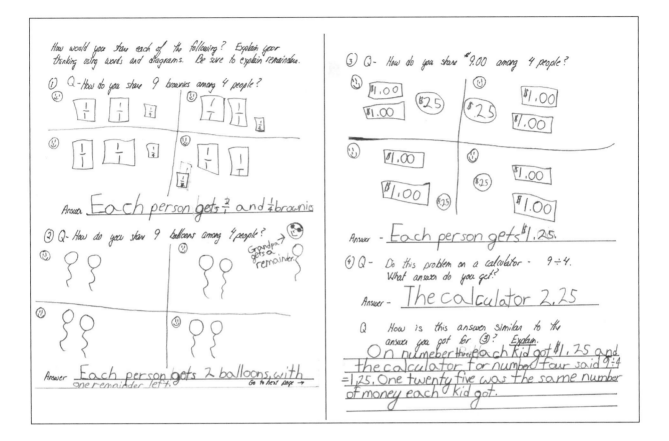

- *Explain 9 ÷ 4 in four different situations.* (See Figure 5–23.)
- *Explain what 20 ÷ 4 = 5 means to a younger student.* (See Figure 5–24.)

FIGURE 5–23 ▲

Eun-Jin explored 9 ÷ 4 from four perspectives.

One-on-One Student Interviews

Few of us have time to interview every child in our classroom for assessment purposes. For this reason, consider interviewing a small number of students to gain a sense for how your class is understanding sharing and grouping problems. Select one who you believe firmly understands division, one child who has a less secure understanding, and one child has not yet grasped the concept. Don't be surprised if your original judgments about each student's division sense changes during your interviews.

As you introduced division, you presented your students with problems in which they had to manipulate papers, pencils, and other everyday objects as you asked questions. Try following a similar format during your one-on-one interviews. Be sure to include some questions that lead to sharing and others that lead to grouping, some that lead to remainders and some that do not. Here are some possibilities:

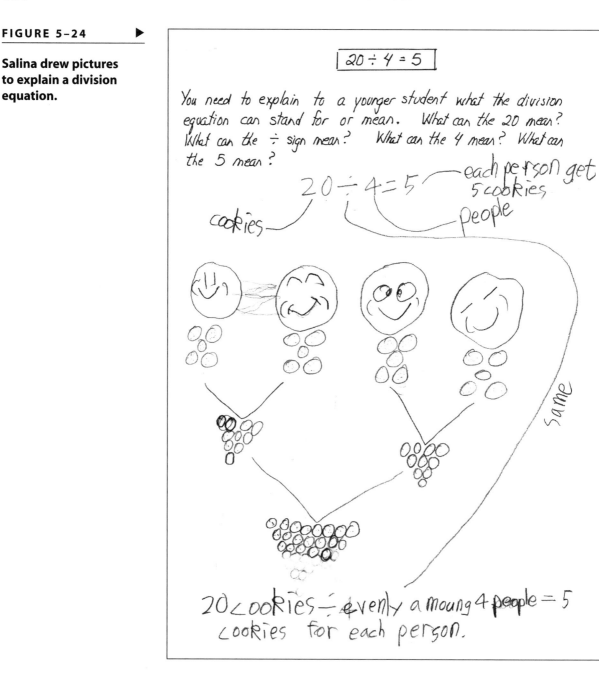

$20 \div 4 = 5$

You need to explain to a younger student what the division equation can stand for or mean. What can the 20 mean? What can the ÷ sign mean? What can the 4 mean? What can the 5 mean?

$20 \div 4 = 5$ — each person get 5 cookies

cookies   people

same

20 cookies ÷ evenly amoung 4 people = 5 cookies for each person.

Sharing Situations

"Here are eighteen cubes. How many cubes do you estimate each of us will get if you share them fairly between us? Will there be leftovers? Why do you think that? Hand out the cubes and see."

"Here are twenty-three cubes. How many cubes do you estimate each of us will get if you share them fairly between us? Will there be leftovers? Why do you think that? Hand out the cubes and see. What can you to do with the leftovers?"

Grouping Situations

"I have some pencils here. Please group and count them so I can see and hear your thinking. Now group and count them another way so I can see and hear your thinking. Did you get the same total each time? If not, what will you do next?"

"You've figured out that there are thirty-five pencils here. Suppose you wanted to tie the pencils in bundles of four to give away as gifts. How many bundles do you estimate you would have? How did you figure that out? Now go ahead and put your pencils into bundles of four. How many do you get? Do you have leftovers? What are you going to do with them? How could you write an equation with words to represent what you just did? How could you write an equation without words? What multiplication equation helps you make sense of this division situation?"

Chapter 6

EXPLORING FRACTIONS

"An important step in communicating mathematical thinking to others is organizing and clarifying one's ideas. When students struggle to communicate ideas clearly, they develop a better understanding of their own thinking."

Principles and Standards for School Mathematics
NCTM 2000, 129

Many children find fractions exciting when you remind them what fraction experts they already are in their own lives. For example, most third graders routinely use phrases such as "half past" the hour when telling time, "a quarter moon," "half a candy bar," and "a quarter in change." They may have measured an eighth teaspoon of salt or three-fourths of a cup of flour, and they have had many experiences dividing desserts and other everyday things into fair shares at home and in the classroom. At the beginning of this unit, ask your students and their parents to think about ways they use fractions at home. Then use this list of ideas to generate conversations about fractions in class. (See Figure 6–1 on the following page.)

During this unit, your children will revisit sharing paper cookies and begin sharing paper brownies. They'll also explore fractions through games that use concrete models that make fractions visible. ▪

The Learning Environment

Remind yourself that this chapter presents exploratory *work with fractions.*

Even though the second semester of the school year has begun, resist any pressure to cover curriculum quickly. Stay committed to helping your students uncover the meaning of fractions at their pace through many hands-on experiences. The children can bring these concrete, early experiences to the few fraction problems found on standardized tests.

Take time for "math talk."

Provide your students with many opportunities to talk about fractions in both whole-class and small-group discussions. As children play with fraction models and explain their understanding orally, they'll move toward numerical notations representing their thinking. By this time of year, you should be able to sit with a small group while the rest of the class members independently focus on their own mathematics problem solving. However, in both large- and small-group discussions, keep in mind that your students are just beginning to explore fractions. Enjoy the journey with them, and don't feel pressured to move them quickly from naming groups of people or fractional parts of manipulatives to adding and subtracting fractions. They will have many opportunities to revisit fractions as fourth and fifth graders.

Tonight, talk to the adults in your home and think of at least three and possibly four ways fractions are used in their or your everyday life or how the language of fractions is used in our everyday lives. List and explain these ways on the lines below. Write complete sentences that begin - We use fractions when we . . . or I use fractions when I . . .

1. I use fractions when I eat cookies with my 4 friend. If we had one large cookie, I'll eat $\frac{1}{4}$ of cookie.

2. I use fractions when I buy game. Since I have $40.00 in my saving, I spend $\frac{1}{2}$ of my money.

3. I use fractions when I read book. If the book contained more than 60 pages, I read $\frac{1}{2}$ of the book.

4. _____

Give children opportunities to build their fraction understanding with manipulatives.

Children build their understanding of fractions by using manipulatives. Pattern blocks are useful for this purpose, but students also gain a strong sense for fractions when they make their own colored-paper models of circular cookies and square brownies divided into pieces, and when they use handmade kits to play games and solve problems involving fractions.

Help children continue making connections between fractions and division.

Through the activities in Chapter 5, students find that they can divide leftovers of paper cookies into fractional parts to share the food equally among a specific number of people. They learn that some leftovers, such as pencils, can't be divided into fractional parts. The lessons in this chapter provide additional division experiences through which students represent the problem using three forms of notation: $14 \div 4 = 3$ R2; $4\overline{)14}^{3\text{ R2}}$; and $\frac{14}{4} = 3\frac{1}{2}$. This last form of notation has a direct link to fractions.

The Mathematics

Children realize that fractions describe equal parts of a whole.

A "whole" can be one thing—e.g., a shape (such as a round cookie, a rectangular candy bar, a square brownie)—or a group of things (a packet of pencils, a group of children). Children need experiences dividing both a whole shape and a group of things into fractional parts. (See below.)

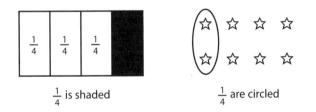

$\frac{1}{4}$ is shaded $\frac{1}{4}$ are circled

Children understand that the bottom number in a fraction shows the number of equal parts into which the whole is divided. The top number shows the number of those parts we are talking about.

Over time, some children begin to notice that the more equal pieces a whole is cut into, the smaller these equal pieces become. Among those children, a few begin to realize that that is why the larger the bottom number becomes the smaller the fractional part is. Remind yourself that many of your students may need a lot more fraction experiences before this makes sense to them. Use the words *numerator* and *denominator* in discussions about the top part and the bottom part of the fraction notation, so children hear these words in context. But remember: Children don't need to master these big words in order to gain a sense of fractions at this point in their learning.

Children need experience comparing fractions by referring to "landmarks" such as one-half and one whole.

When children talk about a fraction being less than or greater than one-half, they have a referent that helps them think about the size or relative magnitude of that fraction. They begin to order fractions by size with the referent in mind.

Children make sense of fractions by exploring their equivalent relationships.

Through concrete experiences with manipulatives, children begin to "see" that two halves, three thirds, four fourths, and so on make one whole. They also grasp that two-fourths, three-sixths, or four-eighths are equivalent to one-half.

Using fraction kits, students begin to understand the equivalent relationship between halves, fourths, and eighths. Using pattern blocks, they explore the equivalent relationship between thirds and sixths, and between halves and sixths.

Children have exploratory experiences combining (adding) and comparing and taking away (subtracting) fractions with like denominators.

When combining $\frac{1}{4} + \frac{1}{4} + \frac{1}{4}$, the children use fraction kits or paper cookies to understand that the sum is $\frac{3}{4}$, not $\frac{3}{12}$. When comparing $\frac{5}{6}$ to $\frac{1}{6}$, they can use pattern blocks or paper brownies to see that $\frac{5}{6}$ is $\frac{4}{6}$ greater than $\frac{1}{6}$.

Mathematics Throughout the Day

When children use fractions to describe equal-size groups of people in their classroom, they are applying fraction thinking to sets of things. The following routines can support this learning.

Lunch Count and Attendance Revisited

During attendance and lunch count, the language of fractions comes up naturally. For instance, suppose you have twenty students in your classroom, and ten of them wish to purchase a school lunch for that day. In this case, the fraction is $\frac{10}{20}$—ten out of twenty people want a school lunch. After having these sorts of conversations over many days, you may want to bring all twenty children to the front of the room. Divide them into two groups of ten, and tell them that one out of these two groups is buying a school lunch. Discuss the idea that $\frac{1}{2}$ is the same as $\frac{10}{20}$.

TEACHER-TO-TEACHER TALK   Your students have probably used the expression *one-half* often when talking about food. But they likely have not seen the numerical representation $\frac{1}{2}$. Thus they may find this notation confusing. They may also be unfamiliar with some of the inconsistencies that characterize conversation about fractions. For example, we say "one-third" for $\frac{1}{3}$ and "one-fourth" for $\frac{1}{4}$, but we say "one-half" (not "one second") for $\frac{1}{2}$. Consider spending a brief amount of time explaining these inconsistencies and notations.

On a day when the fraction of class members who wish to purchase a school lunch doesn't fall so neatly into the one-half category—e.g., fifteen out of twenty students want to buy a lunch—you may want to do something different. In this example, you could bring your students up and make a group of five who do *not* want to buy lunch. Divide the group of fifteen who do want a school lunch into groups of five as well. Suddenly you have four equal-size groups, each comprising five people. Three of these four groups want a school lunch (three-fourths), and one of them does not (one-fourth).

Groups of Children

This activity continues to offer valuable lessons.

Instructions

1. Have a group of four children come up to the front of the room.

2. Ask the class to give fraction statements that are true for this group. For instance, someone might say that girls make up one-half of the group.

3. Write the corresponding fraction on the board. Explain what the denominator tells you. In this example, the denominator tells you to divide the group into two equal-size groups and that one of those equal parts has girls in it.

4. Ask the children in the group to arrange themselves to match this fraction statement. If they group themselves into two groups that each have a boy and a girl in it, repeat the fraction statement in 2 above. Ask if the groupings match this statement. Take suggestions. Eventually, your students will help you group the four children into two groups—one consisting of two girls, and the other consisting of two boys.

5. Continue asking for fraction statements about the group of four. Draw stick figures capturing these statements. For instance, if someone has pointed out that one-fourth of the group is wearing glasses, and one-fourth is wearing wristwatches, draw the corresponding picture. (See below.)

$\frac{1}{4}$ of this group have glasses

$\frac{1}{2}$ of this group are boys

$\frac{1}{4}$ of this group wears a wristwatch

Note that one child in this group may have overlapping characteristics—e.g., he is a boy and he's wearing glasses. Exaggerate these characteristics in your drawing.

This idea is adapted from *Name That Portion, Grades 5 and 6*, by Joan Akers, Cornelia Tierney, Claryce Evans, and Megan Murray.

After many experiences with grouping their classmates and seeing you represent fraction statements through drawings, your students will be ready to draw exaggerated stick figures themselves to represent a class-generated list of fraction statements about a group. Eventually, have them write their own fraction statements and do stick drawings for their table groups. (See Figures 6–2 and 6–3.)

Extensions

■ *Goofy Groups*: This activity really appeals to children, as they love drawing a goofy group of four aliens with different characteristics. Ask them to draw one-fourth of the group with purple polka dots on their cheeks, one-half of the group with antennae, and three-fourths of the group wearing magic wristwatches. Eventually, have the children put their own goofy group together and write their own fraction statements. Depending on how familiar the children are with using pattern blocks to work with thirds and sixths, they might explore having groups of three and possibly six "aliens" or people.

FIGURE 6–2 ◀

Deon's drawing represents three fraction statements.

FIGURE 6–3 ◀

Rebecca's drawing captures four additional fraction statements.

- *Groups of Eight*: If your students are ready for it, you may want to have a group of eight children come to the front of the class. Then you can group them according to fourths and halves. If you do group these children into *two* equal-size groups indicated by the denominator in the fraction $\frac{1}{2}$, each of those two groups will have four children ($\frac{1}{2} = \frac{4}{8}$). If you divide the eight children into *four* equal-size groups, the groups will each have two children ($\frac{1}{4} = \frac{2}{8}$). Three-fourths of the group will equal six children ($\frac{6}{8} = \frac{3}{4}$). Again, children can represent fractional parts of eight with fraction statements connected to stick-figure drawings. (See Figure 6–4.)

FIGURE 6–4 ▶

Sasha's drawing showed various ways in which a group of eight people could be categorized.

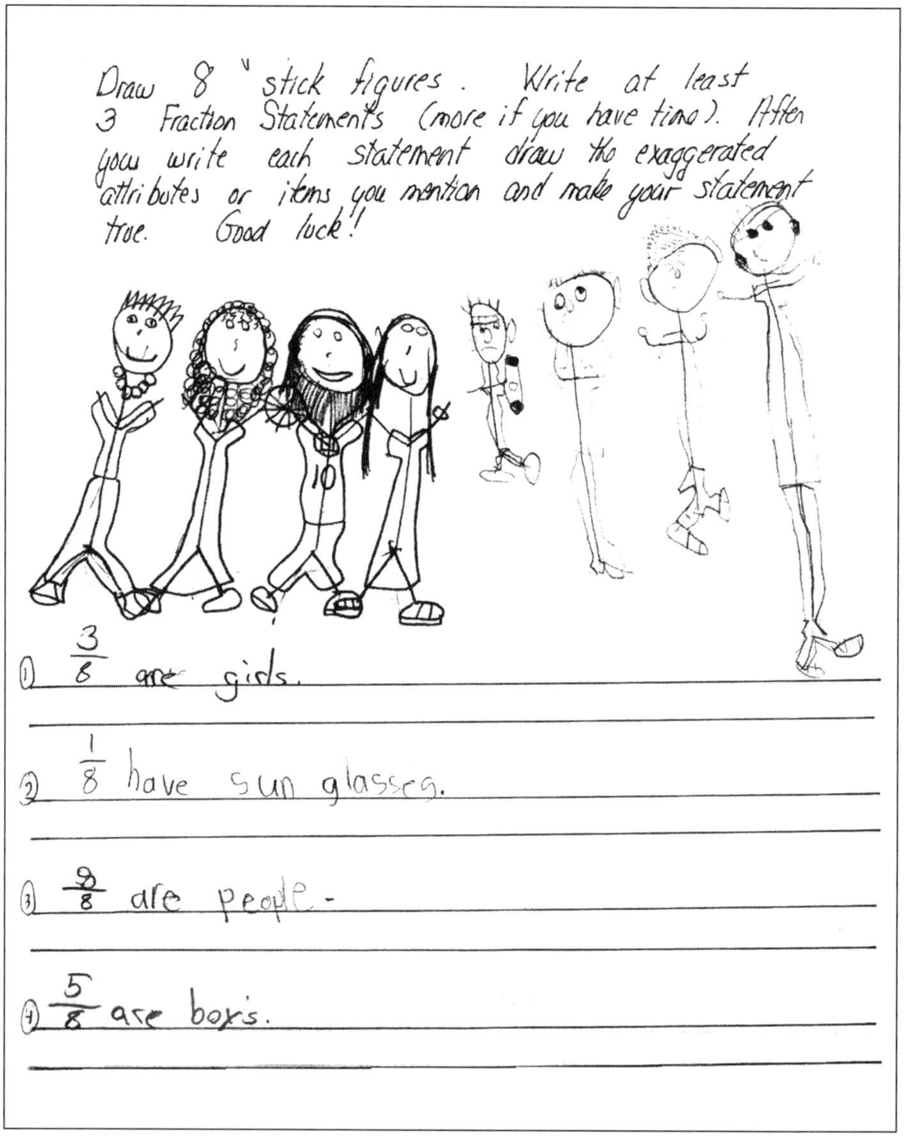

Draw 8 "stick figures. Write at least 3 Fraction Statements (more if you have time). After you write each statement draw the exaggerated attributes or items you mention and make your statement true. Good luck!!

① $\frac{3}{8}$ are girls.

② $\frac{1}{8}$ have sun glasses.

③ $\frac{8}{8}$ are people.

④ $\frac{5}{8}$ are boys.

Games

To play the games described below, children can first make fraction kits. (The instructions for making the kits appear below.) As your students make their kits, conduct numerous whole-class discussions about fractions that are equal to other fractions; for example, $\frac{1}{2} = \frac{2}{4}$, $\frac{1}{8} = \frac{2}{16}$. Once the kits are complete, invite children to play games with them in the classroom and at home. Students can then use pattern blocks to explore thirds and sixths in another series of games. In both of these game situations, children experience the area model of fractions—that is, fractions as parts of a whole rather than parts of a set.

> **TEACHER-TO-TEACHER TALK** When I first began using fraction kits in my classroom, the children and I cut straight to the games. Now we stop along the way to have meaningful fraction discussions as we make the kits and as we write *more than, less than,* and *equal to* statements about the fractions in the kit. In many ways, these discussions offer the most meaningful learning as children make and use their fraction kits.

Making Fraction Kits

Children need a model to look at while they make their fraction kits. So, before you begin, display a completed fraction kit on the board. Attach each piece with a small segment of masking tape, so you can easily move them. (See below.)

1 whole							
$\frac{1}{2}$				$\frac{1}{2}$			
$\frac{1}{4}$		$\frac{1}{4}$		$\frac{1}{4}$		$\frac{1}{4}$	
$\frac{1}{8}$	$\frac{1}{8}$	$\frac{1}{8}$	$\frac{1}{8}$	$\frac{1}{8}$	$\frac{1}{8}$	$\frac{1}{8}$	$\frac{1}{8}$
$\frac{1}{16}$ $\frac{1}{16}$	$\frac{1}{16}$ $\frac{1}{16}$	$\frac{1}{16}$ $\frac{1}{16}$	$\frac{1}{16}$ $\frac{1}{16}$	$\frac{1}{16}$ $\frac{1}{16}$	$\frac{1}{16}$ $\frac{1}{16}$	$\frac{1}{16}$ $\frac{1}{16}$	$\frac{1}{16}$ $\frac{1}{16}$

Materials

- 3-by-12-inch construction-paper strips, in 5 different colors; 1 strip of each color per student
- 1 scissors per student

- 1 dark pen per student
- 1 business-size envelope per student

Instructions

1. Cut the colored construction paper into the strips and give them to the students. (Each child gets five strips, one strip of each color.)

2. Select a color of paper (e.g., brown) to represent one whole. Have the children label this strip with a *1* in dark pen. If you wish to connect this discussion to food, you could invite the children to think of the whole strip as a candy bar.

3. Then select another color of paper (such as yellow) to cut into halves. The children fold this strip in half by matching the strip's ends. Then they cut or tear along the crease in as straight a line as possible. Discuss the fact that students have divided a whole into two equal-size pieces. Have the children label the two halves of the cut strip $\frac{1}{2}$. Make sure the students talk about the *why* behind this label. (It's labeled $\frac{1}{2}$ because each piece is *one* out of *two* equal parts of the whole.)

4. Ask how the children might fold the "candy bar" into four equal parts. Someone might state that a fourth is half of a half. Have the children take a third strip (perhaps blue), fold then cut it in half, then fold each half and cut it. They label each of the resulting fourths $\frac{1}{4}$ (*one* out of *four* equal-size parts). (See below.)

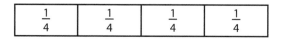

5. Follow the same procedure for creating eighths (by first making fourths) and sixteenths (by first making eighths). This process helps students realize that $\frac{1}{8}$ is one half of $\frac{1}{4}$ and is equal to $\frac{2}{16}$.

6. Have each child put his or her initials on the back of each piece and then place the pieces into an envelope with his or her name on it.

Discussing Fractions: Part 1

Instructions

1. After the children have made their fraction kits, invite students to gather on the rug, and display your fraction kit on the board. Conduct a class discussion about relative sizes of fractions, equivalency of fractions, and any other characteristics of fractions that students have noticed.

    Begin with a general question: "What are some things you notice about the fractions?" If a child says that $\frac{6}{8}$ equals $\frac{3}{4}$, ask him how he knows that. He may come up to the board and show his thinking by cupping his hands around $\frac{3}{4}$ then around $\frac{6}{8}$. Point out that the child is measuring the distance from the beginning of the "candy bar" to the end of the fractional part that equals $\frac{3}{4}$. He is also measuring the distance from the beginning of the candy bar to the end of the fractional part that equals $\frac{6}{8}$. The child finds that these two distances are the same.

Then you might ask: "Does anyone have another way of showing that six eighths equals three fourths?" Perhaps someone will add that $\frac{2}{8}$ equals $\frac{1}{4}$, $\frac{2}{8}$ more equals another $\frac{1}{4}$, and, $\frac{2}{8}$ more equals still another $\frac{1}{4}$. If you and your class have done fractional groupings of eight children, you can connect these latest comments with those findings. Say, "Remember when we grouped eight children at the front of the room, and six out of the eight children were wearing tennis shoes? Let's have eight people come up now—six with tennis shoes and two without. Now group yourselves to see if six eighths is the same as three fourths." Let the children struggle a bit with this.

If the students can't work this out, have them look at the denominator of $\frac{3}{4}$. Ask what the 4 means. (It means there are four equal-size groups.) Ask how the eight children can make four equal-size groups. (There would be two children in each group.) Then ask, "Do three out of these four groups have tennis shoes on? Does one out of these four groups *not* have tennis shoes on?"

2. Refocus students' attention on the fraction kit displayed on the board. Ask, "What else do you notice?" Perhaps a child will say that the smaller the pieces a candy bar is cut into, the larger the number at the bottom of the fraction. In other words, a candy bar cut into eight equal-size pieces has 8 as the bottom number (denominator). A candy bar cut into sixteen equal-size pieces has 16 as the bottom number. And $\frac{1}{16}$ of a candy bar is smaller than $\frac{1}{8}$ of a candy bar. Ask why the children think this is so.

Let the children's responses guide your questioning, and keep asking open-ended questions (queries that do not require a "yes" or "no" answer). For example, "What else do you notice about the fractions on the board?" "What are you thinking about fractions right now?" "What questions do you have?"

TEACHER-TO-TEACHER TALK As I reflect on these suggestions for a class discussion, I realize that I have packed in too many ideas for one day. After winter break, teachers are apt to do this as they feel the pressure to *cover* rather than *uncover* the curriculum. They begin to worry about their students meeting all the district's third grade standards and doing well on standardized tests.

Remember to stop and take time to listen to the children. Follow their lead and pursue only those ideas presented for this class discussion which make sense for your students. Certainly children can handle class discussions longer than ten minutes now that it is second semester, but I recommend twenty minutes at the most. You may decide to have this fraction-kit discussion take place over two days.

3. Begin asking more directed questions about equivalency: "How many sixteenths equal one fourth? How many sixteenths equal two fourths?" "Using the fraction kit on the board, what equations can you write that equal one whole?" Some child might respond that $\frac{1}{2} + \frac{1}{4} + \frac{1}{16} + \frac{1}{16} + \frac{1}{16} + \frac{1}{16} = 1$. You or the child can demonstrate this by moving those pieces from the kit directly above the "1 whole" piece. Discuss the fact that $\frac{1}{16} + \frac{1}{16} + \frac{1}{16} + \frac{1}{16}$ can be combined into $\frac{4}{16}$. This simplifies the equation to $\frac{1}{2} + \frac{1}{4} + \frac{4}{16}$. Then ask, "Does someone else have another equation that equals one whole?" If a child suggests $\frac{1}{8} + \frac{1}{16} + \frac{1}{16} + \frac{1}{8} + \frac{1}{8} + \frac{1}{4} + \frac{1}{4}$, ask, "How can we combine the fractions with like denominators and simplify this equation?" With help from the children, rewrite the equation as $\frac{3}{8} + \frac{2}{16} + \frac{2}{4} = 1$.

TEACHER-TO-TEACHER TALK   Some children may be fascinated by the process of simplifying equations by combining fractions with like denominators. Referring to the equation $\frac{3}{8} + \frac{2}{16} + \frac{2}{4} = 1$, a student might realize that she knows that $\frac{2}{16} = \frac{1}{8}$ and that $\frac{2}{4} = \frac{4}{8}$. Thus she can write $\frac{3}{8} + \frac{1}{8} + \frac{4}{8} = \frac{8}{8}$ and $\frac{8}{8} = 1$. You might encourage this kind of individual exploration, but remember that at this exploratory stage, most children are not ready to take these steps.

When children have frequent experiences combining fractions with like denominators—and when they manipulate models instead of numbers—they begin to understand that $\frac{1}{16} + \frac{1}{16} + \frac{1}{16} + \frac{1}{16}$ does *not* equal $\frac{4}{64}$. Ensure that your students have plenty of time and opportunity to build their understanding of fractions by manipulating models such as fraction-kit pieces, pattern blocks, or paper cookies and brownies.

---

4. Ask, "Can we write an equation for one whole using all the same-size fraction pieces?" If some child suggests that $\frac{1}{4} + \frac{1}{4} + \frac{1}{4} + \frac{1}{4} = 1$, write this equation on the board. Then ask how these fractions can be combined. Next write $\frac{4}{4} = 1$. If a child wrongly says that $\frac{4}{16} = 1$, ask him or her to line up four $\frac{1}{16}$ pieces above the 1 whole piece. Emphasize that mistakes like this happen all the time—even in middle school and high school. These mistakes constitute great opportunities for your students to realize that when they're combining four fourths, the fourths stay fourths and do not become sixteenths.

5. Consider nudging students' thinking beyond the fraction-kit model. For instance, ask, "Do you see a pattern in the equations with the same-size fraction pieces that equal one whole?" (e.g., $\frac{2}{2} = 1$; $\frac{4}{4} = 1$; $\frac{8}{8} = 1$; and $\frac{16}{16} = 1$). "Can you make a similar fraction statement that is true for fractions that are *not* represented in our fraction kit? How did you figure this out?"

Discussing Fractions: Part 2

Instructions

1. The following day, gather your students on the rug again, in front of the fraction kit pieces taped to the board in their original configuration. Today you'll help the children explore fraction statements that use words such as *greater than*, *less than*, and *equal to*. Students will use $\frac{1}{2}$ and 1 whole as landmarks, or referents, to figure out the relative sizes of the fractions in the kit.

2. Write the following statements on a chart posted next to the fraction kit on the board:

   __ *is less than* __ *because* _____.

   __ *is greater than* __ *because* _____.

   __ *is close to* $\frac{1}{2}$ *because* _____.

   __ *is equal to* __.

TEACHER-TO-TEACHER TALK When I first wrote the above sentence frames to work from, I left out the word *because*. The children's fraction statements were often correct, but "why" the statements made sense was missing. When children explain "why," their answers make sense to them, they develop a deeper understanding of their own thinking, and they broaden their classmates' learning.

---

3. Establish a common meaning for the terms *less than, greater than,* and *equal to*. Use concrete examples if you have students whose first language is not English. For example, put two different-height stacks of same-size books side by side. Ask, "Which stack is greater than the other? How do you know? Which stack is less than the other? How do you know?"

   Have children figure it out by eyeballing the stacks and then counting the books. If there are eight books in one stack and five books in the other, write down student-generated statements such as *8 books is greater than 5 books*. Push for further explaining by adding the word *because*. For instance, *8 books is greater than 5 books because* $5 + 3 = 8$. Someone might also say that five books is less than eight books because five is three less than eight $(8 - 3 = 5)$.

4. When the children understand *less than, greater than,* and *equal to* in concrete counting situations, ask, "Yesterday we wrote equations that equaled one whole. Using our fraction kit, what equations using the same-size fraction can we write that equal one half?" ($\frac{2}{4} = \frac{1}{2}$; $\frac{4}{8} = \frac{1}{2}$; $\frac{8}{16} = \frac{1}{2}$).

5. Now ask, "Can you make some *greater-than*-one-half statements using the fraction kit? Remember: We need to hear *why* you think your statement is true, so use the word *because*." Someone might offer that $\frac{9}{16}$ is greater than $\frac{1}{2}$ because $\frac{8}{16} = \frac{1}{2}$. Another child may suggest that $\frac{3}{4}$ is greater than $\frac{1}{2}$ because $\frac{2}{4} = \frac{1}{2}$. Write both statements on the board, and label them with the names of the children who suggested them. Have these students come to the model on the board and show why their statements are true.

6. When you have written two or three such statements on the board, ask, "Now can you make some *less-than*-one-half fraction statements?" The range of answers might include: $\frac{3}{8}$ is less than $\frac{1}{2}$ because $\frac{4}{8} = \frac{1}{2}$, and $\frac{2}{16}$ is less than $\frac{1}{4}$ because $\frac{4}{16} = \frac{1}{4}$.

7. Ask, "Can you make some close to $\frac{1}{2}$ statements looking at the fraction kit?" Responses might include: $\frac{7}{16}$ is close to $\frac{1}{2}$ because it only takes one more sixteenth to equal $\frac{1}{2}$, and $\frac{5}{8}$ is close to $\frac{1}{2}$ because $\frac{5}{8}$ is close to $\frac{4}{8}$ and $\frac{4}{8}$ equals $\frac{1}{2}$. If someone offers that $\frac{1}{4}$ and $\frac{1}{8}$ and $\frac{1}{16}$ is close to $\frac{1}{2}$, suggest that the children use only one fraction instead of a combination of fractions.

TEACHER-TO-TEACHER TALK At this stage of your students fraction work, consider digressing a bit. Point to the fractions that equal $\frac{1}{2}$ on the board: $\frac{1}{2}, \frac{2}{4}, \frac{4}{8},$ and $\frac{8}{16}$. Ask the children if they notice a relationship between the numerator and the denominator in each equivalent fraction for $\frac{1}{2}$. If someone realizes that the numerator is one-half of the denominator or that the denominator is double the numerator, write that child's name and the idea down on the paper where you've been recording students' problem-solving strategies. Then suggest that the children use that idea to think of fractions that equal one-half and are *not* represented in the fraction kit on the board.

If the students don't notice a relationship between the numerator and the denominator, accept that they're not quite ready, and move on.

Writing Fraction Statements

Instructions

1. Send pairs of students to their desks. Ask them to write five fraction statements using the sentence frames posted next to the fraction kit. Invite them to use their own fraction kits to figure out if the statements they have written are true. Or, have partners write four statements (one less than, one greater than, one equal to, one free choice) and explain their thinking through statements beginning with "We know this because _____." (See Figure 6–5.)

2. Ask questions to help children focus their reasoning, especially on the "because" sections of their statements. For those pairs who com-

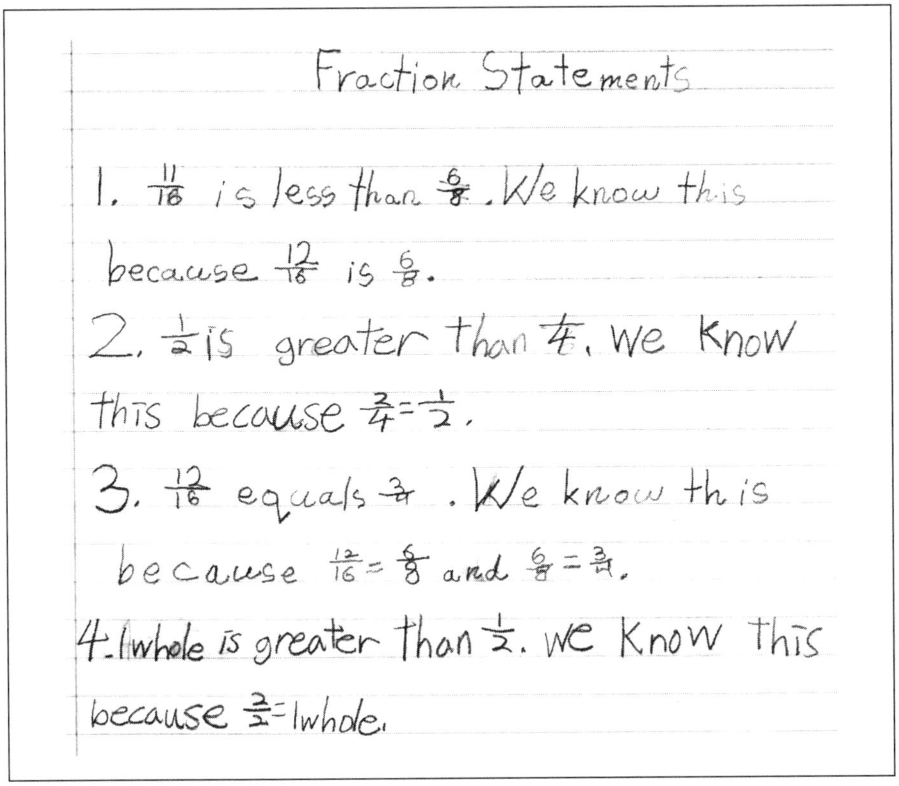

FIGURE 6–5   ◄

Fraction Statements

1. $\frac{11}{16}$ is less than $\frac{6}{8}$. We know this because $\frac{12}{16}$ is $\frac{6}{8}$.

2. $\frac{1}{2}$ is greater than $\frac{1}{4}$. We know this because $\frac{2}{4} = \frac{1}{2}$.

3. $\frac{12}{16}$ equals $\frac{3}{4}$. We know this because $\frac{12}{16} = \frac{6}{8}$ and $\frac{6}{8} = \frac{3}{4}$.

4. 1 whole is greater than $\frac{1}{2}$. We know this because $\frac{2}{2} = 1$ whole.

Ray and Eun-Jin used four sentences to explain their thinking behind their fraction statements.

plete their statements early, check whether the statements make sense. Then have an extension in mind: The children write more fraction statements using the format on the board, they write some fraction statements of their very own, or they try writing fraction statements that are not represented by the fraction kit on the board.

3. Consider copying a fraction statement from each pair and including them in homework assignments over the next several days. The children can take their fraction kits home to complete these assignments. (See Figure 6–6 on the following page.)

TEACHER-TO-TEACHER TALK   Children take pride in seeing the problems they created become part of class homework. They feel that "Yes, I am a mathematician, and what I have to say is important." This practice sends another powerful message as well: "We are all thinking about mathematics together."

Fraction-Kit Games

Children can play several games with their fraction kits, including *Cover Up* and two versions of *Uncover* (described below). If you teach the games during small-group discussions or station time, listen to the children's reasoning. In these settings, you can easily ask follow-up questions that help

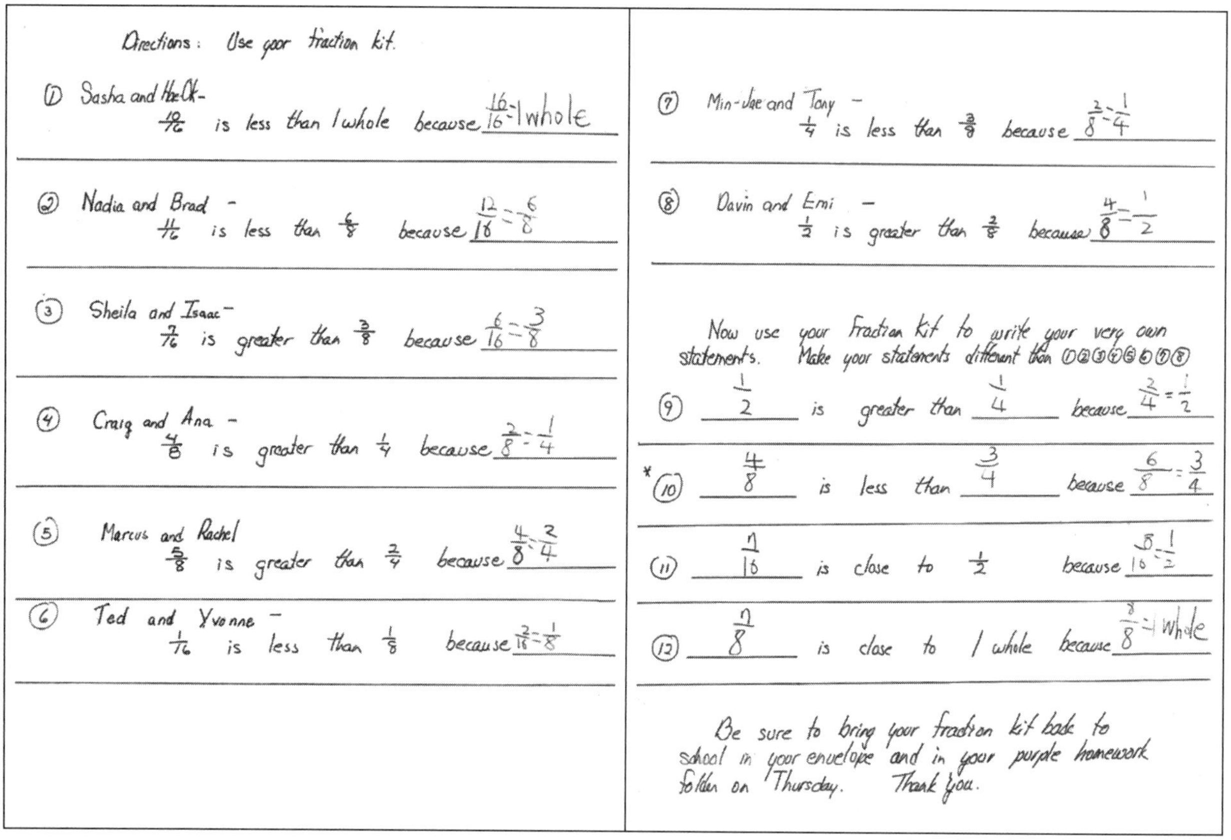

FIGURE 6–6 ▲

Jaime made sense of the fraction statements written by his classmates.

children sort out their fraction thinking. Small-group or station-time settings also encourage quieter children to speak up and ask questions.

Cover Up

Materials

- number cubes with faces marked $\frac{1}{2}, \frac{1}{4}, \frac{1}{8}, \frac{1}{8}, \frac{1}{16}, \frac{1}{16}$, 1 cube per pair of students

Instructions

1. Have the children pair up, and ensure that each student has his or her fraction kit readily available. Give each pair a number cube.

2. Each player lays out his or her "1 whole" piece from the fraction kits. Then they take turns rolling the cube and placing that fraction piece on top of their 1 whole strip. The first player to cover his or her whole strip exactly wins. If a player needs only a small piece to cover the strip (e.g., $\frac{1}{8}$ or $\frac{1}{16}$) and rolls a larger fraction (such as $\frac{1}{2}$ or $\frac{1}{4}$), the child must pass.

3. After both players have covered their whole piece exactly, have them write an equation showing that their fractions do add up to the whole. For example:

> Nadia wrote $\frac{1}{16} + \frac{1}{8} + \frac{1}{4} + \frac{1}{16} + \frac{1}{2} = 1$.
>
> Marcus wrote $\frac{1}{16} + \frac{1}{16} + \frac{1}{16} + \frac{1}{8} + \frac{1}{2} + \frac{1}{16} = 1$. (Note that these fractions don't actually add up to 1.)

4. During whole-class discussion, write some of these *Cover Up* equations on the board. Combine fractions with the same denominator or simplify the equations. For example, Nadia's equation could become $\frac{2}{16} + \frac{1}{8} + \frac{1}{4} + \frac{1}{2} = 1$ and Marcus' might end up being $\frac{4}{16} + \frac{1}{8} + \frac{1}{2} = 1$. See whether anyone notices that Marcus' equation does not equal one whole.

5. Have the students who created the equations take the corresponding fraction kit pieces and line them up above the whole. This process will quickly reveal whether an equation does indeed add up to one whole.

Extensions

Write down a fraction kit *Cover Up* equation from each student, then have the children combine like fractions to simplify each equation.

Uncover: Part 1

This game familiarizes students with the language of equivalent fractions as they exchange fraction pieces such as a $\frac{1}{2}$ piece for two $\frac{1}{4}$ pieces.

Materials

■ number cubes with faces marked $\frac{1}{2}$, $\frac{1}{4}$, $\frac{1}{8}$, $\frac{1}{8}$, $\frac{1}{16}$, $\frac{1}{16}$, 1 cube per pair of students

Instructions

1. Have students pair up, and make sure each player has a fraction kit and that the pair has a fraction number cube to share.

2. Each player covers his or her 1 whole strip with the two $\frac{1}{2}$ pieces. The goal is to be the first to *uncover* the strip completely.

3. Players take turns rolling the number cube. Let's say Player 1 has a roll of $\frac{1}{16}$. She can exchange one of her $\frac{1}{2}$ pieces for eight $\frac{1}{16}$ pieces, but she needs to explain her entire move to the other player. "I know that one half is the same as eight sixteenths so I'm exchanging my one half for eight sixteenths. Now I'll remove the one-sixteenth I rolled

on the number cube." Player 1 is left with a $\frac{1}{2}$ piece and seven $\frac{1}{16}$ pieces on her whole. Player 2 listens and watches carefully to be sure his or her partner is making fraction sense. (As the game progresses, if a player already has a piece that matches the fraction rolled, she or he does not need to do an exchange.)

4. Then Player 2 rolls and exchanges in similar fashion. Suppose that Player 1, on her next turn, rolls $\frac{1}{8}$. This time the player exchanges two $\frac{1}{16}$ pieces for a $\frac{1}{8}$ piece. Then she removes the $\frac{1}{8}$ piece, saying, "I know that two sixteenths equal one eighth, so I am going to exchange here. Now I will remove the one eighth."

5. The game continues until one player removes his or her last piece exactly. If Player 1 has a $\frac{1}{16}$ piece left toward the end of the game, she must wait until she rolls a $\frac{1}{16}$.

Uncover: Part 2

You may want to play this version of the game yourself, before your students do—so that you understand the three options. In this version, each player again covers his or her "1 whole" strip with the two $\frac{1}{2}$ pieces. With each roll of the number cube, the player has three options:

- Remove a piece only if the player has a piece the size indicated by the fraction facing up on the number cube.
- Exchange any of the pieces on the whole strip for equivalent pieces.
- Do nothing.

Players cannot exchange *and* remove a piece on the same turn as they did in the first version of *Uncover*. In this Part 2 version, they can only do one *or* the other. As partners play, they check with one another to be sure they agree with what is being done. The first player to uncover his or her whole piece exactly wins. If a player has only one piece left and rolls a fraction that is larger than the remaining piece, he or she may not remove the piece.

Extensions

The children make a second fraction kit, so they have two sets to take home to play the various games with their parents. Assign construction of the second set as homework. For the games, send home a set of instructions. Be sure the instructions explain that the talking that happens during this game is the most important part. (See Blackline Masters.) Here are some questions that stimulate thinking and talking during the games:

Why are you exchanging __ for __?

Show me how those two fractions are equivalent.

Pattern Blocks

With fraction kits, children work with fourths, eighths, and sixteenths. With pattern blocks, they explore thirds and sixths. You will want your students to have many experiences using both models of fractions.

The whole in a pattern-block set is a yellow hexagon. Your class can use it to represent one cookie. The green equilateral triangle represents one-sixth of the whole cookie, the red trapezoid equals one-half, and the blue parallelogram equals one-third. If you don't have pattern blocks, you can use the Blackline Master in the back of the book to make cardstock models. The children can then color them to match the above descriptions.

These pattern-block fraction activities are also explained in *About Teaching Mathematics, Second Edition* by Marilyn Burns (2000) and in *Fair Shares* by Cornelia Tierney and Mary Berle-Carman (1995).

Build the Yellow Hexagon

Instructions

1. Have the children cover the yellow hexagon in their pattern-block set with the green triangles. It takes six triangles, so the children need to understand that one out of the six triangles is one-sixth of the whole hexagon.

2. Repeat this process with the two red trapezoids and then the three blue parallelograms, establishing the fact that one trapezoid is half of the whole hexagon and one parallelogram is one-third of it.

3. Have the children build all the possible whole hexagons using the triangles, trapezoids, and parallelograms. Remind them that different arrangements of the same pieces do not equal a different hexagon. If a hexagon is covered with two triangles and two parallelograms, that counts as one whole—even though the pieces may be arranged in different ways. (See below.) There are seven different arrangements that cover the hexagon.

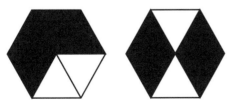

These count as one way to build a whole hexagon.
They each have two blues and two greens.

4. When everyone agrees on the seven possible arrangements, the children draw each arrangement on a sheet of blank hexagons. (See Blackline Masters.) They then label each fractional part. They place the pattern-block shapes on the hexagons and trace around the shapes.

5. Students next write equations for their pattern-block arrangements. For example, for the hexagon covered with two parallelograms and two triangles, the equation would be $\frac{1}{3} + \frac{1}{3} + \frac{1}{6} + \frac{1}{6} = 1$.

6. Early finishers explore further with their pattern blocks.

7. When all students have completed the investigation, discuss the seven equations that represent the arrangements. Write these equations on the board or a chart:

$$\frac{1}{2} + \frac{1}{2} = 1$$

$$\frac{1}{3} + \frac{1}{3} + \frac{1}{3} = 1$$

$$\frac{1}{6} + \frac{1}{6} + \frac{1}{6} + \frac{1}{6} + \frac{1}{6} + \frac{1}{6} = 1$$

$$\frac{1}{2} + \frac{1}{3} + \frac{1}{6} = 1$$

$$\frac{1}{6} + \frac{1}{6} + \frac{1}{6} + \frac{1}{2} = 1$$

$$\frac{1}{3} + \frac{1}{6} + \frac{1}{6} + \frac{1}{6} + \frac{1}{6} = 1$$

$$\frac{1}{3} + \frac{1}{3} + \frac{1}{6} + \frac{1}{6} = 1$$

8. Ask students how they would combine or add some fractions in the equations on the chart to create shorter equations. Record these shorter equations next to the original ones:

$\frac{1}{2} + \frac{1}{2} = 1$	$\frac{2}{2} = 1$
$\frac{1}{3} + \frac{1}{3} + \frac{1}{3} = 1$	$\frac{3}{3} = 1$
$\frac{1}{6} + \frac{1}{6} + \frac{1}{6} + \frac{1}{6} + \frac{1}{6} + \frac{1}{6} = 1$	$\frac{6}{6} = 1$
$\frac{1}{2} + \frac{1}{3} + \frac{1}{6} = 1$	
$\frac{1}{6} + \frac{1}{6} + \frac{1}{6} + \frac{1}{2} = 1$	$\frac{3}{6} + \frac{1}{2} = 1$
$\frac{1}{3} + \frac{1}{6} + \frac{1}{6} + \frac{1}{6} + \frac{1}{6} = 1$	$\frac{1}{3} + \frac{4}{6} = 1$
$\frac{1}{3} + \frac{1}{3} + \frac{1}{6} + \frac{1}{6} = 1$	$\frac{2}{3} + \frac{2}{6} = 1$

Extensions

In *Fair Shares, Grades 3 and 4,* by Cornelia Tierney and Mary Berle-Carman (1995), children use their seven hexagon arrangements to explore the following questions involving take-away subtraction:

"On your hexagon with three thirds, if you took away one third, what would you have left? Look at all your hexagons. Is there another way you can give away one-third of a hexagon?"

"On your hexagon with six sixths, if you took away two sixths, how much of the hexagon would you have left? Is there another way you could say this fraction?"

"On your hexagon with two halves, if you took away one half, what would you have left? Now look at all your hexagons. Is there another way you could take away half of a hexagon? What equations can you write that equal one-half?"

"Can you give away one-fourth of a hexagon? Why or why not?"

Hexagon Exchange

Play this early fraction game (adapted from Tierney and Berle-Carman 1995) with a small group of four to six children, perhaps during station time.

Materials

- 1 "Build the Yellow Hexagon" sheet per student (see Blackline Masters)
- 1 die per group, marked $\frac{1}{2}, \frac{1}{2}, \frac{1}{3}, \frac{2}{3}, \frac{1}{6}, \frac{5}{6}$

Instructions

1. Players take turns rolling the die and placing the corresponding pattern-block piece on a blank hexagon. For example, if Susan rolls $\frac{1}{3}$, she places a blue parallelogram on her hexagon.

2. After everyone has had one turn, players roll the die again. If Susan rolls $\frac{5}{6}$ on her second turn, she keeps her $\frac{5}{6}$ at the side of the hexagon page and does some exchanges before placing her pieces on the page. She must talk through her moves: "I am exchanging two sixths for one third because two sixths equals one third. I am also going to exchange another two sixths for one third. Now I have two thirds to add to the one third already on my hexagon." She moves the $\frac{2}{3}$ piece onto the first cookie to join the $\frac{1}{3}$ already there. "Now I am going to exchange three thirds for one whole hexagon, and I'll put my extra one sixth on the next hexagon."

This "trading up" is a basic part of the game. Players trade two or three pieces for a larger piece. The goal is to have each hexagon represented by the fewest pattern blocks by the end of the game.

During the game, you and the other children listen and watching to make certain that each player's "fraction talk" and moves make sense. The idea of mixed number comes up quite naturally in this game, so point out, for example, that Susan has $1\frac{1}{6}$ hexagons. Explain that this is called a *mixed number* because it contains a whole number followed by a fraction. Remind the children that even though Susan has "one and one-sixth hexagons," we do not write the "and." On the other hand, if including the "and" helps your children master fraction work, they can say "one hexagon and one-sixth of a hexagon."

After you and the children have played several rounds of *Hexagon Exchange*, try asking "more than" and "less than" questions. For instance, you could say, "Look at our papers. Ray has two and one-sixth hexagons and I have two and two-sixths. Who has more? How much more?" Here the children can use comparison subtraction to solve the problem.

Once students seem comfortable talking about their exchanges, explaining fractions that are equivalent, naming the mixed number, and comparing one mixed number to another, they are ready to play this game in pairs. The pairs decide how many hexagons a player needs to complete in order to win the game.

Extensions

Have your students play *Hexagon Exchange* at home with their parents. You could send home card-stock copies of the yellow hexagon, red trapezoid, blue parallelogram, and green equilateral triangle pieces. The children could color these pieces before cutting them out and take them home in an envelope. You would need to provide a hexagon sheet for each player (see Blackline Masters) and a die marked with $\frac{1}{2}, \frac{1}{2}, \frac{1}{3}, \frac{2}{3}, \frac{1}{6}, \frac{5}{6}$.

Besides sending home the game rules, consider sending a list of questions parents could ask to encourage fraction talk while playing the game. For example:

"Why did you exchange one green triangle and one blue rhombus for a red trapezoid?"

"How many hexagons do you have now?"

"What is the difference between your number of hexagons and mine right now? How do you know that?"

"How many more hexagons do you have than I have?"

"How does four sixths equal two thirds? Show me?"

Wipeout

The object of this partner game is to be the first player to discard one's pattern blocks. It is similar to *Uncover, Part 2*.

Materials

- a pattern-block set per student

■ 1 number cube per pair of students, with faces marked $\frac{1}{2}$, $\frac{1}{3}$, $\frac{1}{3}$, $\frac{1}{6}$, $\frac{1}{6}$, and $\frac{1}{6}$ (**Note:** this die differs from the die for *Hexagon Exchange* and the die for the fraction kit games.)

Instructions

1. Have children pair up.

2. Each player begins by covering one hexagon from his or her pattern-block set with other pieces (green triangles, blue rhombi, red trapezoids) using one of seven patterns explored on page 205 in *Build the Yellow Hexagon.*

3. Player 1 rolls the number cube and has three options:

   Remove one of the fraction pieces from the top of the hexagon (but only if it represents the fractional part of the hexagon indicated by the fraction face up on the cube).

   Exchange any of the remaining blocks for equivalent blocks.

   Do nothing and pass the number cube to Player 2.

   Players cannot remove a block and exchange on the same turn. They must do only one or the other. As they play, the children pay attention to each other's trades to make sure they are done correctly.

4. The game ends when one partner has cleared all his pieces from the top of his or her hexagon.

Measurement

Using Fraction Kits for Linear Measurement

When children use their fraction kits in their original configuration, they measure the space from left to right starting at the edge of the "candy bar" as they compare $\frac{1}{4}$ of the whole to $\frac{2}{8}$ or to $\frac{2}{16}$. Thus fraction kits provide opportunities to practice measurement. (See pages 195–96.)

Have students cut out a 3-by-12-inch strip of paper, fold it into four equal parts, and use it as a paper ruler to measure things in the room. Their goal? To see if the objects they're measuring are closer to one-fourth of a foot, one-half of a foot, or three-quarters of a foot long. If your district standards insist on standard measurement tools, students could eventually measure off inch markings on their paper rulers. If they do this, they'll soon realize that the one-quarter-foot section would include markings for three inches. From the beginning of the ruler to the half-foot fold would include six inches. From the beginning of the ruler to the three-quarters-foot fold would include nine inches. The entire ruler would include twelve inches. (See Figure 6–7.)

FIGURE 6–7   ▶

Here's how the paper rulers would look with folds and inch markers.

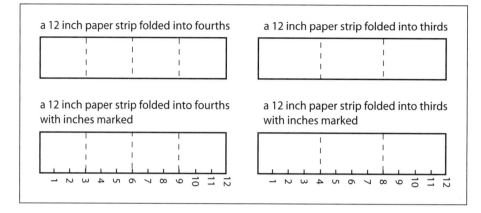

Telling Time

As children tell time throughout the school day, help them connect their words to fractional parts of the clock face. A quarter hour is one-fourth of the clock face, or fifteen minutes. A half hour is one-half of the clock face, or thirty minutes. Three quarters of an hour is three-fourths of the clock face, or forty-five minutes.

Money

Whenever you introduce activities involving money from this point forward in the school year, be sure to point out that a quarter is twenty-five cents—one-quarter of a dollar (which is one hundred cents). Thus the children can think of a quarter as the fraction $\frac{25}{100}$, or $\frac{1}{4}$. Remind students of the $.25 notation. Clarify the value of a half-dollar similarly ($\frac{50}{100}$, $\frac{1}{2}$, and $.50. Show how three-quarters of a dollar can be represented as $\frac{75}{100}$, $\frac{3}{4}$ and $.75.

Literature-Based Activities

Sharing Cookies

In *Little House in the Big Woods* by Laura Ingalls Wilder, Laura and Mary visit their neighbor, Mrs. Peterson. At the end of the visit, Mrs. Peterson gives each girl a cookie. The girls each eat half of their cookies and take the remaining halves home to Carrie. Owing to their generosity, Carrie ends up with two halves, or one whole cookie. Ask your students, "How could the two girls each divide up their two cookies into fractional parts so that each of the three girls would have fair shares?"

Dividing Lemon Cakes

In *One Hungry Cat* by Joanne Rocklin (see page 167 in Chapter 5), Tom bakes a square lemon cake and divides it into four equal pieces. Then he eats one of the pieces, leaving three pieces for himself and two friends. Invite your students to figure out how Tom might have shared all four fourths fairly among three people. In the next part of the story, Tom eats half of each of the three remaining fourths. Say to your students, "Hmmm, I wonder what fractional part of the original whole cake these remaining pieces are now?"

Sharing Remainders

Using *The Doorbell Rang* by Pat Hutchins (see page 163 in Chapter 5), your students can brainstorm some problems that involve cookie remainders that need sharing.

Making Noodle Soup

Revisit *Too Many Cooks!* by Andrea Buckless (see page 101 in Chapter 3). This time, focus on the recipe for noodle soup in the back of the book. The fractions $\frac{1}{2}$ and $\frac{1}{4}$ are part of the recipe. You and the children could discuss halving and doubling the recipe.

Story Problems

The activities below provide additional opportunities for students to divide pretend food into fractions and perhaps write their own food problems.

Dividing Cookies Revisited

If you have not already done so, have your students do the cookie-sharing problems described on pages 170–74 in Chapter 5. In those activities, the children experience sharing six, five, four, three, two, and one paper cookies fairly among four or two people. In *The Doorbell Rang* activity in that chapter (page 163), they share twelve cookies with different numbers of children, then they share thirty cookies with twelve children. Again, see the Blackline Masters for circular paper cookies.

> **TEACHER-TO-TEACHER TALK** Think about having students fold an $8\frac{1}{2}$-by-11-inch sheet of copy paper into eight equal sections, as they do for *Circles and Stars*. The children could label each section $\frac{1}{8}$. Then you could have a class discussion about how many eighths equal one-half of the whole sheet of paper. How many eighths equal one-fourth of the whole sheet of paper? This activity connects students' previous folding experiences to their present fraction work and provides a lead-in for brownie-sharing investigations.

Sharing Brownies

Give each student several copies of the brownies worksheet. (See Blackline Masters.) Have them practice cutting out and folding brownies to get a feel for fractional parts of squares.

Next have the children figure out how to share seven brownies with two people, with three people, and so forth. Or they could share eight, nine, and ten brownies with three or four children. Based on your students' experi-

> **TEACHER-TO-TEACHER TALK** Children enjoy sharing square paper "brownies" and discovering how to fold the brownies into fractional parts for leftovers. Dividing squares is different from dividing circles. Yet you might find children making the circle connection when they think of thirds. A circular cookie divided into thirds looks like a circle with a Y inside. (See below.)
>
>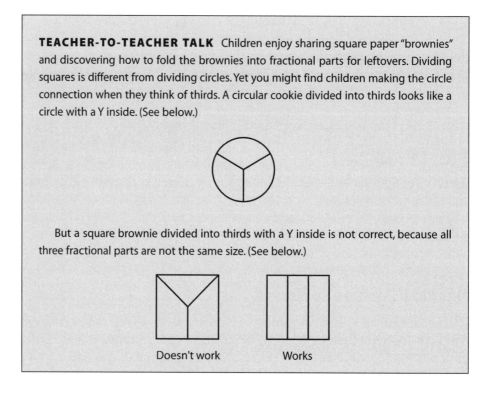
>
> But a square brownie divided into thirds with a Y inside is not correct, because all three fractional parts are not the same size. (See below.)
>
> Doesn't work   Works

FIGURE 6–8 ◄

Jarod showed how he would share eight brownies among three people.

ences with sharing cookies, you'll know which of these problems makes the most sense at this point in your students' learning. Make sense of each problem ahead of time before presenting them to the children. (See Figure 6–8.)

Deciding Which Is More

After your students have many experiences sharing brownies, encourage them to work on problems that require them to figure out which is more. Remember: The children did "which is more?" problems while working with multiplication—when they compared the number of windowpanes in various arrays or the number of cookies in several trays.

See *Fair Shares* (Tierney and Berle-Carman 1995) for more details on problems where children have to figure out who gets the larger share and who gets more.

First, you could assign two different brownie-sharing problems and ask the children who gets more brownies. If your children are ready for this, you could ask, "How much more?" As the children problem-solve, they use paper brownies and/or drawings labeled with numbers to show how the brownies are shaded. (See below.)

Problem 1: How do 2 people share 5 brownies?

Person A 😊 | 1 | | 1 | | $\frac{1}{2}$ |

Answer: Each person gets $2\frac{1}{2}$ brownies.

Person B 😊 | 1 | | 1 | | $\frac{1}{2}$ |

Problem 2: How do 4 people share 5 brownies?

Person A 😊 | 1 | $\frac{1}{4}$

Person B 😊 | 1 | $\frac{1}{4}$

Person C 😊 | 1 | $\frac{1}{4}$

Answer: Each person gets $1\frac{1}{4}$ brownies.

Person D 😊 | 1 | $\frac{1}{4}$

The people in Problem 1 got more brownies.

Next, you might ask two different cookie-sharing problems, followed by the question, "Which group gets more cookies?" (See below.)

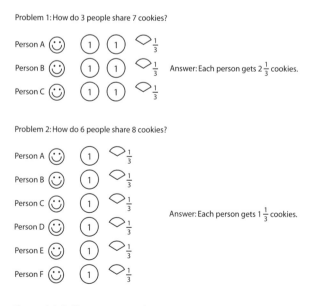

Problem 1: How do 3 people share 7 cookies?

Person A 😊 1 1 $\frac{1}{3}$

Person B 😊 1 1 $\frac{1}{3}$ Answer: Each person gets $2\frac{1}{3}$ cookies.

Person C 😊 1 1 $\frac{1}{3}$

Problem 2: How do 6 people share 8 cookies?

Person A 😊 1 $\frac{1}{3}$

Person B 😊 1 $\frac{1}{3}$

Person C 😊 1 $\frac{1}{3}$

Person D 😊 1 $\frac{1}{3}$ Answer: Each person gets $1\frac{1}{3}$ cookies.

Person E 😊 1 $\frac{1}{3}$

Person F 😊 1 $\frac{1}{3}$

The people in Problem 1 got more cookies.

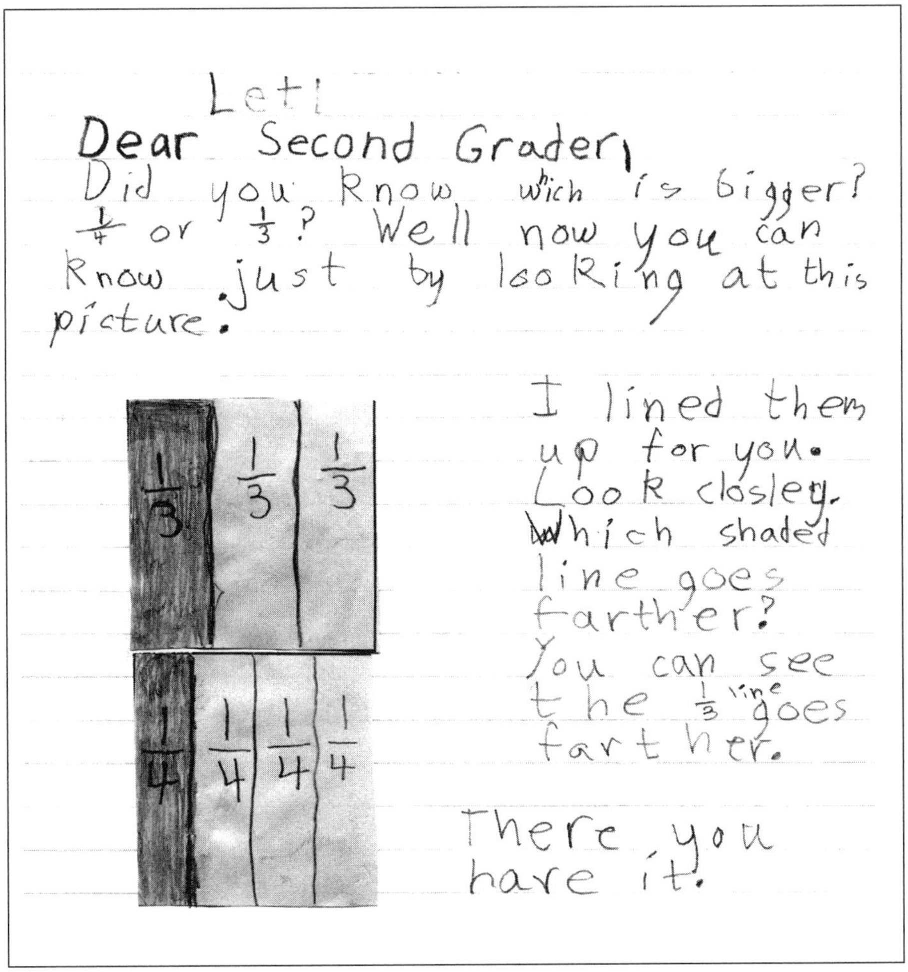

FIGURE 6-9 ◄

Susan explained to second graders how to tell whether a third or a fourth is bigger.

Let!

Dear Second Grader,
Did you Rnow which is bigger?
¼ or ⅓? Well now you can
Rnow just by looRing at this
picture.

I lined them up for you. Look closley. Which shaded line goes farther? You can see the ⅓ line goes farther.

There you have it!

The children could also write a letter to a second grader explaining which is greater—a third of a brownie or a fourth. (See Figure 6–9.)

Assessment

Continue to assess your children's understanding by listening during whole-class and partner discussions (see Chapter 2), by looking at their written classwork and individual written assessments (Chapter 3), and by having student interviews whenever possible (Chapter 5). Do this throughout the rest of the school year in spite of the time needed to prepare for and take standardized tests.

Standardized-Test Preparation

If you feel the need to do so, this is a good month to begin daily, short standardized-test-preparation exercises, perhaps on the overhead projector. Continue with the strong math program you have built up over the past five months and go lightly on the test prep—ten to fifteen minutes daily.

To mimic the testing environment, have students work alone on these exercises without talking over their strategies with one another and without using manipulatives. They can write numbers and draw pictures on scratch paper. If they are ready to do so, the children will reason mentally by occasionally jotting down certain numbers as signposts.

Remember: In the multiple-choice format, the test makers do not want too many children to figure out the problems correctly. So advise your students to examine the answer choices for tactics meant to confuse. Often, two answers will be completely unreasonable, so the youngsters can eliminate those. Then the children can focus on the other two possible answers and spend time figuring out which of the two is more correct and why. During test-prep practice sessions, have a class discussion about each correct answer after everyone has had time to make sense of the problem in his or her own way. Encourage a relaxed atmosphere and be excited about the children's powerful math thinking. Be reassuring and low key about it all.

If you can, wait for a month or two before timing these practices. Most children have plenty of time to grapple with the problem-solving sections of standardized tests. They are allotted less time and hence feel much more rushed in the sections that require them to compute numbers that are alone on a page.

During this month, present a couple of multiple-choice problems to your students daily. Vary the problems so the children have to think about whether to add, subtract, multiply, or divide. Present problems with two addends and more than two addends. And give them both take-away and comparison subtraction problems. For division, provide a balance of grouping and sharing problems. If you do not have time to create problems, look for ideas in textbooks or in test-prep materials.

Chapter 7

March

REVISITING ADDITION AND SUBTRACTION

"When students are challenged to think and reason about mathematics and to communicate the results of their thinking to others orally or in writing, they learn to be clear and convincing. Listening to others' explanations gives students opportunities to develop their own understandings."

Principles and Standards for School Mathematics
NCTM 2000, 60

By this time of the school year, many of your students are using numerical and mental reasoning as they increase their computational efficiency. Some children are continuing to reason more concretely by using manipulatives or drawings. Others use numerical reasoning by mapping their number understandings on paper. You will want to encourage all these groups of students as they work to make sense of problems. In spite of the pressures end-of-the-year testing brings, continue to help your students make sense of mathematics in ways they understand.

Before you begin introducing the problem solving suggested in this chapter, reread Chapter 2 to see if there are some problems your students did not have a chance to do and might benefit from doing now. ∎

The Learning Environment

Revisit and extend familiar problem situations from Chapter 2.

Many of the problems described in this chapter are extensions of problems the children thought about as they added and subtracted last fall. In *Estimate and Measure Revisited*, students use standard measurement units such as centimeters and inches instead of interlocking cubes. In *Handfuls of Beans Revisited*, they use pinto beans or lentils instead of lima beans to group, count, compare, and combine. In *Alexander, Who Used to Be Rich Last Sunday,* the children spend from $2.00 to $5.00 instead of $1.00. You may decide to revisit only those problems that particularly interested your students.

Help students who are ready to move toward more numerical and mental reasoning.

Increasingly, you'll see more and more students feeling eager to make sense of addition and subtraction problems in their minds without much figuring on paper. For example, a child might say that he knows in his head that after spending $1.58 and giving the cashier a $5.00 bill, the change would be $3.42. Each time you see this happening, take delight in the moment and ask how the student worked out the solution. In this case, the child might say that he thought $1.58 plus $.02 is $1.60, then $.40 more equals $.42 in change so far. So that gets him to $2.00. He quickly wrote $.42 on his paper as a signpost. It takes $3.00 more dollars to get to $5.00, so he wrote $3.00. When he looked at these signposts, he just knew he had $3.42 in change.

Remind yourself that all pathways to making sense of this problem are valid. The child who uses coins from his money bag to grapple with the problem is thinking and reasoning in a way he or she understands.

Some children might use the traditional procedure to figure the change.

$$
\begin{array}{r}
{}^{4\,9\,1} \\
\$\cancel{5}.\cancel{0}0 \\
-\;\;\;1.58 \\
\hline
\$3.42
\end{array}
$$

If you insist that each child use at least two strategies, students will be able to think and reason more flexibly. They will also feel more mathematically powerful.

Broaden your program with more extensions, menu time, and a monthly math area.

By this time of year, some students are feeling confident in addition and subtraction problem-solving situations. Others may not be there quite yet. If you have a meaningful extension ready for each problem, you can use it to engage the more confident students. You can also free yourself to support the learning of those students who need more time. Give these latter students time to work through their thinking without feeling inadequate. Support them by helping them focus on the original problem without feeling pressure to do the extensions.

During menu work, those children who need more time to problem solve can do the "dinner menu" problems only. Make certain these problems are directly connected to problems already done in the whole-class setting. Remind these students that mistakes are opportunities to learn and that a dinner menu completed in a convincing way is something to be proud of. Send this message: "I know you can do it, and I'm here to help you."

Give the more confident problem solvers a "dessert menu" of problems that extend their thinking to new situations after they have completed the dinner menu. Encourage them to work in pairs with the thought that "two heads are better than one." If they have questions, they can help one another instead of coming to you.

If you decide to designate an area in the classroom for monthly math problem solving (where students can go when they finish their assigned work), reread Chapter 1 for suggestions.

TEACHER-TO-TEACHER TALK As teachers, we need to remember that the child who struggles to make sense of addition or subtraction situations may shine when making sense of geometry or fraction problems. The reverse is true as well. The student who is a confident addition or subtraction problem solver may not be so confident when doing geometry or fraction work, because his or her spatial reasoning may not have developed yet.

The Mathematics

As children work with numbers greater than 100, they continue to make sense of the numbers by going to nearby familiar or friendly numbers (also known as landmarks or referents). They also break numbers into familiar or friendly parts.

Even though your students are working with larger numbers, they still use friendly-number strategies in their meaning making. For example, if a child is adding 348 apples to 267 apples, she might break the numbers into familiar parts: 300 + 200 = 500; 40 + 60 = 100; and 8 + 7 = 15. The total is 500 + 100 + 12 = 615 apples. Or, she might go to nearby familiar numbers by taking 3 from 348 to get 345, then adding the 3 to 267 to make 270. Finally, she adds 345 + 270 by breaking the numbers into familiar parts.

Friendly-number strategies are also useful for solving take-away or comparison subtraction problems. For example, consider this problem:

500 birds are perched in a tree, then 275 birds fly away. How many birds are left in the tree?

A child might go to a nearby familiar number and think of 275 as 300 by adding on 25. Then he reasons that 500 − 300 = 200 and compensates by adding on 25 to this answer as well. So his answer is *225 birds are left in the tree.* Another student might "count down" by breaking the smaller number, 275, into familiar or friendly parts: 200 + 70 + 5. This child then thinks 500 − 200 = 300; 300 − 70 = 230; and, finally, 230 − 5 = 225. A different student could decide to "count up" by thinking 275 + 5 = 280; 280 + 20 = 300; and finally 300 + 200 = 500. 5 + 20 + 200 = 225. Again, celebrate the strategies you see and hear in your classroom. Do not explicitly teach the strategies mentioned above; just be alert to when they might

TEACHER-TO-TEACHER TALK Some school-district standards suggest that third graders work with numbers in the thousands. But you'll know best what your students are ready for. Children must know how to break numbers into friendly parts or go to nearby friendly numbers between 0 and 100 while adding and subtracting before they can apply these understandings to larger numbers.

present themselves. That way, you can help students share their strategies with their classmates.

Children need experiences solving a variety of result-known *addition and subtraction problems.*

Chapter 2 featured numerous problems in which the result of an operation was the unknown. Now your students need experiences adding and subtracting in problem situations where the result *is* known. For example:

In the morning, there were 120 birds in a tree. In the afternoon, 80 birds remained in the tree. How many birds flew away?

The result is known: There were 80 birds still in the tree. Thus the equation would look like this: 120 − __ = 80. It's the change that's unknown.

Some take-away subtraction questions deal with the onset, or the original quantity. For instance:

The principal gave away 150 pencils to the students at her school. She had 225 pencils left. How many pencils did she have to begin with?

This is a result-known subtraction problem. The equation would look like this: __ − 150 = 225. Students can often solve these sorts of problems by counting up or adding, just as they do with comparison subtraction problems. (See Chapter 2.).

There are result-known addition problems, too. Consider this one:

At 9:50 there were 200 children waiting inside the cafeteria for the principal. By the time he arrived at 10:00, there were 350 children in the cafeteria. How many children came to the cafeteria between 9:50 and 10:00?

The corresponding equation would be: 200 + __ = 350. Children could solve this problem using subtraction, but many of them might choose to add up from 200 to 350 children.

Children continue to add with more than two addends.

Children hone their math skills by solving many problems with more than two addends. For example, they can do this by adding the lunch count for four classrooms at their grade level and for four classrooms at another grade level. And if you assign each letter in the alphabet a dollar value—from A = $1 to Z = $26—they can figure the monetary value of their first name by using more than two addends. These and other activities are described in various sections of this chapter.

Mathematics Throughout the Day

Lunch Count Revisited

When you and the children add the lunch count for all the classrooms at your third-grade level, you can compare the count to another grade level that has the same number of classrooms. For instance, if there are four third grades at your school and four second grades, your students might calculate on one day that 14 + 16 + 13 + 15 third graders ordered lunch and 11 + 12 + 16 + 9 second graders ordered school lunch.

> **TEACHER-TO-TEACHER TALK**   By the end of third grade, many children can make sense of the numbers mentally by simply jotting down numbers as signposts to remember. For example, on the third-grade data, children could mentally figure that four 10s = 40 and write down the 40. Then they could reason in their heads that 4 + 6 = 10 and 3 + 5 = 8, so 10 + 8 = 18. They might jot down the 18 and quickly reason that 40 + 18 = 58. Instead of writing down every step in their thinking, many students may be doing more mental figuring supported by some writing. This kind of sign-post reasoning might be especially helpful in whole-group situations, because it saves time. You may still want students to document all the steps in their thinking during individual work. It's your call.

For the second-grade data, the children might reason that three 10s equal 30 and jot down the 30. Next they reason that 9 + 1 = 10 (they go for a familiar number), then 2 + 6 = 8. Finally, they mentally reason 10 + 8 = 18. They jot down the 18 and get 30 + 18 = 48.

After your students have finished this process, you can ask, "Which grade level is ordering more school lunches today? How many more lunches? How do you know that?"

Extensions

- Students chart lunch-count information for second and third grade over time, then look for days when more students at both grade levels buy school lunches. They also examine which selections children are making from the lunch menu for the month.

- Students track attendance data for second and third grade. They continue to figure out the totals and the differences between the two totals. They try to determine whether there are more absences on some days than there are on other days.

How Old Is the Coin?

Children can find many opportunities to figure out the age of something—whether it's coins in their money bags or characters in a book. For example, if class members notice that several quarters in their money bags were minted in 1974, have them first estimate the age of the coins. Then give them quiet time to figure out the solution step by step on paper. Next, they can share their strategies with one another. (See Figure 7–1.)

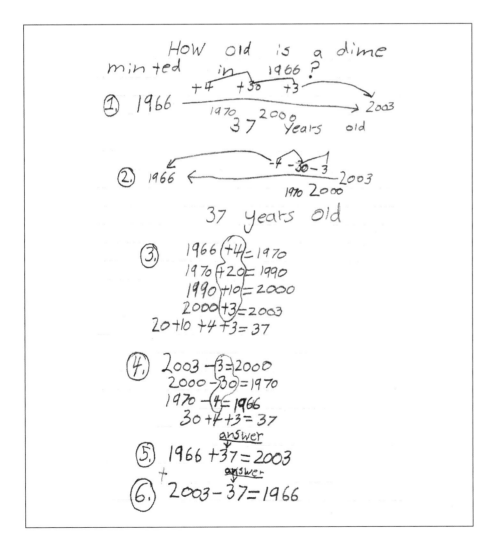

FIGURE 7–1 ◄

Marcus figured out the age of a dime that was minted in 1966.

Extensions

- Children find three different coins at home and record each coin, its mint date, and the age of the coin today. They show how they figured out the age of each coin.

- At home, students look for the oldest U.S. coin they can find. They then figure out the age of the coin, showing their reasoning in a clear and convincing way.

How Old Is the Character?

When you and the children read books together, you'll find many opportunities to figure out how old a character might be. For example, in the book *Ramona the Pest*, Ramona is in kindergarten, which makes her about five years old. According to the copyright date, the book was written in 1968. How old would Ramona have been in 2001? (See Figure 7–2.)

How Long Ago?

Reading books in the classroom also gives you plenty of opportunities to ask "How long ago?" questions. For instance, *Caps for Sale* was first written in 1940. Ask your students how long ago 1940 was. (See Figure 7–3.)

FIGURE 7–2 ▶

Nan calculated Ramona the Pest's age in 2001.

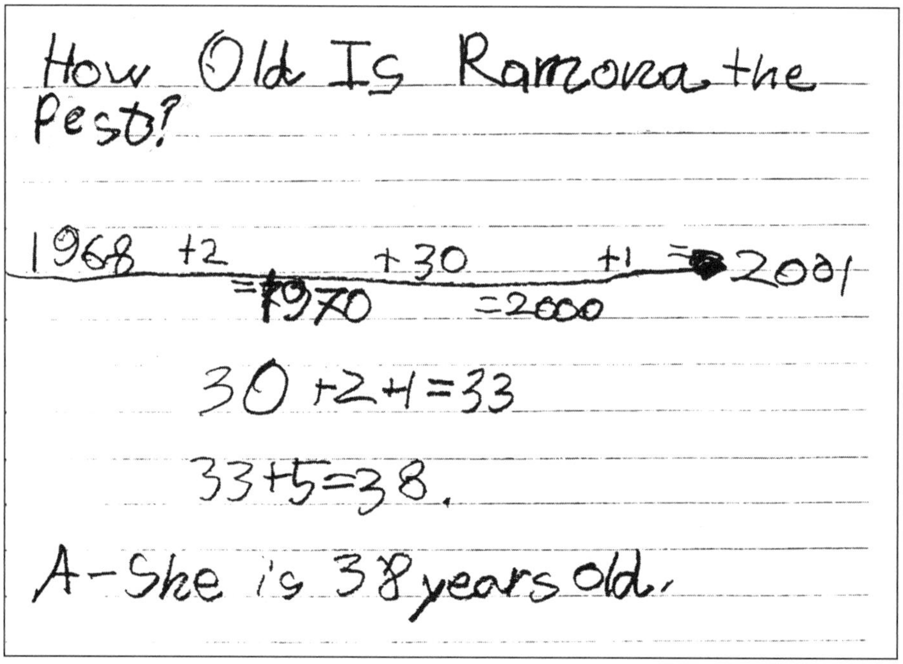

How Old Is Ramona the Pest?

1968 +2 +30 +1 = 2001
    =1970   =2000

30 +2+1=33

33+5=38.

A—She is 38 years old.

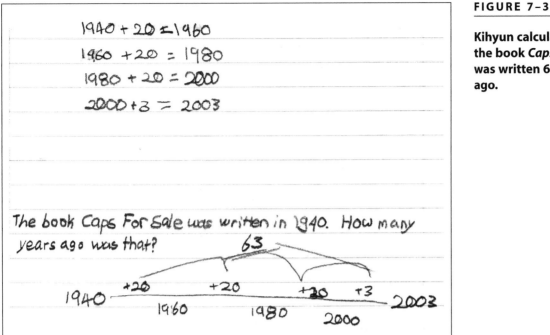

FIGURE 7–3   ◄

Kihyun calculated that the book *Caps for Sale* was written 63 years ago.

Extensions

In my class, I meet individually with four children each day to discuss the book they are reading as part of their weekly homework. If your students do weekly one-on-one book conferences with you on the books they are reading at home, ask how long ago their book was published.

School-Days-So-Far Equations

By March, your students have been in school for more than 100 days. As the children write equations showing how many days school has been in session, give them freedom to write equations without constraints (such as "Use addition only" or "Use subtraction only"). Then you can assess the breadth of children's numerical understanding, and you can follow their lead. Based on what you see and hear, you can decide on constraints that make sense; for instance, "Today, use three addends, one of which is eighty-five, in your equations." Sometimes, limiting the options in this way pushes students to new understandings of a large number such as 125.

School-Days-So-Far Story Problem

Once children have written equations for the number of school days so far, they can figure the number of school days left in the year. (First find

out how many school days children are attending school in your district.)
(See Figure 7–4.)

Calendar Days So Far

At the bottom of CNN's television picture, the rotating words often include
information on the number of days in the calendar year so far. You can
use this information to design interesting problems for your students. (See
Figure 7–5.) For example:

On October 1, 2002, it was the 274th day of the calendar year.

There were 365 days in the calendar year of 2002.

What is the difference between 274 and 365 days?

You may wish to discuss the fact that each year really has $365\frac{1}{4}$ days.
So every fourth year, we add one day to February to catch up with accu-
mulated four $\frac{1}{4}$ days. The fraction $\frac{4}{4}$ equals 1.

FIGURE 7–4   ▶

**Yousif calculated the
number of school days
left in the year.**

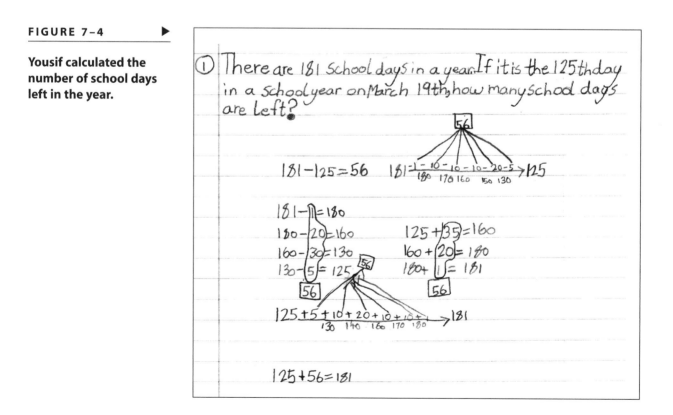

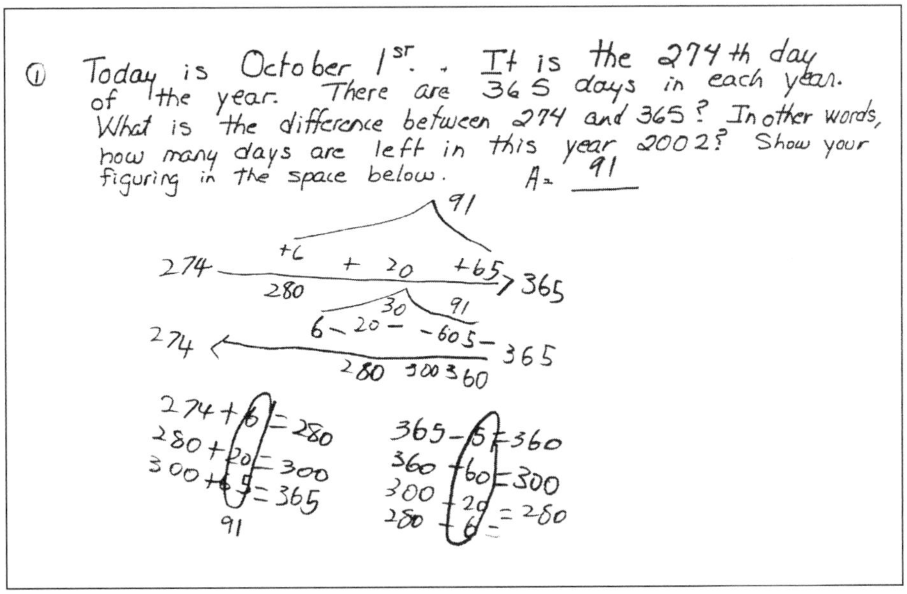

FIGURE 7–5   ◀

Sasha showed how she found the difference between day 274 of the calendar year and 365 days.

Pages Left to Read in a Book

Suppose you and your students have read some pages in a chapter of a book. You can ask the children how many pages are left to read.

Extensions

When children bring the book they are reading to their weekly book conference with you, they figure out how many pages they have left to read in the book.

Games

You may want to revisit games that the children played during September and October. (See Chapters 2 and 3.) Here are some additional possibilities.

Pig

A game of strategy and chance, *Pig* provides addition practice. The object of the game is to reach a score of 100 or more. Players take turns rolling two dice and mentally keep a running total of the sums that come up.

A player may roll as many times as he likes and then record the total score, adding it to the total from previous turns. However, if a 1 comes up before the player decides to "stick" (stop rolling), the player scores 0 for that turn. Also, if two 1s come up, the player scores 0 for that turn and loses his entire score so far. He must start again from 0!

You can introduce this game by playing it with the entire class. Use the board to record scores for yourself and the class. Make manipulatives and 1–100 charts available to the students. After the children become familiar with the game, have them share their strategies for adding mentally as they go. Then they can play in pairs at their desks.

Extensions

After playing many rounds of *Pig* at school and at home, children write an answer to one of the following questions:

> "How did you decide when to keep rolling and when to stop and keep your score?"
>
> "Suppose your score was nineteen and you rolled eleven. What would your new score be, and how did you figure that out?"
>
> "What is your strategy for winning this game?"

How Close to 0?

This partner game comes from *Teaching Arithmetic: Lessons for Addition and Subtraction, Grades 2–3* by Bonnie Tank and Lynne Zolli (2001). *How Close to 0?* is appropriate to play after the children have had many experiences playing *Pig*. As with any game involving counting and addition of larger numbers, students might wish to use the 1–100 chart. (See Blackline Masters for the chart, game rules, and recording sheet.)

Materials

- 1 die per pair of students
- copies of game rules, 1–100 chart, and recording sheet per pair of students

Instructions

1. Player 1 rolls the die. She decides whether to use the number as a 10 place value or a 1 place value. (For example, a 5 could be 50 or 5.)

2. Player 1 subtracts the number from 100 and writes the equation and result on the recording sheet.

3. Player 2 does the same—rolls the die, decides whether to use the number as a 10 or 1 place value, subtracts the number from 100, and records the play.

4. Play continues until each player has rolled seven times. The player closest to 0 after seven rounds wins and receives a score of whatever number is left by the opposing player.

5. If a player reaches 0 or below before the seventh round, the game ends. The other player wins and scores the points left over from the opponent's previous round. The goal is to get 0 on the seventh round of each game and to win the most points after playing more than one game with the same partner.

TEACHER-TO-TEACHER TALK Games play an important part in children's efforts to make sense of numbers. They are as meaningful at the *end* of the third-grade year as they were at the beginning. Consider sending games home for family math time. To do this, you might want to look at *Close to 100* in *Combining and Comparing, Grades 3 and 4* by Jan Mokros and Susan Jo Russell. In this game, each player draws four numeral cards and puts the four numbers into two double-digit numbers that, when added together, get very close to 100 as a total. In another game, *Capture Five*, found in *Putting Together and Taking Apart, Grades 2 and 3* by Karen Economopoulos and Susan Jo Russell, each player places twelve markers on a 1–100 chart then draws five change cards such as these: +3, +10, −1, +2, and −30. The player uses all or some of these cards put together in an equation to move his game piece to one of the twelve markers he placed on the 1–100 chart. For example, to move his game piece from 36 to 19, a player might use the above-mentioned change cards then write this equation: *36 − 30 + 3 + 10 = 19*.

Two games that involve classroom conversations about number (not games to be sent home) are found in *Developing Number Sense, Grades 3–6* by Rusty Bresser and Caren Holtzman. In *Guess My Number*, you choose a secret number in a range such as 1–50, 50–100, or 1–500, and tell the children the range ahead of time. The children guess your secret number; if their guess is incorrect, you announce whether your number is greater or less than the number guessed. In *Tell All You Can?* you write an arithmetic problem such as *45 + 45 + 45* horizontally on the board. Give children time to think about the problem, then ask them to tell you what they know about the answer *without* actually revealing the answer. A student might say, "I know the answer will be between one hundred and one hundred fifty, because three forties equal one hundred twenty, and three fifties equal one hundred fifty." In this problem, the children get valuable estimation practice.

Measurement

The following activities build on those in Chapter 2 by encouraging students to work with larger numbers as they count, combine, separate, and compare.

Fill the Cube (Volume)

Materials

- 1 interlocking cube per student, with hole taped over
- a handful of popcorn kernels and lentils per student

Instructions

1. Students fill the cube with popcorn kernels and record the number of kernels.

2. Based on this data, they then estimate how many lentils will fill the same cube.

3. They fill the cube with lentils and record the number.

4. They figure out how many more lentils than popcorn it took to fill the cube.

Extensions

Children play a version of *Fill the Cube* with larger containers that hold more kernels and lentils.

Handfuls of Beans Revisited (Volume)

In Chapter 2, *Handfuls of Beans* activities were suggested as an extension to *Cubes in a Jar* and as a menu problem. The children used lima beans; this time they use smaller beans.

Materials

- a bowl of lentils or pinto beans per student

Instructions

1. Students grab a handful of lentil or pinto beans with their right hand.

2. They group, count, and record the total number of beans they grabbed.

3. They do the same with their left hand.

4. They figure the difference between the two handfuls and the sum when the handfuls are combined. (See Figure 7–6.)

Extensions

- Students examine one another's data from *Handfuls of Beans Revisited* and record the largest right handful and the smallest right handful of beans in the class. They figure the difference between these two

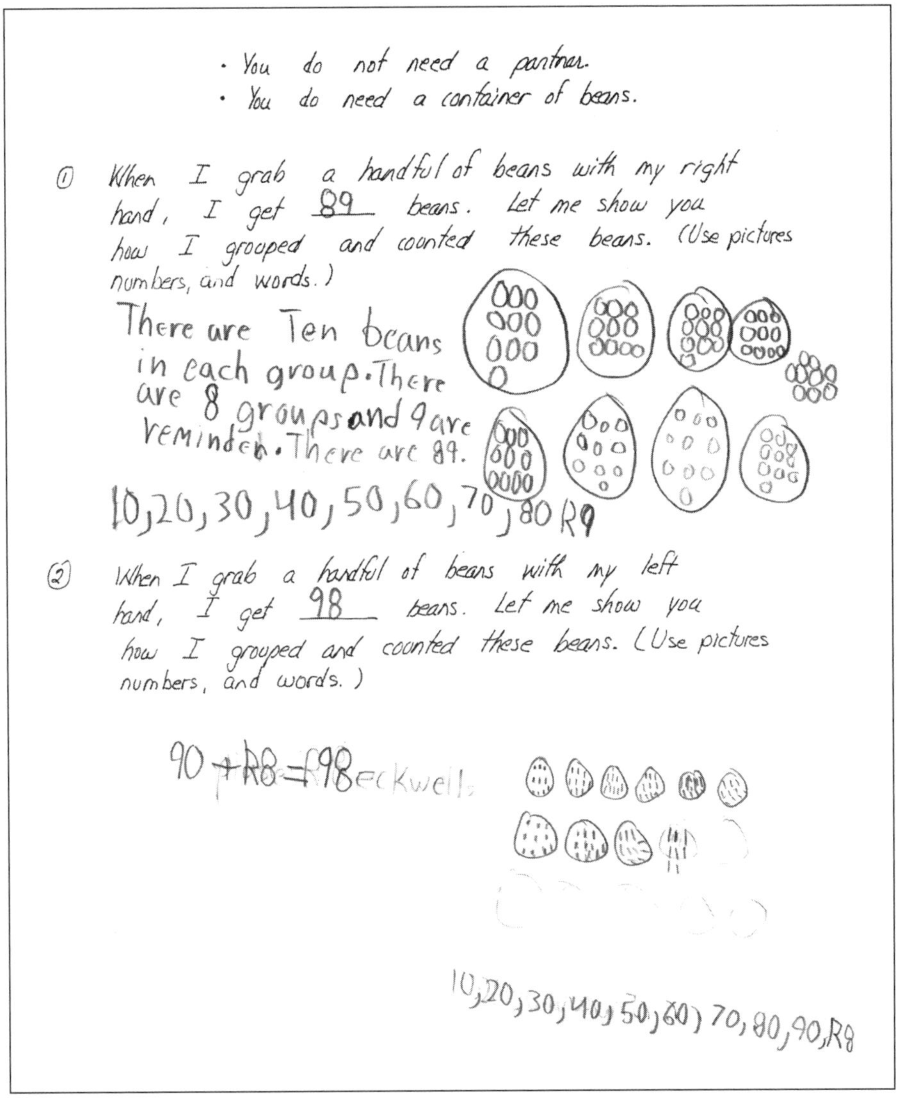

FIGURE 7–6 ◀

Hamid recorded his
Handful of Beans
figuring.

handfuls and then calculate the sum when these two handfuls are combined. Or, each child compares his or her right-handful data to the largest right handful data for the class. Then students do the same with their left-handful data.

- At home, children find and grab two handfuls of some small item. Then they count, compare, and combine the handfuls.

Estimate and Measure Revisited (Linear)

Materials

- the book *How Big Is a Foot?* by Rolf Myller
- standard measuring tools (e.g., yardsticks, meter sticks, rulers with inches on one side and centimeters on the other)

Instructions

1. Read *How Big Is a Foot?* to your students. Stop when you come to the point in the story at which the apprentice is sent to jail for making a bed too small for the queen. Have the children write letters to the apprentice, telling him how to solve the problem of the "too small bed." This activity reveals the usefulness of using standard measurement units and tools.

2. Introduce the children to standard measuring tools, such as yardsticks, meter sticks, rulers with inches on one side and centimeters on the other side, and so forth. Explain that most people around the world use the metric system (centimeters, meters, etc.) but that people in the United States use both the metric and the standard system (inches, feet, yards, etc.).

3. Choose several books, and explain that students will measure the books' lengths, widths, thicknesses, and weights. Review the meaning of each of these words and add to a chart of Measurement Words.

TEACHER-TO-TEACHER TALK Using a clear ruler, model on the overhead how you line up the ruler next to the object you are measuring by aligning the first measurement mark next to the end of the object. You can do this with both the centimeter and inch side of the ruler using common classroom items such as erasers, pencils, and paperclips. Spend time on this until all the children understand. Then rotate to check as the children do their own practice measuring.

First have the children estimate the above measurements in *centimeters*. To prepare them for estimating, have them use their rulers to measure things that are about one centimeter long (e.g., the width of a little finger, width of a paperclip). With these referents in mind, their estimates will make more sense to them. Decide ahead of time how you want students to handle fraction measurements. For example, should they record $14\frac{1}{2}$ cm as 14 or 15 cm? Have students record their estimated measurements (in centimeters) for each book you've selected, the actual measurements, and the differences between the two. (See Blackline Masters.)

Have students follow the same process with a foot-long ruler marked with inches. This time, they find referents for one inch, then they estimate and measure using inches.

Extensions

- Students measure parts of one another's bodies in centimeters and inches.

- Students use rulers and tape measures to find the dimensions of larger objects in the classroom, such as bookshelves and white boards. Decide if you want students to use centimeters, inches, or both.

Money

Name Values

In their book *Teaching Arithmetic: Lessons for Addition and Subtraction, Grades 2–3* Bonnie Tank and Lynne Zolli suggest attaching a dollar value to each letter in the alphabet, starting with A = $1.00. First, you may want to read aloud *The Case of the Backyard Treasure* (see page 237). Students can then figure out the "value" of their first names. For example, Sam would calculate the dollar value of his name as $19.00 + $1.00 + $13.00 = $33.00.

First the children reason numerically as they figure the value of their own name using various strategies. Then they find the difference between their name value and that of other students' names.

Students can also figure out the difference between their own name value and $100.00.

Spending Dollars

Materials

- the book *Alexander, Who Used to Be Rich Last Sunday* by Judith Viorst
- 1 money bag per pair of students
- 1 18-by-24-inch piece of paper per student

Instructions

1. Reread *Alexander, Who Used to Be Rich Last Sunday* to your class. In the fall, your students may have used this story to write their own accounts of spending $1.00 over seven days. In this activity, they'll write stories about spending $2.00 , $3.00, $4.00, or $5.00 over seven days.

2. The same day that you reread the story, have the children (individually or in pairs) figure out how much money each of Alexander's brothers has before their grandparents visit. Anthony has two dollars, three quarters, one dime, seven nickels, and eighteen pennies. Nicholas has one dollar, two quarters, five dimes, five nickels, and

thirteen pennies. Suggest that students use their money bags if needed to solve the problem.

3. The next day, have the children prepare a recording sheet for their new story about spending money. They first fold the 18-by-24-inch piece of paper into eight sections. Then they include a title at the top of the sheet that follows this format: *Michael, Who Used to Be Rich Last Friday*.

4. Have students draw pictures and write text in each of the eight sections of the paper showing how they spent their $2.00, $3.00, $4.00, or $5.00. By the eighth day, they should have no money left.

5. Ask each child to add up all the money spent to see if it equals the amount he or she began with.

Extensions

See *Teaching Arithmetic: Lessons for Addition and Subtraction, Grades 2–3* (Tank and Zolli 2001) for extension and class-discussion ideas. Here's one example: Students figure out how many items in their story at one price can be purchased for one dollar and how much would be left over. For example, if the child spent $.15 for a comic book, how many comics could that child buy for $1.00, and how much money would be left over from the transaction?

Pennies in a Jar Revisited

See Chapter 2 for a more detailed description of this activity. In that version, students use two strategies to group and count the number of pennies filling half a pint jar. Now have students group and count using one strategy. Then, based on their results, ask them to estimate how much money would fill the entire jar.

Extensions

- Students figure out how many dollars, how many quarters, and how many dimes are represented in their total number of pennies estimated for the full jar.

- Students calculate which bills and coins could be used to "shrink" the amount of money in half of the pint jar. For example, if there are 350 pennies in the jar, what bills and coins would take up less space but have the same monetary value as the pennies? (This extension connects to the book *The Case of the Shrunken Allowance* in the "Literature-Based Activities.")

Making Change

You can also introduce the children to the concept of making change for $5.00, $10.00, and $20.00—common situations in everyday life. Ask your students which small objects they regularly buy for less than $5.00, $10.00, and $20.00 outside of school. Use their responses to generate problems that require the children to *add* to get totals and *subtract* to make change.

Also consider posing problems that relate to the children's school lives. For instance, if the daily school lunch costs $2.35, and a child pays with a $5.00 bill, what change will he or she receive? (See Figure 7–7.)

Students may think of other interesting questions for this situation. For instance, could a student purchase two school lunches with the $5.00? If so, how does he or she know this? If the child uses $10.00 to pay for three school lunches ahead of time, what change will he or she receive?

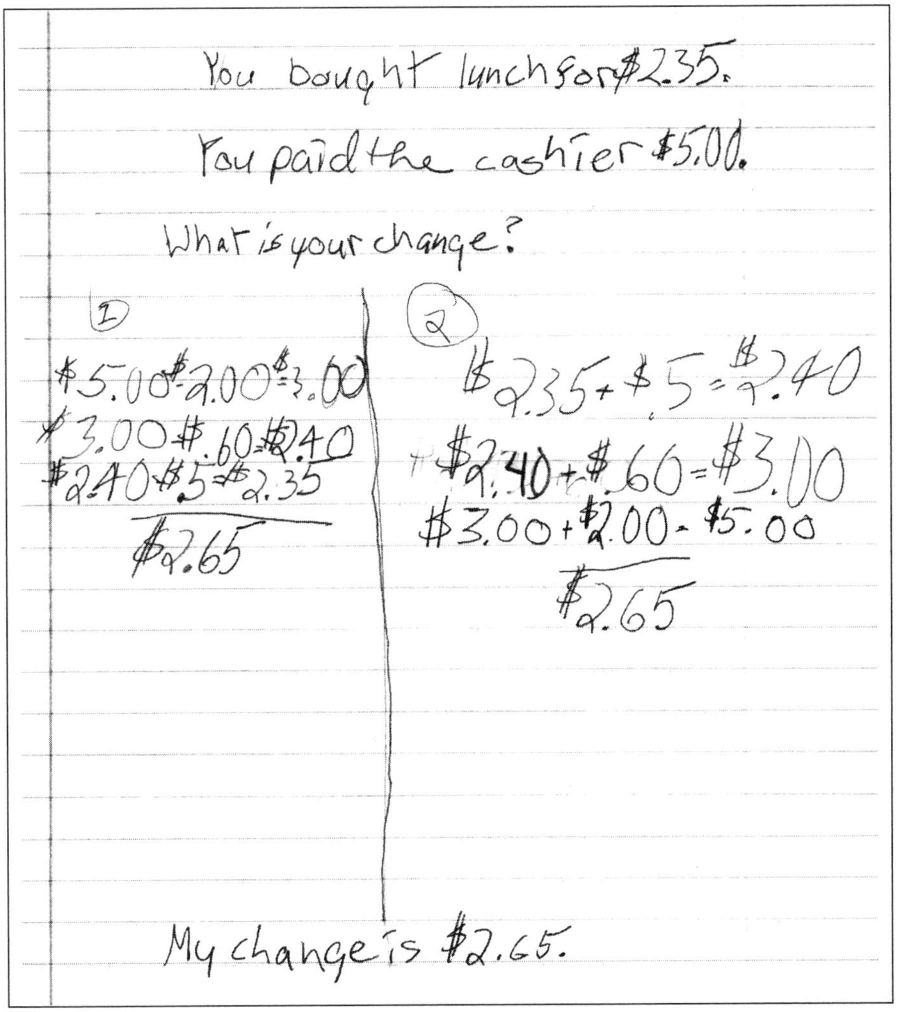

FIGURE 7–7

Janet calculated how much change she would receive if she paid for a $2.35 lunch with $5.00.

Besides school lunches, book orders or special classes can inspire intriguing money problems. To illustrate, if six weeks of one-hour chess lessons cost $12.50, and a youngster pays with a $20.00 bill, what is the change? How did the student make sense of that?

Literature-Based Activities

Comparing Prices

In my classroom, we read *Henry Huggins* by Beverly Cleary. The book is a bit dated, and the chapter titled "The Green Christmas" needs a caring discussion about the way Native Americans are briefly portrayed in a school play and the fact that Christmas is not the only winter holiday. Different cultures and religions have other celebrations.

But the book does open a window onto how children lived fifty years ago and presents many opportunities to solve math problems. For instance, Henry needs to buy a football to replace Scooter's new one. The prices of footballs and other things fifty years ago pique the children's interest. This problem comes directly from the situation in the book. (See Figure 7–8.)

My students also worked on the following problem, comparing the cost of things in the book's time period to the cost of the things today.

Henry took advantage of the Special Offer from the Lucky Dog Pet Shop. He got 1 pair of guppies, 1 fish bowl, 1 snail, and 1 aquatic plant plus 1 package of fish food. The whole thing cost him just $.79!

This week, your teacher bought 2 guppies for $7.99, 2 snails for $.50, 1 aquatic plant for $1.98, and fish food for $2.99 for fish food.

Here are two questions for you:

How much did your teacher spend altogether?

What is the difference between what your teacher spent this week and what Henry Huggins spent fifty years ago? (Show your figuring for each answer.)

Coin and Bill Combinations

In the book *The Case of the Shrunken Allowance* by Joanne Rocklin, P. B. gets a $.50 allowance each week plus additional money for extra chores. His three-month allowance totals $10.05. Have your students combine their bags to figure all the different coin and bill combinations that have the value of $10.05.

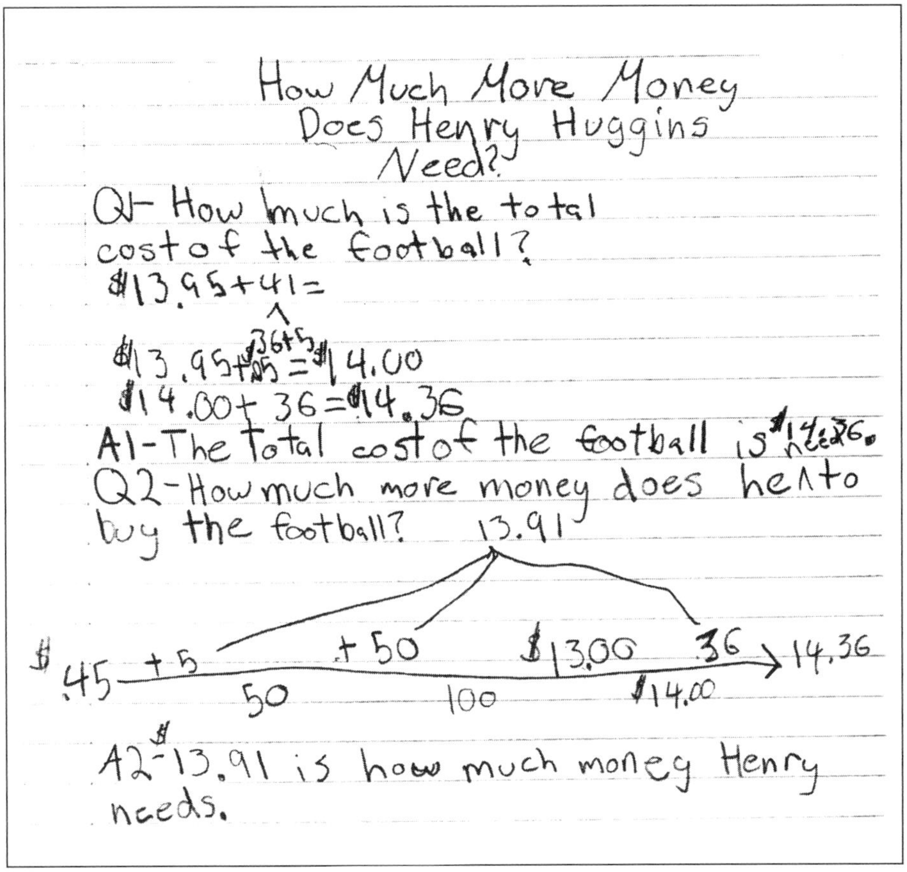

FIGURE 7–8 ◀

Latasha calculated how much money Henry would need to buy a football.

Finding Hidden Treasure

In *The Case of the Backyard Treasure* by Joanne Rocklin, Liz the Whiz; her brother Henry, who is a Whiz-in-Training; and their dog, Marv love to solve problems. A neighbor boy, Zack, needs their help in finding a hidden treasure. First, Liz the Whiz uses the Alphabet Code to decide that 19 – 1 – 13 means Sam. From there, they must crack other number clues that involve geometric shapes and that connect to telling time. The trio finally finds the treasure: cookies left by Zack's friend, Sam, who is moving to another town.

This book provides an excellent preview for the *Name Values* activity described earlier in this chapter.

Adding Up Money

In *The Case of the Shrunken Allowance* by Joanne Rocklin, P. B., who loves peanut butter, enlists his two friends, Maria and Mike, in trying to figure out why his allowance (which is stored in an empty peanut-butter jar) is shrinking. On the previous day, his allowance money filled the jar to the top. Today, the money takes up only half of the jar. P. B. gets an allowance of $.50 each week. If he does extra chores, he gets more money.

This story gives children an opportunity to add thirteen weeks of allowance money plus extra money, and to think about the volumes in different-size jars. The book ends with suggestions for estimating how long it takes to do home chores, timing the completion of those chores, and using water to explore volumes of different-size jars. (Other activities using this book include *Pennies in a Jar Revisited* and *Coin and Bill Combinations*.)

Story Problems

As March unfolds, continue to write story problems that are relevant to your students' school and home lives. Also make certain that the children write their own story problems as often as you write problems for them. Before reading this section, you may want to reread the "Story Problem" section in Chapter 2; also revisit page 221 in this chapter.

Teacher- and Student-Generated Problems

You and your students can write problems together that involve adding up the cost of several things to get a total and then making change for $5.00, $10.00, and $20.00 for that total. These result-unknown, two-step problems require both addition and subtraction. As children continue to make sense of these problems using their money bags, gently nudge them toward computing mentally.

For other problems that don't involve money, continue letting children draw pictures, use manipulatives, or refer to a number pocket chart to make sense of numbers larger than 100. Students may start finding these strategies too time consuming and unwieldy with larger numbers. If you see this happening, support numerical reasoning by encouraging students to generate numerical strategies that you've modeled on the board.

Yes, it is late in the school year, but don't panic or give in to any pressure to cover more material in a short amount of time. Remind yourself of how well your children are making sense of story problems with smaller numbers, and help them connect this sense making to larger numbers. Resist any impulse to teach a single abstract procedure for everyone to follow. If children try to follow a procedure they don't understand, they're bound to make mistakes.

Result-Known Problems

As mentioned earlier in "The Mathematics" section of this chapter, children need combining and separating story-problem experiences in which they know the result but not the change or the initial quantity. Below are some ideas for creating such problems and connecting them to school life and books that the children are reading.

School-Connected Problems

Here is a combining problem that is *result known*.

> *The four third grades were having an assembly together. First Mr. R. and Mr. S. brought their 38 students. By the time Mrs. R. and Ms. F. came, there were 77 third graders at the assembly. How many children came from Mrs. R.'s and Ms. F.'s classes?*

Ask the children, "What do we know in this problem? What don't we know?" Then have them help you write an equation to represent the problem: 38 + __ = 77. Finally, ask, "How can we figure out the answer here?" Some children use addition or counting up to solve this problem. Others use subtraction or counting down.

Here's another *result-known* problem:

> *On Monday, Room 33 had 48 new erasers on the shelf. By Friday, there were only 18 new erasers left on the shelf. How many new erasers did the children in Room 33 use during that week of school?*

The equation for this problem is: 48 – __ = 18. Find out how your students make sense of the problem.

Encourage them to write their own school-connected result-known story problems.

Book-Connected Problems

In this chapter, I've frequently suggested that you and your students write story problems based on books you're reading in class. The following problem doesn't come word for word from a particular story. Instead, I've created a pretend problem inspired by a situation in the story.

> *Henry Huggins caught earthworms for Mr. Grumbie. Over two days, he caught 125 earthworms. If he caught 80 earthworms on Tuesday, how many earthworms did he catch on Monday?*

In this problem, the initial quantity is unknown. Ask your students, "What equation can we write to represent this problem? What do we know? What don't we know?" The corresponding equation is __ + 80 = 125.

Now challenge your students to use the equation to figure out the answer. (See Figures 7–9 and 7–10.)

Teacher Provides Result-Known Equation; Children Provide the Story

You may want to switch gears in your class story-problem work by first presenting an equation with the result known. Then children write story problems that make sense for this situation. (See Figures 7–11 and 7–12.)

FIGURE 7–9 ▶

Sarah approached the earthworm problem by using several numerical strategies.

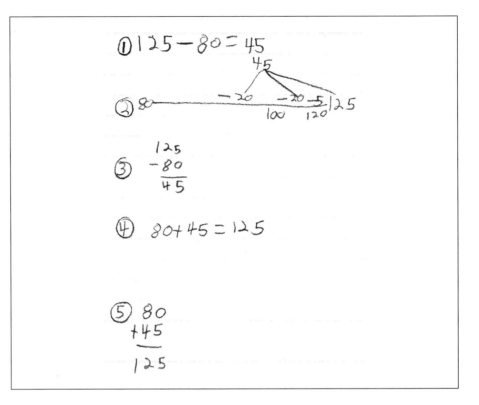

FIGURE 7–10 ▶

Peter counted up from 80 to 125 and down from 125 to 80 by going to friendly numbers.

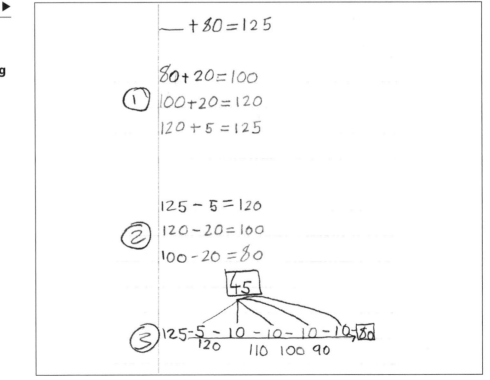

Write a story problem
for 178 - ___ =132. Use two strategies
to solve your problem. Write a sentence
answer to your problem question.

There are 178 dogs.
Some dogs ran away.
There 132 dogs left.
How many dogs ran away?

178 - (8) = 170
170 - (20) = 150
150 - (10) = 140
140 - (8) = 132
46

20 + 18 + 8 = 46

132 ← -18 -20 -8 → 178
        150 170

46 dogs ran away.

Angela wrote a story problem drawn from the equation 178 – __ = 132, provided by her teacher. She used two different strategies to make sense of her problem.

Write a story problem for 27 + ___ = 89
Use two strategies to solve your problem.
Write a sentence answer to your
problem question.

① 89
  -27
  ───
  62

② 62
  27 +3 / +50 / +9 → 89
     30   80

③ 27 + 3 = 30
  30 + 50 = 80
  80 + 9 = 62 → 62
       62

I have 27 balloons.
My friend gave me some.
I ended with 89 balloons.

How many did my friend give me?
My friend gave me 62 balloons.

Ray wrote a story problem that made sense for the equation 17 + __ = 89, provided by his teacher. He used three strategies to solve his problem.

> **TEACHER-TO-TEACHER TALK**   As your students solve various result-known problems, have them continue using more than one strategy. By drawing pictures, using manipulatives, or consulting a number pocket chart, students can connect their numerical strategies to more concrete models. But by now, more and more students understand their numerical strategies without models.

Standardized-Test Preparation

The signpost strategy discussed in "The Learning Environment" section on page 218 may help some of your students deal with the timed aspect of standardized testing. However, children need to feel comfortable with numerical reasoning to use signposts. Continue to encourage those students who need to draw pictures or write out every step in their numerical thinking to use the strategy that makes the most sense to them.

Solving and writing result-known story problems is good practice for the thinking required on standardized tests. Also, children who can combine (add) and then compare or separate (subtract) within the same problem bring this reasoning to problems involving two steps. For example, when they add up the cost of several items and then figure out the change for $5.00 or $10.00, children are using addition in one step and subtraction in the other step.

Besides being timed and including two-step problems, standardized tests are designed to confuse children. For example, some story problems provide extra information or a number that isn't necessary to the solution. Your students need to understand this, and to be aware of such roadblocks to their sense making. Present some problems with this extra information.

Another roadblock is the word *about*. If a story problem includes this word, that's a signal that the children are to round off numbers. For instance, suppose a question contains the figures $1.77, $.98, and $4.56. The problem asks students *about* how much the total of these three amounts would be. In this case, students should think through the solution mentally and quickly with rounded numbers—$2.00 + $1.00 + $5.00—rather than spend time working out the exact figuring on scratch paper.

Children also get confused when they see *none of the above* as a fifth choice in a multiple-choice question. In Chapter 6, I suggested that students practice narrowing four choices down to the two most reasonable-sounding answers. The *none of the above* choice forces them to double-check the correctness of their answer choice. Practice with this format to help your students feel more confident when they face the actual standardized test.

If you have been presenting equations horizontally all year (17 + 26, 95 − 57, 8 × 4, and 36 ÷ 4), have the children work these same problems vertically. Encourage them to use the same sense-making strategies they used with the horizontal format. For example:

For $\quad$ 17 the children still reason 10 + 20 = 30; 7 + 6 = 13, so
$\quad\quad$ + 26 $\quad\quad\quad\quad\quad\quad\quad\quad\quad\quad\quad\quad$ 30 + 13 = 43.

For $\quad$ 95 they can still "count up": 57 + $\underline{3}$ = 60; 60 + $\underline{30}$ = 90;
$\quad\quad$ − 57 $\quad\quad\quad\quad\quad\quad\quad\quad\quad$ 90 + $\underline{5}$ = 95, so $\underline{3}$ + $\underline{30}$ + $\underline{5}$ = 38

Explain to your students again and again that they will do well on the tests, even if the format looks different from what they're used to. Encourage them to use the strong sense-making strategies they have been employing throughout the year in their daily problem solving. Support a "can do" attitude and balance the ten or so days of test taking with singing, art, hands-on math and science projects, relaxing read alouds, and fun!

Station Time

At the end of Chapter 3, there is an extensive discussion of stations as another way to organize your teaching. You may want to review what is explained there.

Here is a sample station schedule for this chapter.

	Write a Result-Known Problem (with the teacher)	*Do* Handfuls of Beans Revisited *(with a table partner)*	*Play* How Close to 0? *(with parent)*	*Figure Values of Names (at team table)*
8:30–9:00	Table 1 with Ray	Table 2 with Sarah	Table 3 with Latasha	Table 4 with Juan
9:00–9:30	Table 4	Table 1	Table 2	Table 3
9:30–10:00	Table 3	Table 4	Table 1	Table 2
10:00–10:30	Table 2	Table 3	Table 4	Table 1

Chapter 8

REVISITING MULTIPLICATION
AND DIVISION

*"But if their learning becomes a process of simply mimicking
and memorizing, they can soon begin to lose interest.
Instruction at this level must be active and intellectually stimulating and must help students make sense of mathematics."*

Principles and Standards for School Mathematics
NCTM 2000, 143

Before you introduce the activities in this chapter, reread Chapters 3 (multiplication) and 5 (division) to see whether they contain any problems or activities that you'd like your students to experience first. In this chapter, the children revisit some of these same activities using larger numbers, plus some new intellectually stimulating problems, as they multiply and divide. ■

The Learning Environment

Continue to support your students as they use models to solve problems involving multiplication and division.

Many textbooks and standardized tests are intended to move children quickly to numerical representations by teaching them to manipulate numbers using a specific procedure for multiplication or division. Resist this intent. Continue to encourage the use of models such as manipulatives or pictures so children bring meaning to these two operations.

For example, if your students have played *Leftovers* (Chapter 5), they shared a given number of colored tiles over a given number of plates. Their division equations showed the sharing of these manipulatives. In a story problem, as children figure out how many eggs there are in three dozen, often they will draw pictures of the egg cartons, then assign number labels (such as skip-counts by 12) before they represent the problem with a multiplication equation.

Encourage students to use words so as to bring even more meaning to their equations for multiplication and division.

Words help children bring sense to the numbers they are using. One child might write, *I know one egg carton has 12 eggs, so two egg cartons have 24 eggs and three egg cartons have 36 eggs.* Another might write a word/number equation: *3 cartons × 12 eggs in each carton = 36 eggs in all.* Using words to explain their thinking step by step helps children make better sense of their problem solving.

By having students use two strategies while solving multiplication and division problems, you nudge them toward numerical reasoning that represents their models. When your students draw a picture of three egg cartons and then skip-count (12, 24, 36) or add (12 + 12 + 12), they are assigning numbers. If you encourage them to present a second strategy, they may bring the concrete reasoning gained from using models to more abstract numerical equations (3 × 12 = 36).

Have children record their step-by-step problem solving on papers they organize themselves.

Provide fewer preformatted recording sheets and support the children in presenting their work completely and convincingly on their own. You may want to review the material on what makes a math paper strong in Chapter 5 (pages 142–43), which recommends placing the title of the problem at the top of the page with the child's name; clearly indicates the question; and includes words, numbers, and/or labeled drawings to explain the reasoning. Most third graders need help in spacing or arranging their work throughout the page instead of squeezing it into a tiny, hard-to-read space. Encourage your students to include number labels on their drawings, to indicate the connection between the drawings and their mathematical reasoning.

The Mathematics

Children make sense of multiplication and division situations by thinking of equal-size groups.

If you've posed a problem to your students such as "How many eggs are there in three cartons?" ask them if they combined equal-size groups to get their answer. If so, how did they do so—and why? Help them understand that this strategy enables them to multiply as well as add.

Or if the children are figuring out how to share fifteen tiles among five plates, ask them, "Are all the tiles being shared in equal-size groups among the five plates? If so, how?" Keep reinforcing the idea that whenever children multiply or divide, they are dealing with equal-size groups.

Some children are ready to break numbers into friendly or familiar parts as they solve multiplication problems involving larger numbers. Others are not.

If your students revisit *The Doorbell Rang* (Chapter 5) to figure out how many cookies are on Grandma's tray, they'll see thirteen rows with six cookies in each row. Most of them will want to make sense of the problem by drawing the tray, then skip-counting or adding. Support these strategies.

Wait until someone suggests 6×13 as a strategy. Take this opportunity to remind students how they decompose double-digit numbers into two addends when they add. Suggest that they try that now, with Grandma's cookie tray. If they think of 13 as $10 + 3$, how can they multiply? Then have the children help you break the two-digit factor 13 into its friendly parts: $10 + 3$. The resulting equation would be: $(6 \times 10) + (6 \times 3) = 60 + 18 = 78$.

Remind yourself that this numerical reasoning constitutes a big step for most third graders. Therefore, guard against teaching this as a procedure they *must* follow. Present it as one possible strategy. To make the distributive property of multiplication more visual or concrete, you could break a 6-by-13 rectangular window array into two arrays. (See Figure 8–1.)

The children who understand the strategy of breaking two-digit factors into friendly parts soon start using it with one-digit times two-digit problems. For example, 4 × 35 becomes 4 × 30 plus 4 × 5. The partial products are 120 and 20, respectively. Children who do not find this numerical thinking meaningful will continue to use pictures, adding, skip-counting, and other ways to reason.

Children use multiplication to make sense of division and to check the correctness of their division thinking.

As students grapple with division problems, they often multiply. For instance, consider this problem: "How many cars are there if the total number of wheels is thirty-two and there are four wheels on each car?" In this case, a child might think, "I know that four times eight equals thirty-two,

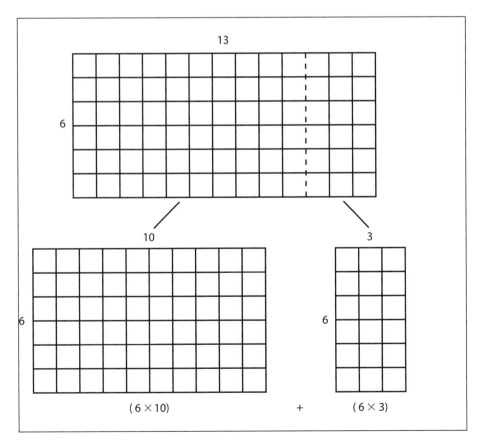

FIGURE 8–1 ◀

Breaking this window-pane array into two separate arrays helps demonstrate the distributive property of multiplication, and may make sense to some of your students.

so there must be eight cars." Another child might draw pictures of cars and carefully group four wheels on each until he or she has used all thirty-two wheels on eight different cars. To check the thinking behind these drawings, the child reasons, "Four wheels times eight cars does equal thirty-two wheels, so this makes sense." Encourage multiplication as a "companion" operation for grasping division.

Some children begin to use multiplication to check their division. For example, they realize that seventy pencils shared among twenty students equals three pencils per child, with ten leftovers. They prove this by checking: $3 \times 20 = 60$ pencils; 60 pencils + 10 leftovers = 70 pencils.

Mathematics Throughout the Day

Daily Attendance Revisited

If your classroom is like many, the students gather attendance for the entire third grade each day. If most classes have up to twenty students, attendance counts might be something like 18, 20, 19, and 20 on any particular day. When the children figure the total of these four numbers, they might think $18 + 19 = 37$ and $2 \times 20 = 40$. Finally, $37 + 40 = 77$. They could also add $20 + 20$. However, if there are two equal-size numbers, encourage students to also use multiplication to get the total and check their thinking.

Using these strategies to calculate attendance totals gives children opportunities to multiply one-digit and two-digit numbers.

Today's Temperature Revisited

If your students record daily temperatures on a bar graph, they can continue to compare temperatures on their own graph or compare results to the temperature elsewhere in the world by looking at a newspaper or online information source. This activity gives them continued practice with comparison problem solving.

Inventory of Classroom Manipulatives

If your students are comfortable working with larger numbers, ask each table group to take a tub of manipulatives (e.g., pattern blocks, colored tiles, Unifix cubes, interlocking cubes, colored wooden cubes) and figure out how many manipulatives there are in that tub. If you do not have all these manipulatives, invite the children to inventory books or other supplies in the classroom. Tablemates work in groups of four over several days as they come up with ways to group and count all these items. Thus you may want them to work at other locations around the room instead of at their desks. As they group and count, they'll find that multiplication comes in handy for figuring out the total number of objects in several equal-size groups. The idea that multiplication saves time or is computationally efficient has real meaning in this investigation. (See Figures 8–2 and 8–3.)

Extensions

Students inventory classroom supplies such as reams of copy paper and boxes of pencils and erasers in the faculty supply room. Consider using the information they compile to order supplies for the next school year.

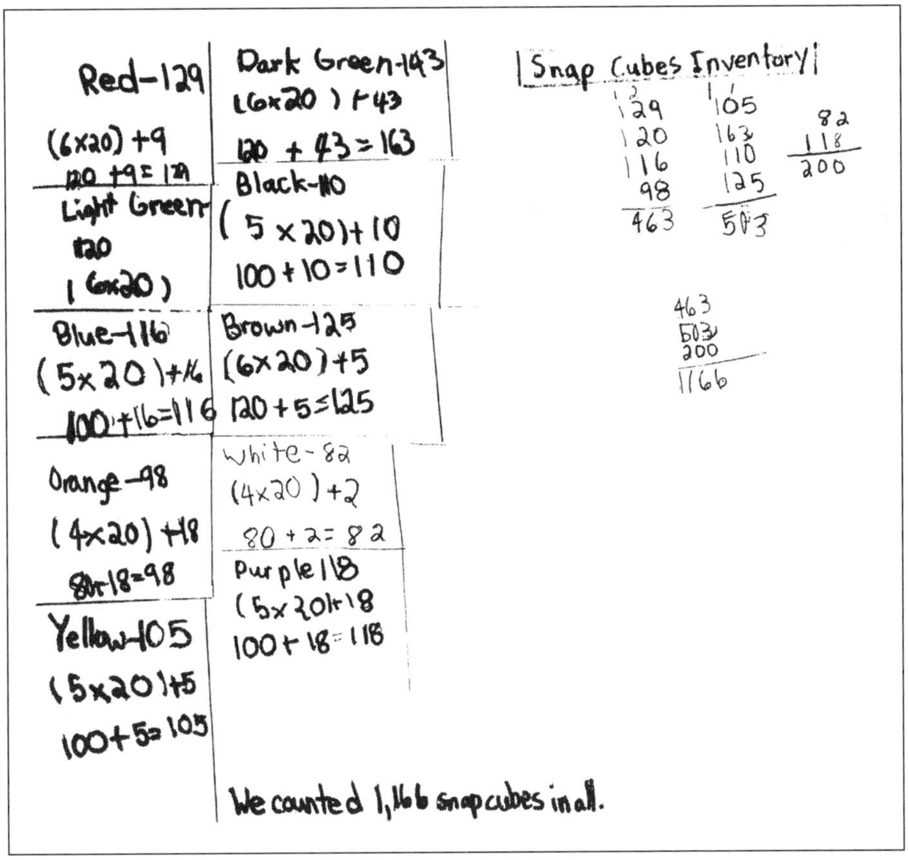

FIGURE 8–2   ◀

Rebecca showed how her table group calculated the number of Snap Cubes in a tub.

FIGURE 8–3 ▶

Kihyun's table group counted Unifix cubes.

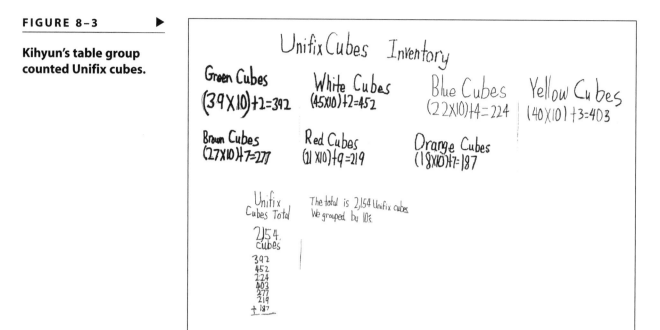

Games

These games are old favorites with new twists. Rather than have children memorize their multiplication combinations in isolation, they use these combinations while playing the games.

Leftovers **Revisited**

In Chapter 5, *Leftovers* involved sharing fifteen tiles among one, two, three, four, five, or six paper plates (depending on the roll of a die.) Now have students play the game with a number cube whose faces are labeled *4, 5, 6, 7, 8,* and *9.* Provide the corresponding number of plates, along with more tiles, such as twenty-four.

Circles and Stars **Revisited**

As mentioned in Chapter 5, instead of having students play this game with a die, give them number cubes whose faces are labeled *4, 5, 6, 7, 8,* and *9.* Before the game begins, ask, "What is the smallest product possible? The largest product? How do you know that?" (The smallest product possible is $4 \times 4 = 16$. The largest product possible is $9 \times 9 = 81$.)

After the children have played many games with the number cube ask them what is the smallest total number of stars possible after seven rounds of this game. Some students may imagine seven recording pages, each with four circles filled with four stars, and then multiply: 7 × 16 = 112. Ask, "What is the largest total possible in all seven rounds?" (The answer would be 7 × 81 = 567.)

Post a new *Circles and Stars* products chart. On the old chart, you put tally marks next to the products that came up most often when students played the game with a regular die. Start a new chart for this different version of the game. This chart would go from 16 to 81.

Also continue encouraging the children to record a division equation as well as a multiplication equation on each round of the game, as you did in Chapter 5.

Multiplication Bingo Revisited

Have students refer to the new *Circles and Stars* products chart to see which products come up most often with the number cube. Ask them to use this information to fill in their *Multiplication Bingo* grid. (See Chapter 3.) Finally, have them use the number cube instead of the regular die as they play this game.

Multiplication Tic-Tac-Toe

This game gives student practice with larger products and with combinations for 7s, 8s, and 9s. See below and also Blackline Masters for instructions with the game board.

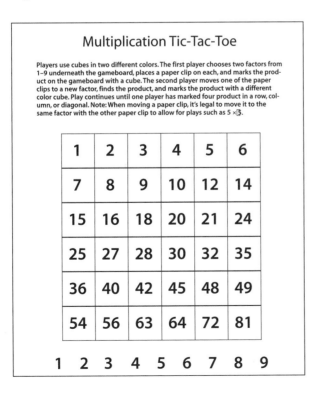

Multiplication Tic-Tac-Toe

Players use cubes in two different colors. The first player chooses two factors from 1–9 underneath the gameboard, places a paper clip on each, and marks the product on the gameboard with a cube. The second player moves one of the paper clips to a new factor, finds the product, and marks the product with a different color cube. Play continues until one player has marked four product in a row, column, or diagonal. Note: When moving a paper clip, it's legal to move it to the same factor with the other paper clip to allow for plays such as 5 × 5.

1	2	3	4	5	6
7	8	9	10	12	14
15	16	18	20	21	24
25	27	28	30	32	35
36	40	42	45	48	49
54	56	63	64	72	81

1 2 3 4 5 6 7 8 9

The instructions for *Multiplication Tic-Tac-Toe* suggest that partners play with counters in two different colors. As an alternative, they can use different-colored beans or different coins as markers. In my classroom, the children circle numbers on the game sheet with different-color pens or pencils for each partner.

Measurement

Estimate and Measure Revisited (Linear)

Last month, did you have your students measure the length, width, and thickness of books using inch and centimeter rulers? If not, consider having them do so now.

Once children feel confident measuring smaller objects in inches and centimeters, they can begin using yardsticks or meter sticks to measure larger objects, such as bookshelves, desks, doors, and so forth. But first they need to understand the number of inches and rulers in a yardstick and the number of centimeters in a meter stick. If it takes two yardsticks plus twenty-eight more inches to span a classroom shelf, the children could figure 36 + 36 + 28. Alternatively, they might think (2 × 36) + 28.

Beans in a Jar Revisited (Volume)

Materials

- 1 pint-size glass canning jar
- 1 one-quarter measuring cup
- 1 bag of kidney beans
- 1 rubber band
- overhead projector

Instructions

1. Wrap the rubber band around the glass jar at the halfway point.

2. Fill a $\frac{1}{4}$ measuring cup with kidney beans.

3. Pour the beans out on the overhead.

4. Have the children help you group and count the beans. (You should get a total of about 80.)

5. Put the beans back in the measuring cup, then pour them into the glass jar.

6. Ask the class to estimate the number of measuring cupfuls it will take to fill the jar halfway. Record the range of estimates on the board.

7. Scoop up another $\frac{1}{4}$ cupful of beans and place them in the jar. Ask if anyone wants to change his or her estimate.

8. Continue until you have used four measuring cups to fill the jar to the halfway point.

9. Have students pair up and explore the following problems:

   It takes four cupfuls of beans to fill the jar to the halfway point. Each cupful holds 86 beans.

   - *How many beans are there in the jar at the halfway point? Show how you arrived at your answer.*

   - *How many beans do you think the entire jar will hold? Show how you arrived at your estimate.*

Cubes in a Box Revisited (Area and Volume)

Materials

- 1 7-by-9-inch box (e.g., for holding a silk scarf or other similarly-sized object) per pair of students
- 1 4 × 4 × 4-inch box (e.g., for holding mugs)
- bag of 2-centimter or 1-inch colored cubes per pair of students

Instructions

See Chapter 3 for more details on this activity, where the children estimate how many cubes it will take to cover the bottom of a box. A 7-by-9-inch box enables students to multiply one-digit and two-digit numbers; e.g., 8 rows times 11 cubes in each row. Then they figure the number of cubes in two layers.

Next, have the children use their mug boxes. Once they have figured the area of one layer, they must figure out how many cubes there are in five layers.

Handfuls of Cubes

This problem comes from *Teaching Arithmetic: Lessons for Introducing Division, Grades 3–4* by Maryann Wickett, Susan Ohanian, and Marilyn Burns (2002).

Materials

- handfuls of small counting cubes per student

Instructions

1. Model the activity by taking nine cubes and grouping them by 2s. You'll get four groups of two, with one remainder.

2. On the board, write the equation that represents this division situation: *9 ÷ 2 = 4 R1.*

3. Ask the children, "If we add ten more cubes to the original nine and then *group* all of the cubes by twos, how many groups of two will we get?"

4. After the class discusses various strategies, write (under the equation mentioned above) the division equation that represents grouping the nineteen cubes by 2s. Have the children check this thinking with multiplication:

$$9 ÷ 2 = 4 \ R1 \qquad 2 × 4 = 8 \qquad 8 + 1 = 9$$

$$19 ÷ 2 = 9 \ R1 \qquad 2 × 9 = 18 \qquad 18 + 1 = 19$$

5. Add ten more cubes, then repeat the above process. The resulting equation is:

$$29 ÷ 2 = 14 \ R1$$

6. Now have the class figure out what will happen when they group thirty-nine cubes by 2s. The corresponding equation is:

$$39 ÷ 2 = 19 \ R1$$

7. Again add ten more cubes, to get 49 ÷ 2 = 24 R1

8. Ask the children what patterns they notice in the list of equations that's growing on the board:

$$9 ÷ 2 = 1 \ R1$$
$$19 ÷ 2 = 9 \ R1$$
$$29 ÷ 2 = 14 \ R1$$
$$39 ÷ 2 = 19 \ R1$$
$$49 ÷ 2 = 24 \ R1$$

They may notice that each equation has a remainder of 1, or they may see that each answer is 5 greater than the previous answer. Discuss and record these and other observations.

9. Now have students complete the following activity:

    Take a handful of cubes.

    Count them and record the total on a piece of paper.

    Figure the number of pairs (groups of 2) in your handful. Record.

    Add ten more cubes. Figure the new number of pairs (groups of 2). Record.

    Do this another four times. Record each time.

    Write about the patterns you notice.

10. When the children have completed this investigation, list the first five equations of half a dozen students and look at the patterns once again. Are they the same or different than the ones the children saw when you listed equations on the board at the beginning of the investigation? You will find a lengthy pattern discussion connected to this problem in *Teaching Arithmetic: Lessons for Introducing Division, Grades 3–4.*

Extensions

Students grab handfuls of cubes and group them into 3s, 4s, 5s, 6s, and so on, and continue to look for patterns when adding ten more cubes repeatedly.

Stars in Several Minutes

This activity gives students practice with larger numbers.

Instructions

1. Have students draw as many stars as they can in one minute, then in two minutes, and then in three minutes.

2. Ask them to group and count their stars in each category.

3. Invite the children to look for opportunities to multiply and divide. For example, if a child drew thirty-five stars in one minute, seventy stars in two minutes, and 105 stars in three minutes, he could begin by working with the results from the one-minute category. The corresponding word/number equation would be: 35 stars grouped so there are 5 stars in each group = 7 groups of stars. The student uses division and multiplication equations to represent his reasoning:

$$35 \div 5 = 7$$

$$7 \times 5 = 35$$

Suppose this student also wanted to work with the 105 stars he drew during three minutes. If the child grouped the stars by 10s, the corresponding word/number equation could read: 105 stars grouped so there are 10 stars in each group = 10 groups of stars and 5 leftovers. He might also use these notations:

$$105 \div 10 = 10 \; R5$$

$$10 \times 10 = 100$$

$$100 + R5 = 105$$

If your children are tired of drawing, grouping, and counting stars, switch to digits, alphabet letters, or dollar signs.

Money

TEACHER-TO-TEACHER TALK Earlier this year, you may have had your students practice grouping 100 ants in one line, then two equal lines, then four, five, and finally ten equal lines. As they did this, they were dealing with the factors of 100: 1×100, 2×50, 4×25, 5×20, and 10×10. As children use multiplication to make sense of division, they can use these factor pairs for 100 to solve money problems. That's because there are two \$.50 in \$1.00, four \$.25 in \$1.00, five \$.20 in \$1.00, and ten \$.10 in \$1.00. Some children grasp the connection between division problems involving 100 and money amounts by using their money bags:

\$1.00 shared equally among 4 children = \$.25 for each child. \$1.00 ÷ 4 = \$.25, and \$.25 × 4 = \$1.00

\$1.25 shared equally among 5 children = \$.25 per child. \$1.25 ÷ 5 = \$.25, and \$.25 × 5 = \$1.25

\$1.35 shared equally among 5 children = \$.27 per child.

\$1.35 ÷ 5 = \$.27, and \$.25 × 5 = \$1.25 R \$.10

\$.10 ÷ 5 = \$.02

\$.25 + \$.02 = \$.27

Lunch Money and Book Orders

Money spent (e.g., on lunch) or raised during the school day offers rich possibilities for multiplication and division practice. Regarding lunch, be sensitive to those children who are on a free or reduced lunch program. Pretend lunch-money problems based on a make-believe school that has just one lunch price. For example:

At Arrow Math School, 8 children brought money for school lunch. Each child brought $2.25. What is the total amount of money these children brought?

Your students can use addition or multiplication to figure this out. In either case, support their thinking for separating dollar amounts from cents amounts:

Strategy One: Multiplication

$$8 \times \$2.00 = \$16.00, \ 8 \times \$.20 = \$1.60, \ 8 \times \$.05 = \$.40$$

then $16.00 + $1.60 + $.40 = $18.00 or

Strategy Two: Addition

$$\$2.00 + \$2.00 + \$2.00 + \$2.00 + \$2.00 + \$2.00 + \$2.00 + \$2.00 = \$16.00$$

$$\$.20 + \$.20 + \$.20 + \$.20 + \$.20 + \$.20 + \$.20 + \$.20 = \$1.60$$

$$\$.05 + \$.05 + \$.05 + \$.05 + \$.05 + \$.05 + \$.05 + \$.05 = \$.40$$

then $16.00 + $1.60 + $.40 = $18.00

Another math opportunity arises when you order books for the classroom. Often you'll order several books that cost the same; e.g., seven books that cost $3.95 each. Present these scenarios to your students and ask them to multiply.

If it seems appropriate, you may initially want to round money amounts for these sorts of problems to a multiple of 10. For example, instead of $3.95 each, make the books $4.00 each, then present students with the following sharing division problem:

The total for the books is $28.00.

There are 7 books that cost the same amount of money.

How much does each book cost?

With school-lunch problems, pretend that one lunch costs $2.00. Then present the following grouping division problem:

The total for the lunches is $16.00.

Each lunch costs $2.00.

How many children bought lunches?

Field trips provide additional opportunities for children to solve multiplication and division problems that connect to their own lives.

Pennies and Dimes

This problem is adapted from Chapter 9 in *Teaching Arithmetic: Lessons for Introducing Division, Grades 3–4*. See that book for more information on the problem and possible extensions.

Materials

- about 1500 pennies if you do the activity as a whole-class lesson; about 300 pennies if you offer it during station time

Instructions

1. Grab a handful of pennies, then group and count them.

2. Show on the board how you grouped and counted your handful. Make the connection between grouping and counting pennies and how the children grouped and counted raisins.

3. Ask the class, "If I wanted to trade all of my pennies for dimes, how many dimes could I get?"

4. On the board, write the word/number equation that would help you solve this problem. For example, if you grabbed twenty-three pennies, write *23 pennies equals 2 dimes R3*.

5. Have the children help you write words showing that this is a grouping division problem:

   23 pennies grouped so there are 10 pennies in each group = 2 groups or 2 dimes with 3 leftover pennies.

   Write two different division equations to represent this thinking:

   $$23 \div 10 = 2 \text{ R3} \qquad 10)\overline{23}^{\,2\text{ R3}}$$

6. Hand out an open container holding at least 300 pennies to each table or group of four or five students. Have each child group and count his or her own handful of pennies. They record their work on paper by circling their equal-size groups and not circling remainders. Inside their circles they draw pennies or put a number for the pennies. They also draw or use numbers to represent remainders. Then they record the total number of pennies they have. Finally, they write two division equations showing how many dimes they could get for their pennies, or they use words and numbers to explain their thinking.

7. As the children work, fill in a T-chart with the students' results using the format shown below. Leave large spaces between each line in the chart.

# of pennies	# of dimes
10	1
20	2
30	3
40	4
50	5

8. Ask the children to state their results. As they respond, fill in the chart with the answers that have remainders. Also include your "penny grab." For example, if you had twenty-three pennies, make the following entry between the "20" and "30" lines on the T-chart:

# of pennies	# of dimes
23	2 R3

9. After filling in the T-chart, ask the children what they notice. Do they see any patterns? Record their responses.

Extensions

- Students pair up with their side-by-side table partners and combine their pennies. Then they count the total number of the combined pennies and the number of dimes they could get for them.
- All four students at a table combine and then group and count the total number of pennies grabbed. Then they figure the numbers of dimes they could get for that total.

TEACHER-TO-TEACHER TALK In *Teaching Arithmetic: Lessons for Introducing Division*, the authors emphasize that children "learn that the remainder from dividing by ten is the same as the number in the ones place in the dividend, and that the dividend with the number in the ones place removed is the quotient. For example, $32 \div 10 = 3$ R2, $163 \div 10 = 16$ R3, and so on" (2002, 85).

Literature-Based Activities

Continue to find math problems in the books you're reading aloud to the class or in the books students are reading on their own. For example, in Roald Dahl's *Matilda*, five-and-a-half-year-old Matilda uses mental math to figure out 2×28 and 2×487 on her first day in Miss Honey's class. You can have your students solve these and other, comparable problems.

> **TEACHER-TO-TEACHER TALK**   Children love to have the same picture book read to them again and again. As you reread *The Doorbell Rang* and *Amanda Bean's Amazing Dream*, you will uncover new mathematics problems with larger numbers to solve.
>
> In *The Doorbell Rang*, Grandma brings in a tray of cookies that have thirteen rows with six cookies in each row. First, have the children figure out the total number of cookies (if you haven't already assigned this activity). Then have them share these cookies equally with the whole class and decide what to do with the leftovers.
>
> Using *Amanda Bean's Amazing Dream*, students can do two-step problems that involve figuring out the number of windowpanes in several windows on the front of each building in the story. First, they figure the number of panes in one window. If one window has six rows with three panes in each row, there are eighteen panes in that window. Second, they figure out how many windowpanes there are in all the windows that have these same arrays. For example, if there are six windows that have eighteen panes in each on the front of a building, how many panes are there in all six windows?

Milk Money

In *Annabelle Swift, Kindergartner* by Amy Schwartz, Annabelle has an older sister, Lucy, who helps prepare her for kindergarten by teaching her fancy stuff—such as geography, the color of Raving Scarlet, and ways to count change past 100. On the first day of kindergarten, Annabelle is embarrassed several times as she shares things Lucy had taught her. Finally, snack time arrives, and she sees an opportunity to demonstrate her knowledge. The teacher, Mr. Blum, asks each child to put his or her $.06 in milk money on the rug. He is very surprised when Annabelle counts all the money, including nickels and pennies, and correctly figures their total value as $1.08. Thanks to her ability with counting change, Annabelle gets to be Milk Monitor.

Stop reading the story aloud at this point and pose this grouping division problem to your students:

Annabelle took $1.08 to the cafeteria.

Each carton of milk cost $.06.

How many milks did she buy?

(See Figure 8–4.)
After the children have figured out the answer, have a whole-class discussion. Then read the rest of the story to see if the class's answer matches the answer from the story.

Extensions

- Students work on milk-money problems based on the number of milks bought each day in kindergarten at your school.

- You generate problems based on how many children are purchasing milk at lunch each day in your classroom. Be sensitive to children who are on the free-milk program.

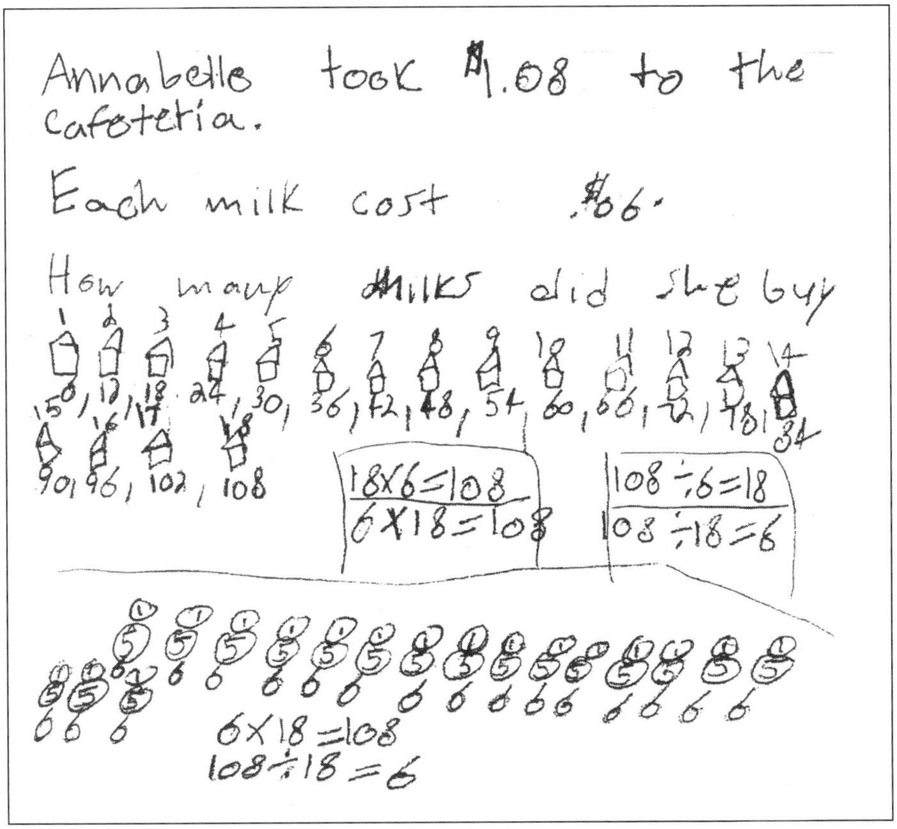

FIGURE 8–4 ◀

Susan used drawings and numbers to figure out the milk-money problem.

Class Pets

In *How Much Is That Guinea Pig in the Window?* by Joanne Rocklin, Mr. Day's class raises $50.00 from a bake sale. They now have enough money to buy a class pet. When they visit Mrs. Piper's Pet Palace, they find that the pet they can most afford is a guinea pig. The story offers many opportunities for children to add, subtract, multiply, and divide. Marilyn Burns provides some problem-solving suggestions at the end of the book:

> *If two bunnies cost $60.00, how much does one bunny cost?*

> *Frogs cost $10.00 for three. Mice cost $5.00 for two. Which costs more: one frog or one mouse? Explain your reasoning.*

> *Since the pet-store owner tells the students that they can purchase one month's supply of guinea-pig food ($5.00) at half price, the water bowl ($2.00) at half price, and the nut treat ($.50) at half price, how much will each thing cost?*

> *How much money will the students in the story need to buy guinea-pig food for a year if one month's supply costs $5.00?*

Ants in a Line

By rereading *One Hundred Hungry Ants* by Elinor J. Pinczes, you can help your students revisit the different arrangements of the 100 ants and the division notations for those arrangements mentioned in Chapter 5. Then, ask the children how they would arrange the ants into three lines. The corresponding word/number equation would read *100 ants divided equally into 3 lines = 33 ants in each line with R1.*

In *Teaching Arithmetic: Lessons for Introducing Division, Grades 3–4,* the authors present the following problem:

> *There are 20 ants going to the picnic in one long line. What would happen if the ants rearranged themselves into two lines? Three lines? Four lines? (and so on up to ten lines)*

If you pose this problem to your students, write on the board:

20 Hungry Ants

1 line of 20
2 lines
3 lines
4 lines
5 lines

6 lines

7 lines

8 lines

9 lines

10 lines

TEACHER-TO-TEACHER TALK If your students did the *Classroom Groups* problem in Chapter 5 and there were twenty children in the class, they'll find this problem familiar.

In *Classroom Groups*, the children do grouping problems. They know the total number of children and the number of children in each group. They have to figure out how many groups are needed.

In the ants problem, the children are doing sharing. They know the total number of ants and the number of groups or lines. They need to figure out how many ants are in each line.

Have the children figure out the twenty ants shared into different numbers of lines, then write their responses on the board.

Extensions

Using their thinking about the factors for 100 and their work with money, students tackle these grouping division problems:

120 ants shared so there are 20 ants in each line equals how many lines?

125 ants shared so there are 25 ants in each line equals how many lines?

Doubling Ants

In *The 512 Ants on Sullivan Street* by Carol A. Losi, a little girl and her family go on a picnic. The girl notices one ant carrying a crumb, then two ants carrying some pieces of plum, four ants with a barbecued chip, eight ants with a crisp bacon strip, and so forth. The story continues until there are 512 ants.

The book gives your students an opportunity to think about numbers that double repeatedly. In the math activities suggested by Marilyn Burns at the end of the book, children are asked to explain what it means to double a number. If the story went on, what number would come after 512, and how do they know that? Have the children record using both addition and multiplication as they double numbers:

Addition	*Subtraction*
1	1
2 = 1 + 1	2 = 2 × 1
4 = 2 + 2	4 = 2 × 2
8 = 4 + 4	8 = 2 × 4
16 = 8 + 8	16 = 2 × 8
32 = 16 + 16	32 = 2 × 16

Extensions

Students decide if the doubling of numbers in this story produces the number 100. (It does not: 2, 4, 8, 16, 32, 64, 128, 256, 512.) Then they figure out whether they would get 100 if they started with the number 3 instead of 2 and kept doubling. They conduct the same investigation with starting numbers of 4, 5, 6, and so forth.

Shared Elephants

In *17 Kings and 42 Elephants* by Margaret Mahy, seventeen kings journey with forty-two elephants through the jungle. The book has gorgeous batik paintings and clever words that take the form of a rollicking nonsense poem. You and your class will love reading this story again and again.

When the children are ready, pose this problem:

If the kings divide up or share the elephants equally, how many elephants would each king get? What would you do with any leftover elephants?

The children can work on the problem individually or in pairs. (See Figure 8–5.)

Extensions

Students solve the following problems:

How many elephants could seventeen kings have so that there would be no leftover elephants? Think of several possible answers.

If there are forty-two elephants, how many kings could have a fair share so that there would be no leftover elephants?

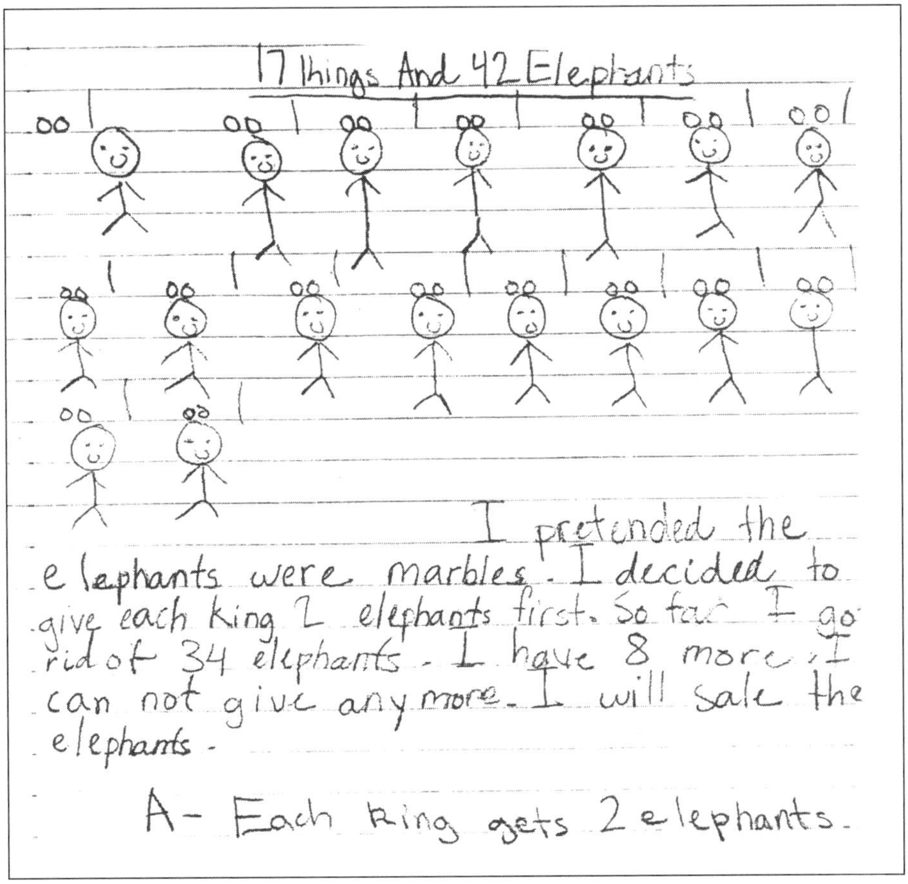

FIGURE 8–5 ◀

Deon showed how seventeen kings would share forty-two elephants—and what he would do with the "leftover elephants."

Story Problems

Teacher-Generated Problems

As you think about division problems as sharing or grouping, you will begin noticing opportunities to provide practice with both using classroom and other situations.

For example, when your students line up for P. E., count off the first three, then let that group run to the end of the school yard to join the P. E. teacher. After a pause, count off the next three youngsters. Suddenly, you've got a handy grouping problem:

When I count you off in groups of three as you go to P. E., how many groups of three are there? How many remainders? What do we do with the remainders? How did you figure all this out?

Here's another classroom situation that lends itself to division problems: One of my students brought in seventy pencils as a gift to the class before winter break. I held onto the pencils, waiting until we began our division discussions in January before handing them out. Then I posed the following problem:

Sarah gave the class 70 pencils.
There are 20 students in the class.
How can we share these pencils fairly?

My students used a wide range of strategies to make sense of the situation. (See Figures 8–6, 8–7, and 8–8.)

After the students finished their problem solving, as a class we came up with the corresponding word/number equations and the multiplication and division equations. The children added these to their work.

FIGURE 8–6 ▶

Juan used pictures to make sense of the problem.

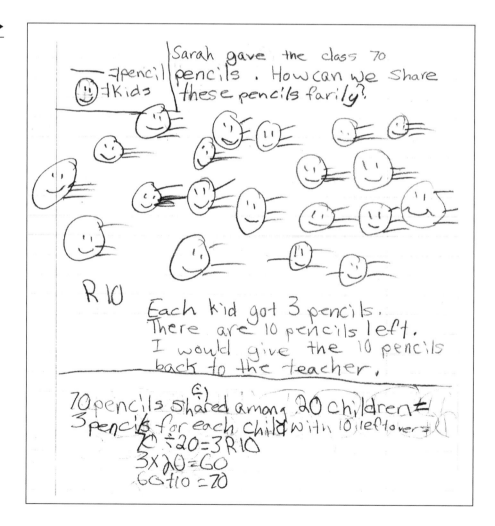

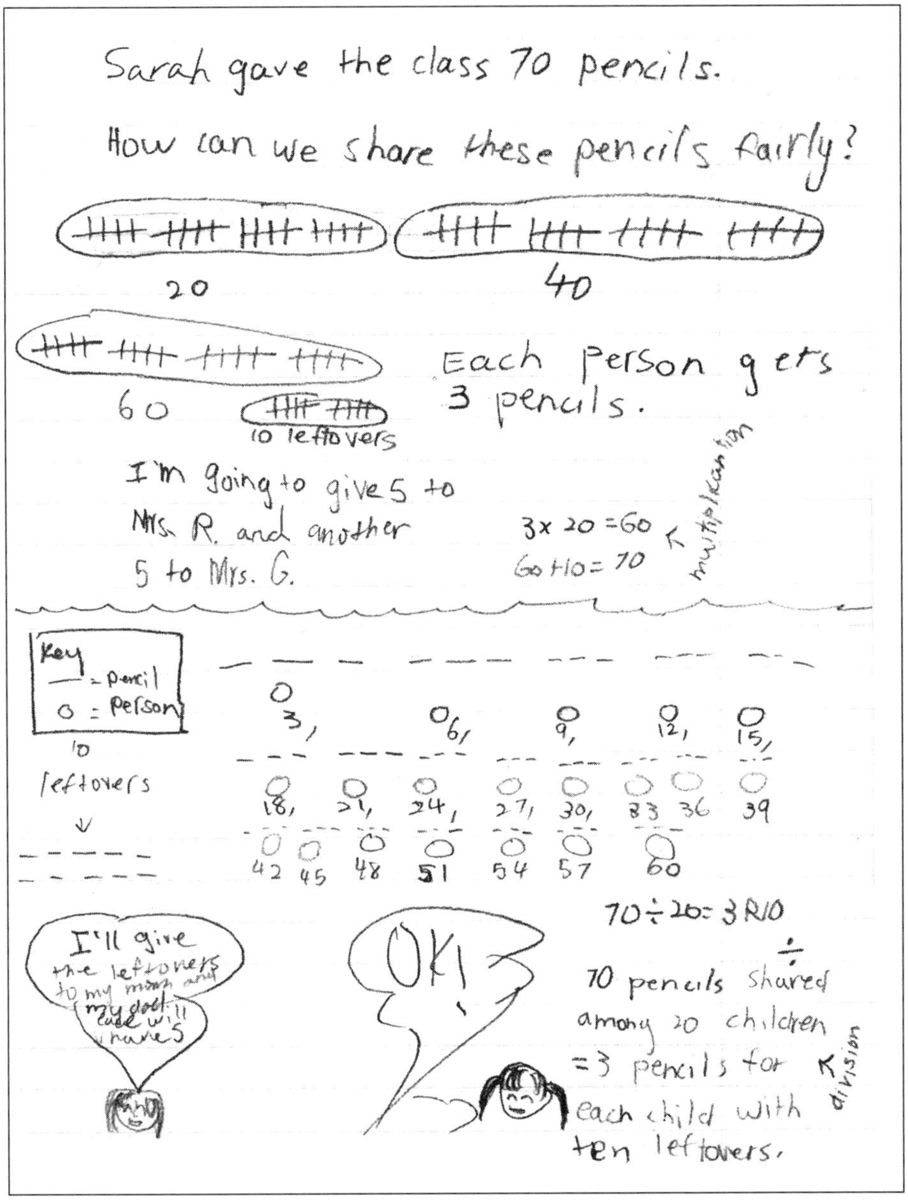

FIGURE 8–7   ◀

First Latasha used tallies to represent pencils grouped in 20s. Then she used numbers to represent pencils.

You can also generate division problems from sources outside the classroom or from extensions of activities you introduced to your students earlier. For example, if your class has figured out how many eggs "three dozen" is during the *Things That Come in Groups* activities, you might want to pose the following problem (as suggested by Marilyn Burns in *About Teaching Mathematics, Second Edition*):

There were two cartons in the refrigerator with a dozen eggs in each plus 3 extra eggs. Mom liked to eat an omelette each day and used 2 eggs to make

FIGURE 8–8   ▶

Peter used numbers to count groups of 20s by 1s.

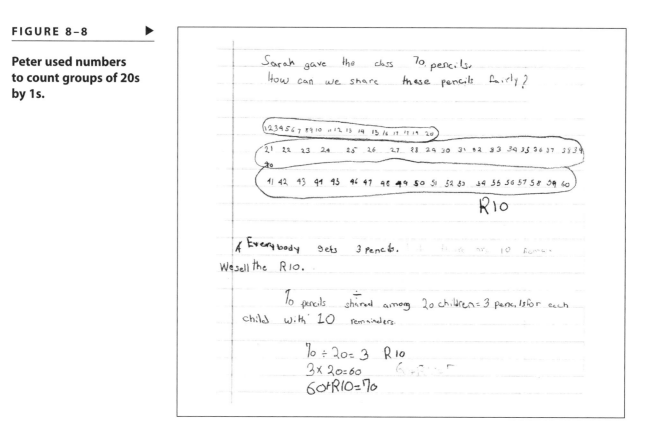

each omelette. How many days could she make omelettes before she had to buy more eggs?

Scenarios involving the sharing or grouping of food serve as excellent sources for problems. For example, your students can share fifty-four raisins equally between two children, three children, and four children as an extension of the raisin-sharing activities described earlier in this book. (See Figures 8–9, 8–10, and 8–11.)

Student-Generated Problems

As in you did in earlier units, provide multiplication and division equations and have the children write problems that make sense for these equations. Then encourage them to solve their own problems using one or two strategies.

At this time of year, it can be interesting to have children pick their own numbers, write their own equations, then write their own problems. For multiplication, some youngsters will continue to use one-digit numbers. Others will venture into situations that require them to multiply one-digit numbers by two-digit numbers. You may also see children drawing on their interests to create problems. (See Figures 8–12 and 8–13.)

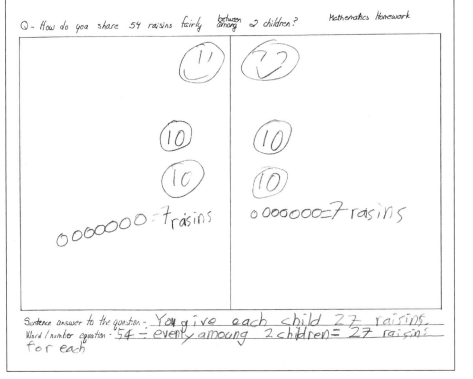

FIGURE 8–9 ◀

Salina showed how she should share fifty-four raisins between two children.

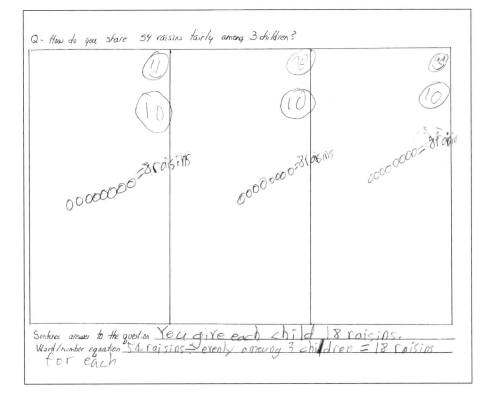

FIGURE 8–10 ◀

Yousif took this activity to the next level: sharing the raisins among three children.

FIGURE 8–11 ▶

Here's how Jarod would share fifty-four raisins among four children.

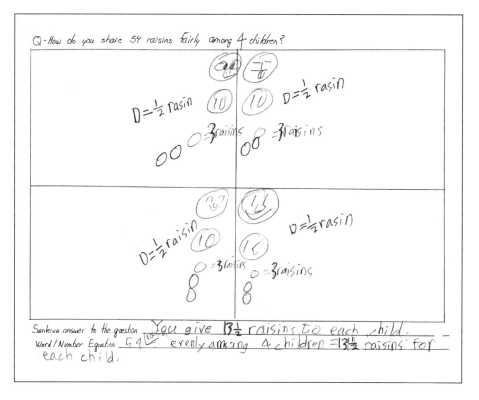

FIGURE 8–12 ▶

Aaron used his interest in chess to create a multiplication problem—using addition to solve it.

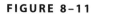

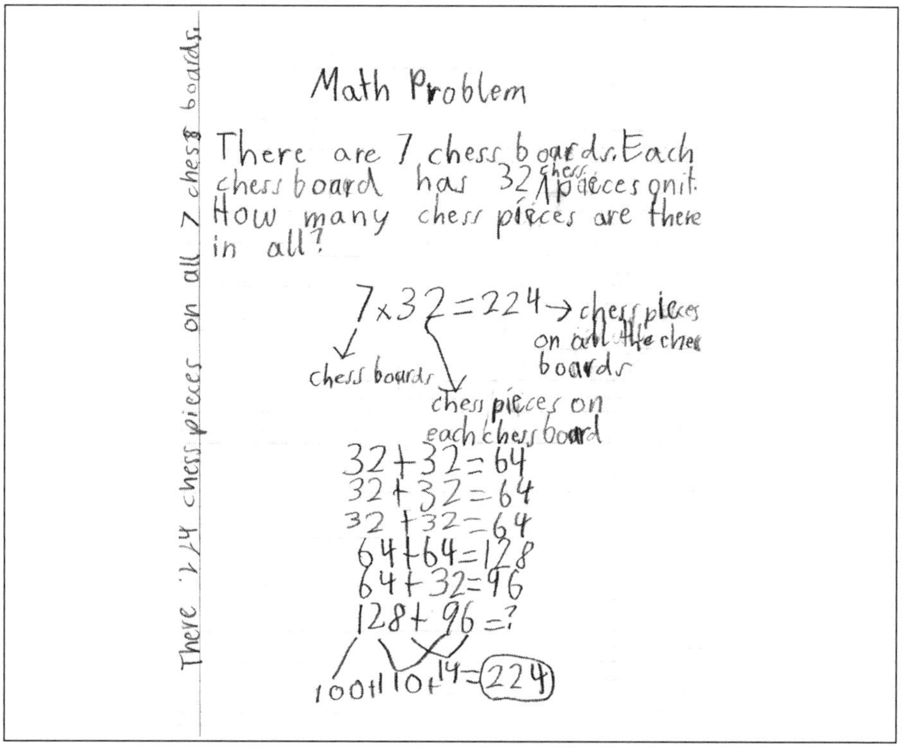

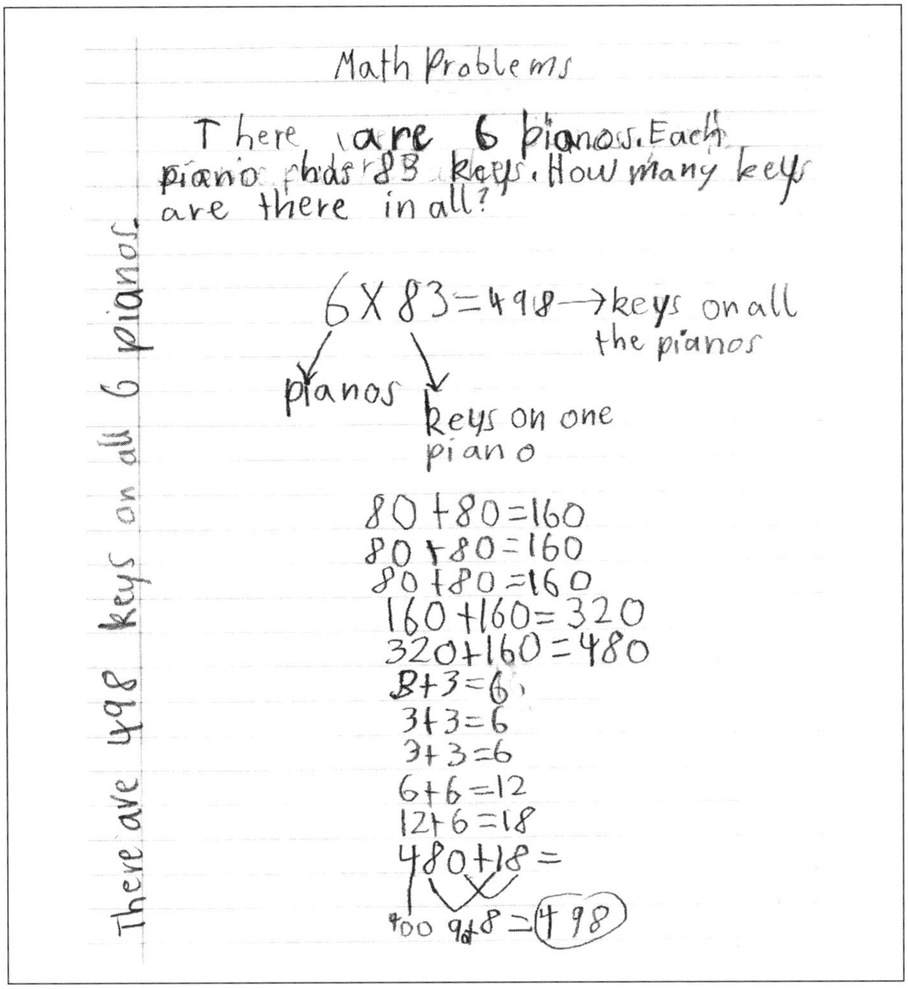

FIGURE 8–13 ◀

Though Aaron mis-
counted the number of
keys on a piano, he cre-
ated another interesting
multiplication problem
based on his interests.

Menu

Menu was first discussed at the end of Chapter 2. You may want to reread that section before you look over these suggestions here. Notice that these problems relate to books we have read and to school routines such as book orders and school lunch. Also, many of these problems have two questions. Some, such as *Cornell School Lunch*, are two-step problems because the answer to the second question depends on the answer to the first.

By this time of year, you expect your students to organize their papers on their own and show how they figured out the answer to each problem after they write the question. For this menu, children will need to provide a sentence answer and an equation for each question as well. (See Figure 8–14.) The students can place a checkmark or an X on the blank before each problem as they complete that problem. They choose the order in which they will do the problems and decide with whom they will work.

FIGURE 8–14 ▶

Angela made sense of the first Book Order question using two strategies.

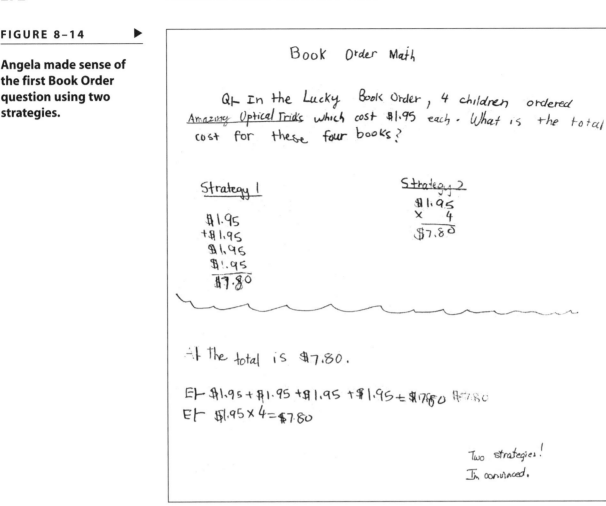

Making Sense of Multiplication and Division: Dinner-Menu Problems

__ *Little House in the Big Woods Questions*

Q1: How old was Laura Ingalls Wilder when she wrote this book in 1932? She was born in 1867.

Q2: How many years ago was this book written?

__ *Henry Huggins Questions*

Q1: Henry caught 1,103 worms. He needed to catch 1,331 worms. How many more worms did he need to catch?

Q2: Let's pretend that over two days Henry caught 1,103 earthworms. If he caught 637 earthworms the first day, how many did he catch the second day?

— *Cornell School Lunch Questions*

  Q1: If each school lunch including milk costs $2.25, how much do 5 school lunches cost?

  Q2: If you paid for these 5 lunches with a $20.00 bill, what would be your change?

— *Days Left in the Calendar Year Question*

  Q1: Monday, May 19, was the 139th day of the calendar year. How many days are left in 2003?

— *Book-Order Math Questions*

  Q1: In the Lucky Book Order, four children ordered Amazing Optical Tricks, which cost $ 1.95 each. What is the total cost for these four books?

  Q2: Seven children bought the Magic Treehouse Dinosaur Pack. *The total was $27.65. How much did each child have to pay?*

— *Pencil Order Questions*

  Q1: Mrs. Ronfeldt needs to order 9 pencils for each child for the next year. She will have 20 students. How many pencils must she order?

  Q2: The pencils come 6 in a package. How many packages will she need to order?

We provided a dessert menu for those children who finished the dinner menu early and who did complete and convincing work on each of their dinner-menu problems.

Making Sense of Multiplication and Division: Dessert-Menu Problems

Children who finished the Dinner Menu early with complete and convincing work on those problems can now begin on the Dessert Menu problems, using addition, subtraction, multiplication, and division. (See Figure 8–15.)

1. Use a separate recording sheet for each incomplete equation.

2. Write a story problem that makes sense for each incomplete equation.

3. Share your step-by-step work in solving the problem.

4. Use two strategies.

5. Write a sentence answer.

FIGURE 8–15 ▶

Nan worked on the 56 × 4 = __ problem from the Dessert Menu.

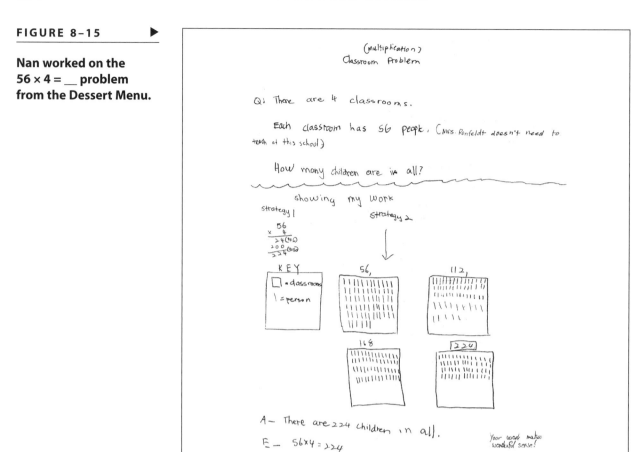

Here are the incomplete equations:

$$364 + 596 = \underline{}$$

$$452 - 198 = \underline{}$$

$$56 \times 4 = \underline{}$$

$$120 \div 10 = \underline{}$$

Chapter 9

TWO- AND THREE-DIMENSIONAL GEOMETRY

"The study of geometry in grades 3–5 requires thinking and doing. As students sort, build, draw, model, trace, measure, and construct, their capacity to visualize geometric relationships will develop."

Principles and Standards for School Mathematics
NCTM 2000, 165

Before you and the children spend time doing the three-dimensional geometry problems in this chapter, you might want to take a second look at any two-dimensional investigations that the class did not get to in December. (See Chapter 4.) ▪

The Learning Environment

Take delight in one another's company and ideas as the school year winds down.

As the school year draws to a close, teachers and students realize how much they care about one another. Celebrate this sense of community by making sure children have plenty of time to problem solve together, either as partners or in groups of four. Step back more and more, letting your third graders take the lead in their own learning.

Introduce long-lasting projects or investigations that build students' mathematical independence and persistence.

As children transition from third grade to fourth grade, they need to rely more on themselves for their learning and less on the adults in their lives. By having them work more independently on investigations, you are helping them prepare for the next school year.

The Mathematics

Children reason systematically as they work with shapes that build on another.

As students construct shapes that follow a rule or pattern (e.g., in each successive four toothpick pattern, one toothpick has been moved), they use "if this . . . then that" thinking. At the same time, they use spatial reasoning as they flip or rotate the shapes.

Children understand that three-dimensional shapes have specific attributes by which they are identified and named.

As children observe two-dimensional shapes (polygons) in their three-dimensional formats (polyhedra), they become familiar with the meaning of edges, faces, and corners. If you or a colleague has a commercial set of geometric shapes such as cubes, rectangular prisms, pyramids, cones, cylinders, spheres, and so forth, you can invite your students to assess what's similar and different about these shapes. For example, some shapes have flat and curved surfaces (cones, spheres, and cylinders), while others—called polyhedra—have only flat surfaces (rectangular prisms, cubes, pyramids).

Different polyhedra have different names; specifically, tetrahedron (four faces), pentahedron (five faces), hexahedron (six faces), heptahedron (seven faces), octahedron (eight faces), decahedron (ten faces), and dodecahedron (twelve faces). However, don't feel that your students need to know all these names. For now, just help them become familiar with the shapes and understand the basic characteristic of a polyhedra.

Children draw on previous measurement experiences.

As students engage in activities that require them to explore area and perimeter, you can remind them of the work they did on windowpane arrays. For example, as they make topless boxes with grid paper, they informally explore the surface area of five out of six faces. When they fit cubes inside these boxes, they are making sense of volume.

Four Toothpicks

In this sequence of activities, the children further develop spatial reasoning as they use rotational and mirror symmetry to discover the sixteen possible two-dimensional shapes that can be made with four toothpicks. In table groups of four, they first figure out how many shapes are possible. See *Math By All Means: Geometry, Grade 3* by Cheryl Rectanus (1994) for more detail on these activities.

Part 1: Discovering the Sixteen Shapes
Materials

- about 80 flat toothpicks per table group
- a shallow cup of white glue per table group
- 24 6-by-9-inch pieces of construction paper or cardstock per table group (a different color per group)
- 1 copy of toothpick dot paper per student (see Blackline Masters)
- overhead projector

Instructions

1. Remind the children how they made fourteen different polygons using four triangles in December.

2. Explain that, today, they are going to be using four toothpicks to make shapes, but that only one of these shapes will be a polygon.

3. At the overhead, demonstrate how to arrange four toothpicks according to these two rules:

    Each toothpick must touch the end of at least one other toothpick.

    The toothpicks must either touch end-to-end in a straight line or make square corners. (See below.)

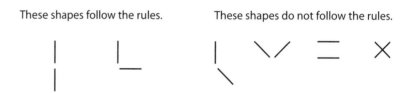

4. Instruct the students to start making shapes, by dipping the ends of their toothpicks into the glue and placing them on a piece of construction paper. Give them plenty of time to explore and to discuss whether the shapes they've created are all unique. (They can check for sameness by rotating their designs and holding them up to the window to see if a particular shape is the mirror image of another shape. (See below.)

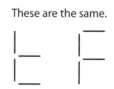

These are the same.

    As you listen to their discussions, be sure to mention if you notice any shapes that are the same.

5. Have the children continue making shapes with the four toothpicks until they've come up with all sixteen possible shapes that follow the two rules above. (See Figure 9–1.)

Extensions

If one table group finishes sooner than the others, have the four students at the table draw each of their shapes on a sheet of toothpick dot paper.

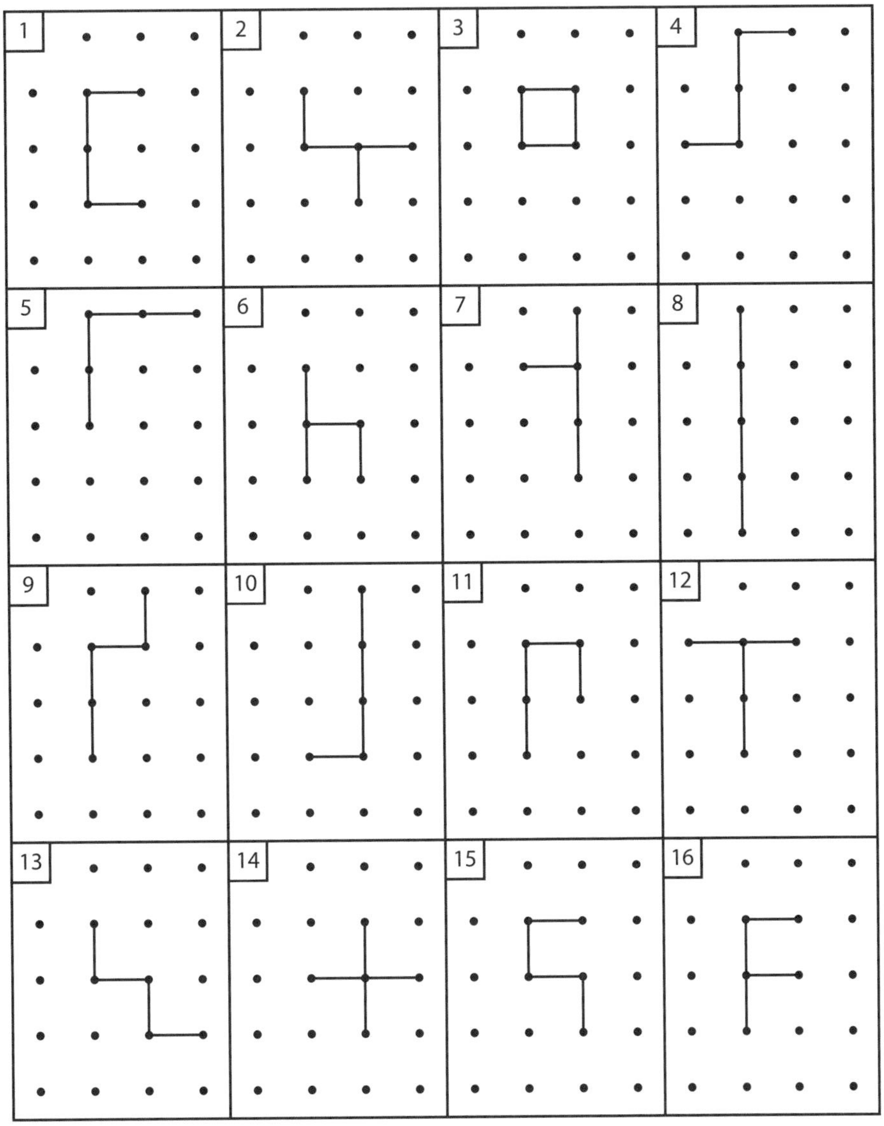

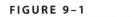

FIGURE 9–1 ◄

These are the sixteen
two-dimensional shapes
that can be made with
four toothpicks.

As they draw, they check again for any repeats. If they discover repeats, they continue their investigation to create any missing shapes.

Part 2: Discussing Our Findings
Instructions

1. At the end of the class period or sometime during the next day, have a whole-class discussion about the children's discovery.

2. As students take turns describing the different shapes they created with four toothpicks, draw those shapes on an overhead transparency of toothpick dot paper.

3. When everyone is satisfied that all sixteen shapes have been recorded, number or name each pattern. (Use those same numbers or names during all future class discussions of these shapes.)

4. Point out that the square is the only polygon among these sixteen shapes. Lead a discussion about the fact that polygons have straight-line segments that connect and enclose a space in the same way a fence encloses a yard. In the other toothpick patterns, the line segments do not enclose a space, so they are not polygons.

Part 3: Playing the Toothpick Card Game

Students will now use their sixteen shapes to play the *Toothpick* card game. First have them make the cards needed for the game.

Materials

- 1 or 2 sheets of toothpick dot paper photocopied onto cardstock per table group
- 1 scissors per student
- 1 rubber band per table group

Instructions: Making the Cards

1. Students copy the sixteen shapes onto their toothpick dot paper and number (or name) them according to the transparency on the overhead.

2. They cut out the sixteen patterns along the lines, creating sixteen square cards.

3. They decorate the back of each toothpick card with a simple design agreed upon by everyone at their table.

4. They use the rubber band to hold the cards together, and give their deck to you.

You may want to write these instructions on the board for students to refer to as they work. Also, suggest that the four children at each table group discuss how they might share the jobs that need to be done. For example, perhaps two children can draw the toothpick shapes while two others decide on the design that will go on the backs of the cards. Or, the children might prefer to work on each step of the directions together or identify some other approach to accomplishing these tasks.

As the children work, circulate and notice whether some children have nothing to do. If you spot such a situation, sit at that table and discuss with the four children how they might divvy up the tasks so everyone has something to do.

When children give you their packet of cards, check to see if all sixteen shapes are there. If they are, teach the four students at that table how to play the *Toothpick* game.

Instructions: Playing the Game

1. Player 1 picks a card randomly from the deck and then builds that shape using four toothpicks. He or she displays the shape in the middle of the table.

2. Player 1 places that card back in the deck, shuffles, then deals *all* the cards out to the four players. (Ask the children in this table group, "If you began with sixteen cards and handed out an even number to each player, how many cards should each player have? How do you know that?")

    If there are only three players at a table, Player 1 leaves the first card face up and deals out the remaining fifteen cards. (Again, ask, "How many cards will each of you get? How do you know that?")

3. Each player places his or her cards pattern side up in a row for all to see.

4. Player 1 looks at the toothpick shape displayed in the middle of the table. He then looks at the cards he has spread out in front of him. In those cards, he looks for a shape that he can make from the shape shown in the middle of the table by moving only one toothpick.

    For example, suppose the shape in the middle of the table is #4 from Figure 9–1 and that Player 1 has shape #1 in his cards. In this case, he places his #1 card next to the original pattern (#4). Then he uses four toothpicks to show how to make that #1 shape by moving one toothpick from shape #4. (See below.)

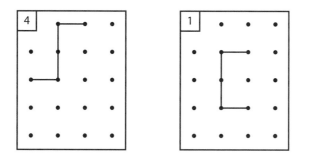

5. Player 2 looks at her cards and does the same: She picks a shape that she could make from the shape put down by Player 1 by moving just one toothpick. (See below.)

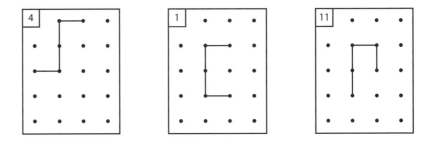

6. Players take turns placing a card and moving a toothpick, each playing a card with a pattern that can be made by changing the position of just one toothpick from the last pattern put down.

This is a game of cooperation, not competition. As the children play, they help one another. If someone can't play a card, he or she says, "I pass." The idea is for the entire group to ultimately place all their cards in the middle of the table.

Sometimes, a group will not be able to play another card. If this happens, the students at the table all have to agree that they are stuck.

After playing several rounds of this game, some children may begin to think ahead and play cards that will enable them to eventually place all their cards instead of getting stuck. If you notice that several table groups have hit on this strategic reasoning, have a class discussion during which the children share their ideas about a "good" card to start with, easier or harder cards to play, etc. Some students will understand such strategies based on their experiences so far. Others will need to play a few more rounds of the game to grasp these ideas.

Extensions

- Students write about the strategies they used when playing *Toothpick*. They explain which shapes are easy to change into others and which are hard to change into others.

- Students make an extra set of *Toothpick* game cards and take them home with four toothpicks. They play the game at home with two or three family members.

Part 4: Putting Toothpick Cards in Order

When your students feel comfortable playing *Toothpick*, they can work individually or in pairs to arrange their deck of cards according to the following one-difference loop pattern:

The cards are arranged in a circle. Each card shows a shape that can be made by moving just one toothpick from the shape shown on the preceding card in the circle. The last card placed in the circle must have a shape that can be made by moving one toothpick from the shape shown on the first card placed in the circle.

Extensions

As a homework assignment, students use their *Toothpick* cards to teach players at home how to arrange the cards following a one-difference loop pattern.

Pentominoes

What are pentominoes? If you're not familiar with these, it helps to think about other related game pieces first. Dominoes have two squares. Triominoes have three squares. Tetrominoes have four squares. And pentominoes have five squares.

Building and manipulating pentominoes gives students practice with two-dimensional shapes. Many of the activities involving pentominoes described below come from *About Teaching Mathematics: A K–8 Resource, Second Edition* by Marilyn Burns (2000).

Building Pentominoes

Materials

- 1 bag of square tiles per table group (around 50 to 60 tiles)
- several sheets of grid paper per table group. (**Note:** Later in this activity, you'll be asking students to make boxes out of their pentominoes, and to fill the boxes with cubes. Select grid paper according to the kind of cubes your students will be working with in that section of the activity. Specifically, if they'll be using Snap Cubes, select $\frac{3}{4}$-inch grid paper. For 1-inch cubes, select 1-inch grid paper. For Cuisenaire cubes, use 2-centimeter grid paper. You can find all these grid formats in the Blackline Masters. If you don't have any of these cubes, students can use sugar cubes for their three-dimensional work. In this case, select $\frac{1}{2}$-inch grid paper, also found in the Blackline Masters.)
- 1 scissors per student

Instructions

1. Ask students to use three tiles to show the two rectangular windowpane arrays they built back in November. (See below.)

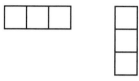

2. Ask what other nonrectangular shapes they could make with three square tiles. (See below.) Draw these shapes on the board.

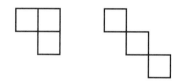

3. State the rules for today's activity: *One whole side of a square must touch one whole side of another square. And the shapes you make with the tiles do not have to be rectangular arrays.* Point out that the first shape you've just drawn on the board follows the rule about squares touching sides, and that the second shape does not.

4. Ask the children to use *four* tiles to build all the shapes possible under the new rules. There are five possible shapes. (See below.) Have the children share their shapes by drawing them on the board or showing them on the overhead with overhead tiles. These shapes are called *tetrominoes.*

5. Ask each group to investigate all the different ways to arrange *five* tiles. Explain that these shapes are called *pentominoes*. Remind the children that they must watch for duplicates as they come up with shapes.

6. Once a group of four thinks they have all the possible pentomino shapes (there are twelve) built with their colored tiles, have them trace their shapes onto the appropriate grid paper (see note in the "Materials" section above) and cut the shapes out.

7. Have the children rotate and flip their paper pentominoes to see if any of their shapes are congruent. Once they've eliminated any redun-

dancies and have created all the possible shapes, have them save their cutouts in a team envelope.

After checking for congruency, the children will likely ask you whether they have all the pentomino shapes. Reply by turning the question back around to them: Ask them if *they* think they have all the pentomino shapes and why they think so. Some children might devise a systematic approach to determining the answer, whereby they try moving one tile at a time. After this discussion, introduce the extension described below.

8. Once all teams have found the twelve pentomino shapes, decide on a number or name for each shape, for clarity of future communication.

Extensions

Each student creates his or her own set of pentomino shapes using grid paper copied onto cardstock. Students write their names on the back of each shape and place it in their own envelope, which also has their name on it.

Pentomino One-Difference Loop

Materials

- sheet of twelve pentomino shapes (see Blackline Masters)
- 1 set of cardstock pentomino pieces per student or pair of students
- 1 scissors per student

Instructions

Have the children work individually or in pairs to arrange one set of the twelve pentomino pieces into a loop such that only one square needs to be moved to change a shape into the one that follows it.

Pentomino Puzzles

Materials

- 1 5-by-12 grid puzzle board per pair of students or table group
- 1 set of cardstock pentomino pieces per pair or table group. (**Note:** Be sure the size of the squares on the puzzle board matches the size of the squares in the pentomino pieces.)

Instructions

Have the children try filling a 5-by-12 grid puzzle board with all twelve pentomino pieces. If they like that challenge, hand out a 6-by-10 or a 4-by-15 grid puzzle board for them to cover with their twelve pentomino pieces.

Extensions

- Two students use a 5-by-12 grid puzzle board with one set of pentomino shapes. As a two-person game, players take turns placing pieces on the board. The object is to be the last player to play a piece, making it impossible for the opponent to fit in another. In this game, all the pieces do not have to be used (Burns 2000, 82).

- Students take their cardstock pentomino sets home and challenge family members to make a pentomino one-difference loop and to try some of the pentomino puzzles described above.

Using Pentominoes to Explore Area and Perimeter

Materials

- sheet of twelve pentomino shapes (see Blackline Masters)
- 1 12-by-18-inch piece of construction paper per pair of students or table group
- 1 scissors for each student
- 1 glue per table

Instructions

1. Remind the children of how they figured the area and the perimeter of each windowpane array.

2. Using input from students, draw a few examples of windowpane arrays on the board and ask students to figure out the areas and perimeters of each.

3. Draw some pentomino shapes on the board or the overhead.

4. Ask the children about the area of these pentomino shapes. Ideally, the children will understand that the area of each pentomino is the same (five squares).

5. Now talk about the perimeter, or "fence," that encloses each pentomino shape. Have the children imagine that a pretend ant is walking around each pentomino. Ask how many sides the ant passes

before he returns to his starting point. Demonstrate this concept with one or two shapes. (See below).

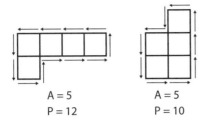

A = 5
P = 12

A = 5
P = 10

6. Give each pair of students a photocopied set of pentominoes. Have them cut out the shapes, then glue them onto a piece of colored 12-by-18-inch construction paper. Next to each shape, they indicate that shape's area and perimeter.

Folding Pentominoes into Boxes

This activity helps children transition from two-dimensional to three-dimensional shapes.

Instructions

1. Hand out each table group's envelope containing the team's paper pentomino shapes.

2. Have students sort the shapes into two groups—those they can fold into a box without a top and those they cannot. Begin by showing the entire class how the Red Cross-shaped pentomino can be folded into a lidless box.

3. Ask students which part of this pentomino will become the bottom of the box.

4. Mark that side with an X, then fold the shape to see if it actually does form a lidless box.

Milk-Carton Pentominoes

This activity gives students practice with transitioning from three-dimensional to two-dimensional shapes.

Materials

- 15 or 16 milk cartons, washed thoroughly and with tops removed, per table group

Instructions

1. Hand out the cartons.

2. Ask each group of four to cut their cartons in such ways that when they lie flat, they form the different pentomino shapes.

Boxes

In this investigation, students have an additional opportunity to see the connection between two-dimensional and three-dimensional shapes. See *Math By All Means: Geometry, Grade 3* for more detail on these activities.

Comparing Boxes

The object of this activity is for students to select two boxes and then describe what is similar and different about them.

Materials

- an array of empty boxes of various shapes (with attached or separate tops) that students bring in from home, supplemented by additional boxes you provide; boxes should be small enough to fit into students' backpacks; aim for about a dozen more boxes than there are students in your class

Instructions

1. Spread out all the boxes on extra tables around the room.

2. Have students pair up.

3. Ask each child to pick out a box, put it on his or her desk, and come to the rug area.

4. Hold up two boxes you have picked. Invite the children to say what they think is the same and different about the two boxes. Write their comments on the board. Make sure the chart of *Geometry Words* is available nearby for the students' reference. Add any new terms to the poster as they come up.

5. As the children talk, help them use the language of polyhedra. For example, if someone mentions the sides of a box, help that child

explain whether he or she is talking about the *edges* or the *faces* of the box. If another youngster talks about a corner on the box, you might introduce the words *vertex* and *vertices*—though you certainly don't have to. Add the following terms to the chart of *Geometry Words*: *polyhedra, polyhedron, rectangular prism, edges, faces, corner*.

Here's how your "Same and Different" chart might look after a class discussion comparing a large cereal box and a smaller cracker box.

Same	*Different*
Both have 6 faces.	One is taller than the other.
Both have faces that are rectangles.	One is black. One is not.
Both have flap lids.	One held cereal. One held crackers.
Both have 8 corners.	One has 2 faces that are squares. One does not.
Both had food inside.	
Both have 12 edges.	

6. Have partners return to their desks and document what is the same and different about the two boxes they selected.

Making Box Puzzles

Materials

- assortment of boxes
- 1 18-by-24-inch piece of construction paper per table group; a different color of paper for each group (post a record of the color coding)

Instructions

1. After school, trace the six faces of one of the rectangular prism boxes onto an 18-by-24-inch piece of paper. Outline these faces with marker so the children will be able to easily see the six faces later. Use a ruler to draw straight lines.

2. Put six or seven different boxes—including the one you traced—on a table in front of the class. Show the class your tracing.

3. Ask the children to guess which box you've traced, and to explain their reasoning. Have several children share their thinking.

4. Now ask them how they could find out the answer for sure. If students suggest that you hold the box to the faces and rotate it face by face, do just that.

5. Distribute several boxes to each table group. Ask each group to select one of the boxes and trace its faces onto the sheet of construction paper. Remind them that they need a system to ensure they have traced each face and that all the faces need to fit on one side of their sheet of construction paper. Encourage the use of rulers for drawing straight lines.

6. Have the students at each table group write their names and the words *Box Puzzle* on the front of the group's construction paper. Then, in tiny letters on the back of the sheet, they write the name of the box they traced (e.g., cereal box, cracker box, etc.). Those who finish early could make a box puzzle for another, different-shaped box at their table.

7. On the following day, spread all the boxes around the classroom, then hand out the box puzzles to table groups other than those who created the puzzles. (Look at the color of the paper used. If one table created their puzzles using yellow construction paper, hand those sheets to another table.)

8. Have the children figure out the puzzles and then sign their names on the front. If they have difficulty making sense of a puzzle, suggest that they go to the children who created the puzzle.

Writing Box Riddles

Materials

- assorted boxes
- 12-by-18-inch sheets of construction paper, in at least three colors, two of each color, per pair of students
- thick yarn in at least three colors per pair of students
- scissors, glue, and rulers per pair of students

Instructions

1. After school, select a rectangular prism box, and trace its faces onto construction paper so that *congruent* faces are traced onto *same-color* paper. Cut out the tracings and glue them onto the box's corresponding faces. Next, glue yarn on each edge of the box, using the same color yarn for edges that are the same length.

2. The next day, show the students your box. Ask them why they think the faces of the boxes are covered as they are. Then ask why you have used different colors of yarn on the edges of the box. Meas-

ure the edges with a ruler to show that some edges are the same length.

3. Next, have the children help you write a riddle about your box. For example, if the box is a cracker box, here are some clues the student could write:

My box has 6 faces.

My box has 12 edges.

Four edges on my box are $8\frac{1}{2}$ inches long.

Eight edges on my box are $4\frac{1}{4}$ inches long.

The top and the bottom of my box are squares.

My box has 8 corners.

4. Now have the children pair up, select a box of their own, and prepare the box in the same way you prepared yours. Remind them to cover the box so that *congruent* faces are the *same* color and *same-length* edges have the *same* color yarn. After they've prepared their box, they write a riddle for it.

5. Have students sign their riddles. When other students believe they have solved the Box Riddle written by Jarod and Angela, they check with them.

Making One-Cube Boxes

This and many of the remaining activities in this section are drawn from *Exploring Solids and Boxes* (Battista and Clements 1995).

Materials

- several Snap Cubes, Cuisenaire cubes, sugar cubes, or other cubes, per table group
- table groups' pentomino shapes (*if* the squares in the shapes have the same dimensions as those of your cubes; *otherwise*, 1 page of pentomino shapes made of grids whose dimensions match those of your cubes) (Refer to page 283.)
- 1 roll of transparent tape per table
- 1 scissors per student

Instructions

1. Hand out each team's paper pentomino shapes. Or if you're using another page of pentomino shapes that match your cubes, hand those out and have the children cut the shapes out.

2. Fold the Red Cross pentomino around a cube to show how you can turn this shape into a topless box. Use tape to fasten the box's edges together.

3. Have the children share their observations about your one-cube box. For example, some may notice that each face is one square unit. Ask, "How many edges and corners are there? How many faces?" Remember: This box is topless, so it has only five faces.

4. Have the children once again find the pentomino shapes that can be formed into topless boxes. This time the children make and tape those boxes with a cube inside.

Making Two-Cube Boxes

Materials

- 2 cubes per student
- sheets of grid paper whose grids' dimensions match those of the students' cubes; 2 sheets per student
- 1 scissors per student
- 1 roll of transparent tape per table

Instructions

1. Invite each student to cut shapes out of the grid paper so as to make a topless box that fits exactly around two cubes. According to *Exploring Solids and Boxes*, each shape the child draws and cuts must fit the following rules:

   It must be made from a contiguous piece of paper.
   It can be folded only along the edges of the grids.
   No sides can overlap.

2. This process may involve some trial and error. After drawing a shape on the grid paper, students can cut it out and fold it to see if it does make a topless box that follows these rules. If it doesn't, they can put the shape aside and try another. Some children have no trouble at all visualizing a two-dimensional shape folded into a three-dimensional shape. Others need lots of time for experimentation. In the end, have the children share their two-cube box patterns and their strategies for figuring them out. Test the patterns.

Making Fill-the-Box Puzzles

Materials

- Snap Cubes, Cuisenaire cubes, sugar cubes, or some other kind of cubes (about 20 per student)
- matching grid paper Fill-the-Box Puzzle sheets A, B, and C (one page of each per student) (see Blackline Masters for Two-Centimeter Squares)
- transparency of each puzzle sheet
- overhead projector
- 1 scissors per student
- 1 roll of transparent tape per table
- a sheet of lined paper for each child

Instructions

1. Show the transparency of the Fix-the-Box Puzzle sheet A.

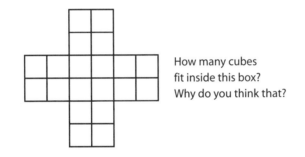

How many cubes
fit inside this box?
Why do you think that?

2. Ask class members how many cubes they think this shape would hold once you've cut the shape out and made it into a box. Ask for the thinking behind the students' predictions. Write their calculations and reasoning on the board. Encourage "math talk," such as "I know that one layer is four cubes because I can see that. Since there are two layers, I know that two times four is eight."

3. Hand out copies of Puzzle A to each student along with a bag of cubes for each table. Have each student cut out the shape, make it into a box, and see if the predicted number of cubes fits in the box.

4. Next, hand out the other two puzzles to each child. Looking at each puzzle sheet, each child predicts the number of cubes that will fit into the resulting box in Puzzle B and explains his or her thinking. He or she does the same for Puzzle C.

5. When all writing is complete, the children construct each topless box, fill each with cubes, and write the answers on their papers.

Extensions

Have the students make some Fill-the-Box puzzles of their own for others in the class to solve.

Building Three-Dimensional Villages

The end of the year is a perfect time for children to build three-dimensional cities that stretch their mathematical thinking.

Materials

- classroom set of cubes
- classroom set of geoblocks
- classroom set of base-ten blocks
- a dozen pieces of 12-by-18-inch cardboard

Instructions

1. Explain to the children that they will be building three-dimensional villages on a base where they can draw roads, paths, and so forth. The children will need to write at least four math questions about some aspect of their village when it is complete. They are to work in groups of four at their team tables.

2. Each team decides which three-dimensional material they wish to work with, and retrieves a bag of that material plus a cardboard base.

3. The children set the pace for this project. You rotate, encourage, and listen to the math questions. Students who use geoblocks might ask questions such as, "How many rectangular prisms do you see in our village?" Those who use cubes might ask, "Three of the buildings are rectangular prisms with twelve cubes in each. How many cubes are there in all three buildings?" "How many square faces do you see in our village?"

4. After two or three days, the children finish drawing the layout of their cardboard base, the buildings, and their four math questions.

5. The class takes another math period or two to rotate by teams. They view one another's villages and answer the accompanying math questions.

Extensions

■ The children may decide to add toy cars, figures, animals, and so forth to their village scenes. They also might wish to make streetlights, signs, and trees. As a group decides how far to take this, always emphasize what math questions can be asked or what story problems can be created that connect to the scene.

■ Refer to *Exploring Solids and Boxes: 3-D Geometry* (Battista and Clements 1995, 69) for ideas on box cities made from grid paper folded into boxes according to this city building code:

1. Each building must have the shape of a rectangular prism.
2. Each building must be made from a box with no bottom.
3. Each building must be made from a single sheet of paper.
4. Only four sheets of graph paper can be used to make all the buildings in the city. You may get more than one building from a single sheet.
5. You must have at least three differently shaped buildings.

Afterword

"Teaching mathematics well is a complex endeavor,
and there are no easy recipes."

Principles and Standards for School Mathematics
NCTM 2000, 17

I was in third grade in 1950. To learn about literature, we read basal readers and filled in workbook-blank questions about vocabulary and the story. Sometimes these exercises were multiple choice. We never discussed the stories, so we had no chance to express our own thoughts about the characters or the problems we found in the books. We simply marked our answers, right or wrong, in our workbooks.

To master writing, we spent long hours learning the rules for capitalization, punctuation, and correct spelling. Again, we filled in workbook pages, some of which contained multiple-choice exercises. We never wrote about moments in our own lives, and we certainly never wrote stories. Again, we simply marked answers in our workbooks.

In learning about mathematics, we watched our teacher show us what to do step by step at the blackboard. Then we followed these same steps on workbook pages filled with numbers. One page had numbers to add. Another had numbers to subtract. There was no discussion about what these numbers meant, and there was only one way to do each problem—the teacher's way. When we finished, our teacher marked our answers right or wrong in our workbook. Sometimes we corrected the wrong answers.

It is now 2003. When I go to local bookstores and look through the education section, I see rows of books on how to help children pass standardized tests that require them to fill in bubbles for right answers. The shelves are filled with workbooks in every subject—workbooks in which children fill in blanks just as I did in 1950.

Today, educators face enormous pressures to "teach to the test." Well-meaning educators are substituting test-preparation materials for their curriculum in every subject. I know you are feeling these same pressures in your classroom. I certainly am in mine.

My hope is that this book will help renew our commitment to the idea that students understand and get excited about mathematics when they are encouraged to make sense of problems using their own strategies. They also find meaning in numbers when those numbers have some connection to objects and routines they encounter in their daily lives and games that they play in class and at home.

> I hear, and I forget;
>
> I see, and I remember,
>
> I do, and I understand.

This Chinese proverb reminds us that it is in the doing that understanding comes. As our children "do" their problem solving and as we "do" our teaching by listening to their meaning making, all of us will grow together in our understanding of and enthusiasm for mathematics.

Blackline Masters

Dice Number Cards
1–100 Chart
Give and Take
Double Give and Take
Supply Order Form
Half-Inch Squares
Circles and Stars with a Parent
  Partner
Multiplication Bingo with a
  Parent Partner
Multiplication Bingo Record
  Sheet
Science Museum Store Price List
Windowpane Chart
T-Chart & 1–100 Chart
Same and Different
Hexagon Fill-In Puzzle
Leftovers
Leftovers Record Sheet
Cookies
Dividing Cookies
Fraction Kit Games
Pattern Block Shapes for
  Hexagons
Build the Yellow Hexagon
Brownies
How Close to 0?
How Close to 0? Record Sheet

Measuring Books
Multiplication Tic-Tac-Toe
Toothpick Dot Paper
Three-Quarter-Inch Squares
One-Inch Squares
Two-Centimeter Squares
Twelve Pentomino Shapes
Fill-the-Box Puzzle, Version 1
Fill-the-Box Puzzle, Version 2
Fill-the-Box Puzzle, Version 3

Dice Number Cards

1	1	1	1	1
2	2	2	2	2
3	3	3	3	3
4	4	4	4	4
5	5	5	5	5
6	6	6	6	6

From *A Month-to-Month Guide: Third-Grade Math* by Suzy Ronfeldt. © 2003 Math Solutions

1–100 Chart

1	2	3	4	5	6	7	8	9	10
11	12	13	14	15	16	17	18	19	20
21	22	23	24	25	26	27	28	29	30
31	32	33	34	35	36	37	38	39	40
41	42	43	44	45	46	47	48	49	50
51	52	53	54	55	56	57	58	59	60
61	62	63	64	65	66	67	68	69	70
71	72	73	74	75	76	77	78	79	80
81	82	83	84	85	86	87	88	89	90
91	92	93	94	95	96	97	98	99	100

Give and Take

You need:
    a deck of playing cards per pair of players (with jokers removed)
    a sign that reads Jack = 11, Queen = 12, King = 13, Ace = 1
    a 1–100 chart

Rules
1. The dealer shuffles the cards and deals them one at a time, starting with the partner.

2. Each player takes the top card off his or her pile and turns the card face up for the partner to see.

3. If Player 1 has a 10 and Player 2 has a 3, Player 1 gets to take both cards *after* he or she explains how much bigger 10 is than 3 by using addition ("I know that three plus seven equals ten.") or by using subtraction ("Ten take away three equals seven so ten is larger than three."). Or the child might place his or her finger on 3 on the 1–100 chart and count up seven spaces to get to 10. Player 2 listens to Player 1's thinking to be sure it makes sense.

4. If both players turn over cards of equal value, they turn over one more card each.

5. Play continues until players have used all the cards in their original pile. The winner is the player with the most cards in their Take pile.

6. Keep the emphasis on the addition and subtraction thinking that is shared between two players.

From *A Month-to-Month Guide: Third-Grade Math* by Suzy Ronfeldt. © 2003 Math Solutions

Double Give and Take

You need:
- a deck of playing cards per pair of players (with jokers removed)
- a sign that reads Jack = 11, Queen = 12, Jack = 13, Ace = 1
- a 1–100 chart

Rules

1. The dealer shuffles the cards and deals them one at a time, starting with the partner.

2. Each player takes the *two* top cards off his or her pile and turns the card face up for the partner to see.

3. Player 1 explains what his two cards equal when added together ("One plus eight equals nine."). Player 2 explains the combining of her two cards ("Thirteen plus four equals seventeen."). Since Player 2 has the larger total, she explains the difference between the two totals of 9 and 17. She could do this in many ways:

   "I know that nine plus one equals ten. Ten plus seven equals seventeen. So nine plus eight equals seventeen. The difference is eight."

   "When I count back from seventeen to nine on the 1–100 chart, it takes eight steps so the difference is eight."

   "Seventeen minus eight equals nine."

   "Nine plus eight equals seventeen."

   Player 1 listens to be sure that Player 2's reasoning is correct, then Player 2 takes all four cards. It is now Player 1's turn.

4. If the players should happen to each turn over cards of equal value, they turn over two more cards for that turn and proceed with the last two draws.

5. Play continues until the players have used all the cards in their original piles. The winner is the player with the most cards in their Take pile.

6. Keep the emphasis on the addition and subtraction thinking that is shared between two players.

Supply Order Form

Quantity	Item Name	Price
		$.
		$.
		$.
		$.
		$.
	Total	$.
	Change	$.

Here is how I figured the total:

Here is how I figured the change:

Half-Inch Squares

Circles and Stars with a Parent Partner

You need:
  2 $8\frac{1}{2}$-by-11-inch sheets of paper per person
  2 pencils, one per person
  1 die to share

Rules
1. Each player folds one of his or her papers into eight rectangles.
2. In the top left rectangle, write *Circles and Stars*. Write your name and the word *total*, your partner's name and the word *total*, and the word *difference*, each followed by a blank. (Seven blank rectangles will be left.)

   Circles and Stars

   Sharon's Total _____

   Sam's Total _____

   Difference _____

3. Player 1 rolls the die and draws that many circles in the first blank rectangle. Then Player 1 rolls the die again and draws that many stars inside each circle. Finally, Player 1 writes an equation with the number of circles as the first factor and the number of stars in each circle as the second factor (for example, $4 \times 3 = 12$).

   Player 2 checks to see if this work makes sense. Then Player 2 has a complete turn with Player 1 checking the work.
4. The game continues for seven rounds until all the blank rectangles are filled in.
5. Then each player takes his or her second sheet of paper and folds it so that the long side is folded in half. After writing their names, each player writes *total* on the left section of their sheet and *difference* on the right section. Next, each player figures the total of their seven products, exchanges papers, and checks each other's work.
6. Finally, the players figure the difference between their own total and their partner's total on the *difference* side of the sheet. Once the partners agree on the difference, they each record their totals and the difference in the first rectangle on their *Circles and Stars* sheet.
7. It helps if each player's two sheets are stapled or clipped together.

Note: The goal of this game is cooperation and making sense of the mathematics (multiplication, addition, subtraction). This is not meant to be a game of competition.

From *A Month-to-Month Guide: Third-Grade Math* by Suzy Ronfeldt. © 2003 Math Solutions

Multiplication Bingo with a Parent Partner

You need:
>*Circles and Stars* Product Chart from classroom data
>2 *Multiplication Bingo* Record Sheets, 1 for each person
>1 die

Rules

1. Look at a copy of the *Circles and Stars* Product Chart from your classroom, and discuss with your partner. Why do some numbers have many tally marks? Why do some numbers have no tally marks?

2. Using the *Multiplication Bingo* Record Sheets (one for each player), fill in the Game 1 grid with products you think will turn up when you roll a die twice. (As in *Circles and Stars*, the first roll is like the number of circles, and the second roll is like the number of stars in each circle.) You may want to write some products more than once.

3. Once the Game 1 grid on each of your record sheets is filled in with your guesses, take turns rolling the die and crossing off the products if they are on the Game 1 grid. If the product appears more than once on the grid, you can only cross it off once. Your partner does the same on his or her sheet.

4. The winner is the first player to cross off four products in a row with the X already filled in. The row can be horizontal, vertical, or diagonal.

Extensions
After you and your child have played several rounds of this game, you might want to discuss which strategy seems to work when filling in the game grid.

Note: If your child makes more sense of the equal-size groups by drawing circles and stars or handling beans to group and count as he or she rolls the die, encourage that strategy. You want your child to bring understanding to the numbers. Some children use their 1–100 chart for their skip-counting approach to multiplication.

Multiplication Bingo
Record Sheet

Game 1

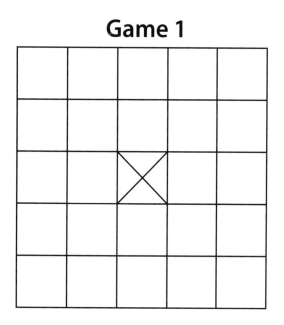

Game 2

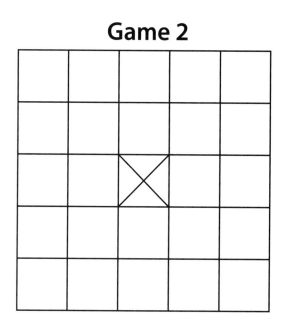

Game 3

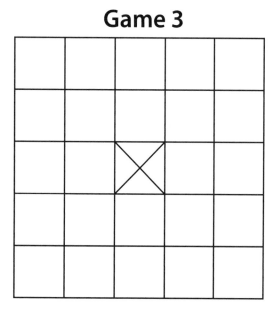

Game 4

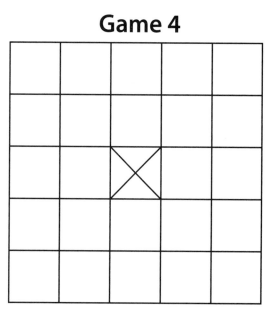

Science Museum Store Price List

$3.00	$4.00	$5.00
1. Origami paper	1. Kaleidoscope	1. Koosh ball
2. Crystal and gem magnets	2. Large magnifying bug box	2. Glow-in-the-dark solar system stickers
3. Furry stuffed seal pups	3. Sunprint kit	3. Inflatable world globe
4. Prism	4. Inflatable shark	4. Wooden dinosaur model kit

Windowpane Chart

Name _____   **Rectangle windows for** _____ **panes**

Factor pairs for these windows.

From *A Month-to-Month Guide: Third-Grade Math* by Suzy Ronfeldt. © 2003 Math Solutions

T-Chart & 1–100 Chart

Name _____

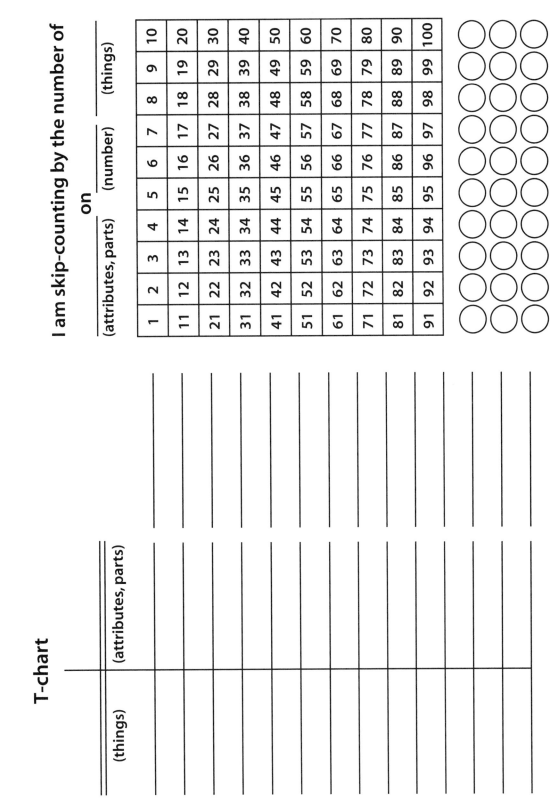

I am skip-counting by the number of

_____ **(number)**

on _____ **(things)**

_____ **(attributes, parts)**

1	2	3	4	5	6	7	8	9	10
11	12	13	14	15	16	17	18	19	20
21	22	23	24	25	26	27	28	29	30
31	32	33	34	35	36	37	38	39	40
41	42	43	44	45	46	47	48	49	50
51	52	53	54	55	56	57	58	59	60
61	62	63	64	65	66	67	68	69	70
71	72	73	74	75	76	77	78	79	80
81	82	83	84	85	86	87	88	89	90
91	92	93	94	95	96	97	98	99	100

T-chart

(things) | **(attributes, parts)**

From *A Month-to-Month Guide: Third-Grade Math* by Suzy Ronfeldt. © 2003 Math Solutions

Same and Different

Name _____

Trace the two four-triangle polygons you are comparing.

Explain what is the *same* and what is *different* about these two polygons.

same	different

Hexagon Fill-In Puzzle

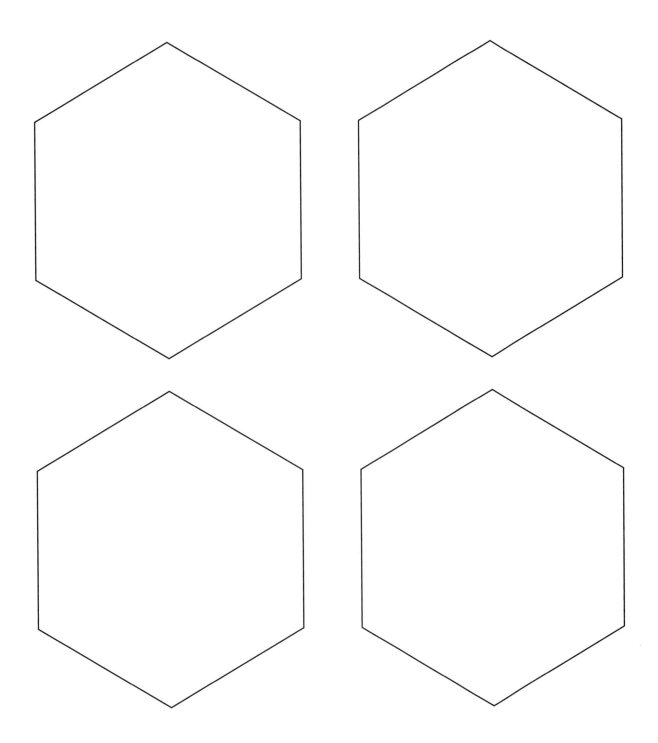

Leftovers

You need:

    15 counters, such as pennies, beans, or paper clips

    6 paper plates, pieces of paper, or napkins

    1 die

Rules

1. Player 1 writes his or her initials on the record sheet, rolls the die (for example, a *4*), and takes that number of paper plates (or pieces of paper or napkins). Player 1 then divides the fifteen counters evenly among the plates, placing any leftover counters to the side.

2. Player 1 then writes on the record sheet the math equation that describes what happened. Record like this: *15 ÷ 4 = 3 R3*

3. Player 1 returns the counters and plates to the center of the table, leaving the three remainders to the side out of the game. (On the next turn after the equation shown above, there would be twelve counters left.)

4. Player 2 repeats steps 1 through 3 above.

5. Players take turns until all the counters are gone.

Extensions

Figure your scores by counting how many remainder counters each player has left on the side. The winner is the player with the most leftovers. Record the score of each player at the bottom of the page.

Note to Parents

Your child has played this game over two weeks in two separate half-hour periods. This game gives children experiences with division as sharing. The children divide counters into equal-size groups, learn about remainders, and record division equations. Please play at least one game this week then continue to play more games in the weeks ahead. You and your child might play with a different number of objects.

    After you and your child play at least one game tonight or tomorrow night, please have your child bring the record sheet back to class the next day. We will spend time discussing the equations with remainders of zero and why that happens.

 From *A Month-to-Month Guide: Third-Grade Math* by Suzy Ronfeldt. © 2003 Math Solutions

Leftovers Record Sheet

Names _____

_____

Initial of Player

_____   _____ tiles shared among _____ plates = _____ tiles per plate R_____

_____   _____ tiles shared among _____ plates = _____ tiles per plate R _____

_____   _____ tiles shared among _____ plates = _____ tiles per plate R _____

_____   _____ tiles shared among _____ plates = _____ tiles per plate R _____

_____   _____ tiles shared among _____ plates = _____ tiles per plate R _____

_____   _____ tiles shared among _____ plates = _____ tiles per plate R _____

_____   _____ tiles shared among _____ plates = _____ tiles per plate R _____

_____   _____ tiles shared among _____ plates = _____ tiles per plate R _____

Cookies

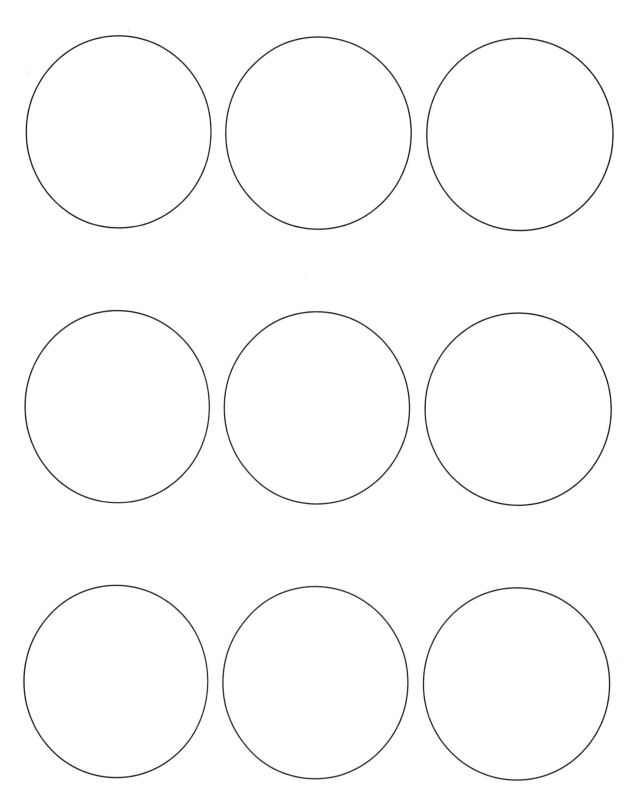

Dividing Cookies

Names _____   _____

_____   _____

Share __ cookies equally among 4 people. Paste each person's share in a box.

How much did each person get? _____

_____

Fraction Kit Games

Cover Up
Each player puts their one whole strip out in front of them. The goal is to be the first player who covers the one whole strip completely with other pieces from the fraction kit. No overlapping pieces are allowed.

1. Players take turns rolling the cube labeled with these fractions: $\frac{1}{2}, \frac{1}{4}, \frac{1}{8}, \frac{1}{8}, \frac{1}{16}, \frac{1}{16}$.
2. The fraction face up on the cube tells what size piece to place on the whole strip.
3. When the game nears the end and a player needs only a small piece, such as $\frac{1}{8}$ or $\frac{1}{16}$, rolling $\frac{1}{2}$ or $\frac{1}{4}$ won't do. The player must roll exactly what is needed.

Uncover, Part 1
This game gives the players experiences with equivalent fractions. Each player starts with the whole strip covered with the two $\frac{1}{2}$ pieces. The goal is to be the first to uncover the strip completely.

1. Players take turns rolling the cube labeled with fractions.
2. After a player rolls the cube, he or she exchanges for pieces that equal the fraction on his or her cube explaining: "My cube shows $\frac{1}{4}$ so I am exchanging my $\frac{1}{2}$ for two $\frac{1}{4}$ pieces. Now I can remove one of these $\frac{1}{4}$ pieces from the whole strip." The other player checks this reasoning. If a player already has a fraction piece matching the fraction on the cube, he or she just removes the piece without an exchange.
3. As in *Cover Up*, the player must roll exactly what is needed before the last piece can be removed.

Uncover, Part 2
In this version of the game, a player can only make one move on a turn, not two as above. After a player rolls, he or she has three options and can *only do one* of them.

1. The player can remove a piece if that exact fraction is indicated on the cube.
2. The player can exchange any of the pieces left for equivalent pieces.
3. The player can do nothing and pass the cube to the next player.

Note to Parents
We have been exploring *the language of fractions and the relationship between fractions*. We make our own fraction kits and have class discussions comparing our fraction kit pieces, asking which piece is greater than another and how we know this; which is less than another and how we know this; and which piece is equal to another. For example, one child might say, "One-fourth is greater than one-eighth because it takes two-eighths to equal one-fourth." Another child might say, "Three-fourths is less than one whole because it takes four-fourths to equal one whole."

Please have conversations such as these as you and your child play the above games. Some questions you can ask include "Why are you exchanging _____ for _____?" and "Show me how those two fractions are equal."

Remind yourself that this is just a beginning step in understanding fractions. Your child will spend the next two school years studying fractions more formally.

 From *A Month-to-Month Guide: Third-Grade Math* by Suzy Ronfeldt. © 2003 Math Solutions

Pattern Block Shapes for Hexagons

Build the Yellow Hexagon

Find all the different ways you can build the yellow hexagon from different assortments of blocks. Count only different combinations of blocks. Have you found them all?

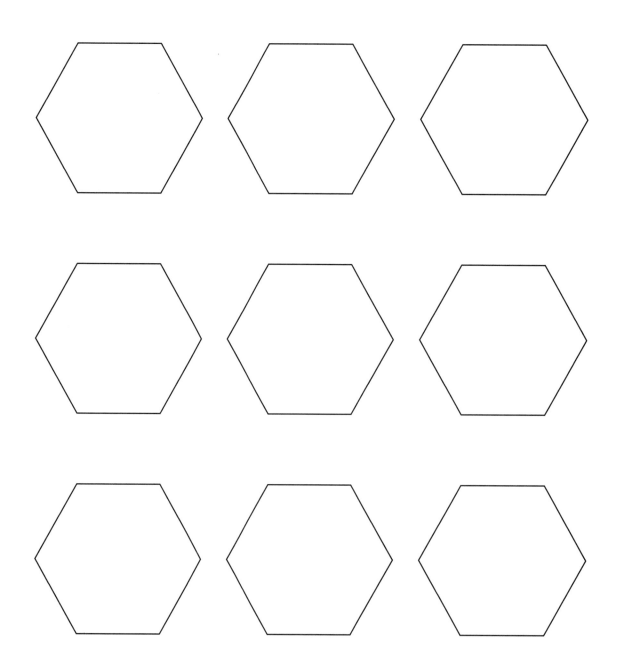

From *A Month-to-Month Guide: Third-Grade Math* by Suzy Ronfeldt. © 2003 Math Solutions

Brownies

How Close to 0?

You need:
   a partner
   a die
   How Close to 0? Record sheet

Rules
1. Player 1 rolls the die, decides whether to use the number as a ten or as a one, and subtracts the number from 100. (Example: a 5 can be 50 or 5.) Player 1 records his or her calculation on the record sheet.

2. Player 2 does the same—rolls the die, decides whether to use the number as a ten or as a one, subtracts the number from 100, and records the play.

3. Play continues until each player has rolled seven times.

4. The player closer to zero after seven rounds is the winner and receives a score of whatever number is left for the opposing player.

5. If a player reaches zero before the seventh round, the game is over. The other player wins and scores the points left over from the opponent's previous round.

   From *A Month-to-Month Guide: Third-Grade Math* by Suzy Ronfeldt. © 2003 Math Solutions

How Close to 0? Record Sheet

	Player 1	Player 2		Player 1	Player 2
ROUND 1	100 – ___	100 – ___	ROUND 1	100 – ___	100 – ___
ROUND 2	– ___	– ___	ROUND 2	– ___	– ___
ROUND 3	– ___	– ___	ROUND 3	– ___	– ___
ROUND 4	– ___	– ___	ROUND 4	– ___	– ___
ROUND 5	– ___	– ___	ROUND 5	– ___	– ___
ROUND 6	– ___	– ___	ROUND 6	– ___	– ___
ROUND 7	– ___	– ___	ROUND 7	– ___	– ___

Measuring Books

Measuring Books Using Centimeters
Book Title: _____

Estimated Length	Actual Measurement	How Far Off?
_____ cm.	_____ cm.	_____ cm.

Estimated Width	Actual Measurement	How Far Off?
_____ cm.	_____ cm.	_____ cm.

Estimated Thickness	Actual Measurement	How Far Off?
_____ cm.	_____ cm.	_____ cm.

Measuring Books Using Inches
Book Title: _____

Estimated Length	Actual Measurement	How Far Off?
_____ in.	_____ in.	_____ in.

Estimated Width	Actual Measurement	How Far Off?
_____ in.	_____ in.	_____ in.

Estimated Thickness	Actual Measurement	How Far Off?
_____ in.	_____ in.	_____ in.

From *A Month-to-Month Guide: Third-Grade Math* by Suzy Ronfeldt. © 2003 Math Solutions

Multiplication Tic-Tac-Toe

Players use cubes in two different colors. The first player chooses two factors from 1–9 underneath the gameboard, places a paper clip on each, and marks the product on the gameboard with a cube. The second player moves one of the paper clips to a new factor, finds the product, and marks the product with a different color cube. Play continues until one player has marked four product in a row, column, or diagonal. Note: When moving a paper clip, it's legal to move it to the same factor with the other paper clip to allow for plays such as 5 × 5.

1	2	3	4	5	6
7	8	9	10	12	14
15	16	18	20	21	24
25	27	28	30	32	35
36	40	42	45	48	49
54	56	63	64	72	81

1   2   3   4   5   6   7   8   9

Toothpick Dot Paper

From *A Month-to-Month Guide: Third-Grade Math* by Suzy Ronfeldt.© 2003 Math Solutions

Three-Quarter-Inch Squares

One-Inch Squares

From *A Month-to-Month Guide: Third-Grade Math* by Suzy Ronfeldt. © 2003 Math Solutions

Two-Centimeter Squares

Twelve Pentomino Shapes

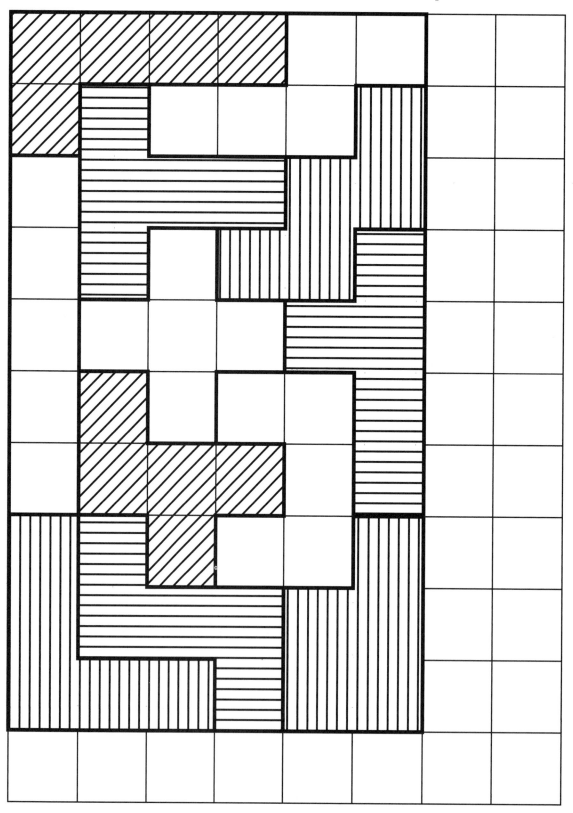

From *A Month-to-Month Guide: Third-Grade Math* by Suzy Ronfeldt. © 2003 Math Solutions

Fill-the-Box Puzzle, Version 1

Fill-the-Box Puzzle, Version 2

Fill-the-Box Puzzle, Version 3

References

Professional Resources

Book Publishers/Distributors

Didax
395 Main Street
Rowley MA 01969
800 458 0024 phone
800 350 2345 fax
www.didaxinc.com

EAI Education
567 Commerce Street
Franklin Lakes NJ 07417
800 770 8010 phone
201 891 5689 fax
www.eaieducation.com

Educators Outlet
P. O. Box 397
Timnath CO 80547
800 315 2212 phone
970 224 3822 fax
www.educatorsoutlet.com

ETA/Cuisenaire
500 Greenview Court
Vernon Hills IL 60061-1862
800 445 5985 phone
800 382 9326 fax
www.etacuisenaire.com

Math Solutions Publications
150 Gate 5 Road, Suite 101
Sausalito CA 94965
800 868 9092 phone
415 331 1931 fax
www.mathsolutions.com

NASCO
901 Janesville Avenue
Ft. Atkinson WI 53538
800 558 9595 phone
920 563 8296 fax
www.enasco.com

Scott Foresman (Dale Seymour
    Publications)
135 South Mount Zion Road
P. O. Box 2500
Lebanon IN 46052
800 552 2259 phone
800 841 8939 fax
www.scottforesman.com

Scholastic Inc.
P. O. Box 7502
Jefferson City MO 65102
800 724 6527 (option #3) phone
800 560 6815 fax
www.scholastic.com

William K. Sheridan & Associates
8311 Green Meadows Drive North
Lewis Center OH 43035
800 433 6259 phone
740 548 0485 fax
www.classroomgoodies.com

Summit Learning
P. O. Box 755
Ft. Atkinson WI 53538-0755
800 777 8817 phone
800 317 2194 fax
www.summitlearning.com

Professional Books

Akers, Joan, Cornelia Tierney, Claryce Evans, and Megan Murray. 1996. *Name That Portion*. Investigations in Number, Data, and Space Series. Palo Alto, CA: Dale Seymour Publications.

Battista, Michael T., and Douglas H. Clements. 1995. *Exploring Solids and Boxes: 3-D Geometry*. Investigations in Number, Data, and Space Series. Palo Alto, CA: Dale Seymour Publications.

Bresser, Rusty, and Caren Holtzman. 1999. *Developing Number Sense: Grades 3–6*. Sausalito, CA: Math Solutions Publications.

Burns, Marilyn. 2000. *About Teaching Mathematics: A K–8 Resource*. 2d ed. Sausalito, CA: Math Solutions Publications.

———. 2001. *Teaching Arithmetic: Lessons for Introducing Multiplication, Grade 3*. Sausalito, CA: Math Solutions Publications.

Economopoulos, Karen, and Susan Jo Russell. 1998. *Putting Together and Taking Apart, Grades 2 and 3*. Investigations in Number, Data, and Space Series. Palo Alto, CA: Dale Seymour Publications.

Mokros, Jan, and Susan Jo Russell. 1995. *Combining and Comparing, Grades 3 and 4*. Investigations in Number, Data, and Space Series. Palo Alto, CA: Dale Seymour Publications.

National Council of Teachers of Mathematics. 2000. *Principles and Standards for School Mathematics*. Reston, VA: National Council of Teachers of Mathematics.

Rectanus, Cheryl. 1994. *Math By All Means: Geometry, Grade 3*. Sausalito, CA: Math Solutions Publications.

Russell, Susan Jo, and Karen Economopoulos. 1995. *Mathematical Thinking at Grade 3*. Investigations in Number Data, and Space Series. Palo Alto, CA: Dale Seymour Publications.

Tank, Bonnie, and Lynne Zolli. 2001. *Teaching Arithmetic: Lessons for Addition and Subtraction, Grades, 2–3*. Sausalito, CA: Math Solutions Publications.

Tierney, Cornelia, and Mary Berle-Carman. 1995. *Fair Shares, Grades 3 and 4*. Investigations in Number, Data, and Space Series. Palo Alto, CA: Dale Seymour Publications.

Tierney, Cornelia, Mary Berle-Carman, and Joan Akers. 1995. *Things That Come In Groups*. Investigations in Number, Data, and Space Series. Palo Alto, CA: Dale Seymour Publications.

Wickett, Maryann, Susan Ohanian, and Marilyn Burns. 2002. *Teaching Arithmetic: Lessons for Introducing Division, Grades 3–4*. Sausalito, CA: Math Solutions Publications.

Children's Books

Buckless, Andrea, with Marilyn Burns. 2000. *Too Many Cooks!* Illus. K. A. Jacobs. Hello Math Reader Series. New York: Scholastic.

Cleary, Beverly. 1950, 1990. *Henry Huggins*. Illus. Louis Darling. New York: HarperTrophy.

Cleary, Beverly. 1968, 1996. *Ramona the Pest*. Illus. Louis Darling. New York: HarperTrophy.

Coerr, Eleanor. 1986. *The Josefina Story Quilt*. Illus. Bruce Degen. New York: HarperTrophy.

Dahl, Roald. 1988. *Matilda*. Illus. Quentin Blake. New York: Puffin Books.

Ernst, Lisa Campbell, and Lee Ernst. 1990. *The Tangram Magician*. New York: Harry N. Abrams.

Flournoy, Valerie. 1985. *The Patchwork Quilt*. Illus. Jerry Pinkney. New York: Dial Books for Young Readers.

Friedman, Aileen. 1994. *The King's Commissioners*. Illus. Susan Guevara. New York: Scholastic.

Holtzman, Caren. 1995. *A Quarter from the Tooth Fairy*. Illus. Betsy Day. Hello Math Reader Series. New York: Scholastic.

Hutchins, Pat. 1986. *The Doorbell Rang*. New York: Mulberry Books.

Ling, Bettina, with Marilyn Burns. 1997. *The Fattest, Tallest, Biggest Snowman Ever*. Illus. Michael Rex. Hello Math Reader Series. New York: Scholastic.

Losi, Carol A., with Marilyn Burns. 1997. *The 512 Ants on Sullivan Street*. Illus. Patrick Merrell. Hello Math Reader Series. New York: Scholastic.

Maccarone, Grace, with Marilyn Burns. 1998. *Three Pigs, One Wolf, and Seven Magic Shapes*. Illus. David Neuhaus. Hello Math Reader Series. New York: Scholastic.

Mahy, Margaret. 1987. *17 Kings and 42 Elephants*. Illus. Patricia MacCarthy. New York: Dial Books for Young Readers.

McDonald, Megan. 2000. *Judy Moody Was in a Mood. Not a Good Mood. A Bad Mood*. Illus. Peter Reynolds. Cambridge, MA: Candlewick Press.

Myller, Rolf. 1962, 1990. *How Big Is a Foot?* New York: Dell Yearling.

Neuschwander, Cindy, with Marilyn Burns. 1998. *Amanda Bean's Amazing Dream: A Mathematical Story*. Illus. Liza Woodruff. New York: Scholastic.

Paul, Ann Whitford. 1991. *Eight Hands Round: A Patchwork Alphabet*. Illus. Jeanette Winter. New York: HarperCollins.

Pinczes, Elinor J. 1993. *One Hundred Hungry Ants*. Illus. Bonnie MacKain. New York: Houghton Mifflin.

Polacco, Patricia. 1998. *The Keeping Quilt*. New York: Aladdin.

Rocklin, Joanne. 1995. *How Much Is That Guinea Pig in the Window?* Illus. Meredith Johnson. Hello Math Reader Series. New York: Scholastic.

———. 1997. *One Hungry Cat*. Illus. Rowan Barnes-Murphy. Hello Math Reader Series. New York: Scholastic.

———. 1998. *The Case of the Backyard Treasure*. Illus. John Speirs. Hello Math Reader Series. New York: Scholastic.

———. 1999a. *The Case of the Shrunken Allowance*. Illus. Cornelius Van Wright and Ying-Hwa Hu. Hello Math Reader Series. New York: Scholastic.

———. 1999b. *Just Add Fun*. Illus. Martin Lemelman. Hello Math Reader Series. New York: Scholastic.

Schwartz, Amy. 1988. *Annabelle Swift, Kindergartner*. New York: Orchard Books.

Slater, Teddy. 2002. *Two Tickets to Ride*. Illus. Ronnie Rooney. Hello Math Reader Series. New York: Scholastic.

Slobodkina, Esphyr. 1940, 1987. *Caps for Sale: A Tale of a Peddler, Some Monkeys and Their Monkey Business*. New York: HarperTrophy.

Smucker, Barbara. 1995. *Selina and the Bear Paw Quilt*. Illus. Janet Wilson. New York: Dragonfly Books.

Tompert, Ann. 1990. *Grandfather Tang's Story*. Illus. Robert Andrew Parker. New York: Random House.

Viorst, Judith. 1978. *Alexander, Who Used to Be Rich Last Sunday*. Illus. Ray Cruz. New York: Atheneum.

Wilder, Laura Ingalls. 1953. *Little House in the Big Woods*. Illus. Garth Williams. New York: HarperTrophy.

Wood, Audrey. 1984. *The Napping House*. New York: Harcourt Brace.

Index